How to Write Better Essays

Fourth edition

Bryan Greetham

 macmillan education   palgrave

First edition 2001
Second edition 2008
Third edition 2013
Fourth edition 2018

First published 2001 by
PALGRAVE

Palgrave in the UK is an imprint of Macmillan Publishers Limited, registered in England, company number 785998, of 4 Crinan Street, London, N1 9XW.

Palgrave® and Macmillan® are registered trademarks in the United States, the United Kingdom, Europe and other countries.

ISBN 978–1–352–00114–3 paperback

This book is printed on paper suitable for recycling and made from fully managed and sustained forest sources. Logging, pulping and manufacturing processes are expected to conform to the environmental regulations of the country of origin.

A catalogue record for this book is available from the British Library.

A catalog record for this book is available from the Library of Congress.

Palgrave Study Guides – Related titles

How to Write Better Essays   *Bryan Greetham*
The Mature Student's Guide to Writing   *Jean Rose*
The Postgraduate Research Handbook   *Gina Wisker*
The Student's Guide to Writing   *John Peck and Martin Coyle*
Research Using I.T.   *Hilary Coombes*
The Study Skills Handbook   *Stella Cottrell*
Teaching Study Skills and Supporting Learning   *Stella Cottrell*
How to Begin Studying English Literature (fourth edition)   *Nicholas Marsh*
How to Study a Jane Austen Novel (second edition)   *Vivien Jones*
How to Study Chaucer (second edition)   *Rob Pope*
How to Study Foreign Languages   *Marilyn Lewis*
How to Study an E. M. Forster Novel   *Nigel Messenger*
How to Study a Thomas Hardy Novel   *John Peck*
How to Study James Joyce   *John Blades*
How to Study a D. H. Lawrence Novel   *Nigel Messenger*
How to Study Linguistics   *Geoffrey Finch*
How to Study Modern Poetry   *Tony Curtis*
How to Study a Novel (second edition)   *John Peck*
How to Study a Poet (second edition)   *John Peck*
How to Study a Renaissance Play   *Chris Coles*
How to Study Romantic Poetry (second edition)   *Paul O'Flinn*
How to Study a Shakespeare Play (second edition)   *John Peck and Martin Coyle*
How to Study Television   *Keith Selby and Ron Cowdery*
Linguistic Terms and Concepts   *Geoffrey Finch*
Literary Terms and Criticism   *John Peck and Martin Coyle*
Practical Criticism   *John Peck and Martin Coyle*

www.palgravestudyguides.com

How to Wri

Acknowledgements

Over the years I have been surprised by how many students have been kind enough to take the time to contact me to tell me how much this book has meant to them. Their generous comments have been more than I could possibly have hoped for when I wrote this book. Although I have told each one of you individually how grateful I am, I would like to express my deep gratitude to you all in the body of the book. Your comments have been a continuing source of support and inspiration. In particular, I would like to thank Frank Possel, Christopher Perkins and Hans de Salas-del Valle for their ideas and encouragement.

By the same token, I owe a considerable debt to all those teachers who have shared with me their ideas on how I could improve the book. I have learnt a great deal from their professionalism and experience in using the book with their students. Their willingness to enter into correspondence with me, at times quite lengthy, is a testimony to their dedication and professionalism. From all of you I have learnt such a lot. In particular, I owe a considerable debt to Phil Hall, whose experience and insights have always been a source of inspiration.

I would also like to thank all of the reviewers, who have, with each new edition, made such valuable suggestions about how the book could be improved and adapted to meet the changing needs of students. I have often wanted to say how grateful I am for all your generous comments, your well-aimed criticisms and for your inventive ideas about how I can improve the book. Thank you for the time you have spent thoughtfully responding to the questions we have asked you. I hope you approve of my responses to your ideas.

I also owe a considerable debt to all those who work behind the scenes at Palgrave Macmillan: those who are responsible for designing the new edition, for marketing it and for creating the website. The one central figure throughout all of this, my editor since the first edition in 2001, has been Suzannah Burywood and now I have a new editor, Helen Caunce. To both of them I owe a considerable debt for the confidence they have shown in me and for their quiet patience, good judgement and professionalism, which has successfully guided the book through each new edition.

Finally, my greatest debt is owed to my partner, Pat Rowe, who has anchored my wavering emotions and steered me gently through each crisis.

Contents

Introduction

About this book

By the time we reach university a surprising number of us are convinced that we should know all we need to know about researching and writing essays. We're inclined to argue that if we've got this far we should know how to analyse the implications of questions, read efficiently, take notes, plan and structure arguments, use evidence, and write light and interesting prose. Indeed, these skills are the very thing that has got us this far in the first place, so to admit that we could be better at essay writing seems to be an admission that we're lucky to have got this far.

Instead of seeking help, then, to improve our skills, we settle for the strategy of just learning by our mistakes, or by example in those rare moments when we might see our tutor think through and analyse a difficult concept, or pull ideas together from different sources and synthesise them into a new way of looking at a problem. If we recognise the significance of the moment, and most of us don't, then we might be lucky enough to retain a small inkling of what went on in the hope that we, too, might be able to do the same.

> Most of us have the abilities to succeed, if only we can unlock and use them by learning simple skills.

But it need not be like this. The two types of skills that we all need to be successful in our courses – *study skills* (reading, note-taking, writing, organisation and revision) and *thinking skills* (analysis, synthesis, discussion, argument and use of evidence) – can be taught. There is nothing mysterious about them. They need not be the exclusive preserve of a few. And there is nothing particularly difficult about them either. Indeed, most of us have the abilities to succeed, if only we can unlock and use them by learning these simple skills.

Learning the skills

In this book you will learn not just the study skills, but the thinking skills too. You will be shown clear and simple ways of overcoming the most difficult problems.

You will be taken carefully through each stage of writing the essay from interpreting the question to the research, planning, writing and revision. In each of these you will be given practice exercises to work on, along with their answers. You will also be given an exercise that you can work on using an essay that you have been set on one of your courses. As you work through each stage you will get practical help right up until the essay has been completed. In this way not only will your work improve, but you'll develop those skills necessary to tackle successfully all your future writing assignments.

All of this means this book is significantly different from any other writing or study-skills book you may have read before:

- **It's an integrated approach**
  It doesn't deal with writing skills in isolation from the thinking skills and the other study skills involved, such as note-taking, reading and organisation. If you've taken study-skills courses before, you'll know that dealing with any skill in isolation results in us just tacking this new skill onto our existing pattern of study. It's not integrated within it. As a result, after a short time we come to realise it's not relevant to the way we use our other skills and we quietly abandon it.

- **It's a purposeful approach**
  Because it's directed at a specific goal of producing a certain essay that you have chosen yourself, it has a clear purpose that's relevant to what you're studying. Unlike more general books and courses, you're not working in a vacuum. In effect you have your own personal writing tutor, who will be by your side to help you with the problems you confront at each stage in the production of an essay that you have to complete for one of your courses.

- **The book takes account of the syllabus objectives of your courses**
  Unlike most books on this subject, this one will help you develop the skills you need to meet the syllabus objectives of the courses you're taking at university. You will develop the skills and techniques that allow you to explore more effectively in your writing those abilities your syllabuses set out to develop. As many of us know from our experience with other books and courses, any book that doesn't do this we are likely to abandon, realising it doesn't address our needs, because it's divorced from the abilities we are expected to use and develop in the courses we are studying.

- **The book is a comprehensive essay writing guide**
  After you've read the book you're left with an invaluable guide that you can use to diagnose and deal with any problem you might have in your writing in the future. As it's broken up into stages it's easy to identify where the problem is and what you need to do to tackle it. To help you in this, the troubleshooting guide can be found on the companion website at www.howtowritebetteressays.com. With this you can diagnose a problem you might be experiencing, so that you can easily locate the relevant section in the book.

Developing your potential

It often seems that developing our potential involves learning complex and difficult things. But this is not always the case. If success in your studies depends upon your ability to write good essays, it will ultimately depend upon learning simple skills that will allow you to use your abilities more effectively. With these unique characteristics this is a book that will ensure you develop the skills and techniques to unlock your abilities and your potential.

Why Write Essays?

For many students the reason for writing essays is a mystery, even though they might have been writing them for years. For others, like science graduates, who may not be used to writing essays as part of their work, and those from different cultures, where there are different assumptions about knowledge and the role of teachers, it can be even more confusing.

So, it helps to make this clear from the start. If we understand why we do something and the value of doing it, we normally find that we're more confident and positive about tackling it. There are two types of reason for writing essays: one general and philosophical, the other more practical.

General reasons

The core aim of all academic work is to get at the truth, to search for greater understanding of our lives and the world. To do this we must exchange ideas with one another, and the best way to do this is by writing essays. Writing is a form of thinking – the most difficult, yet most effective, form. Each time we write we reveal to ourselves and others where our arguments are irrelevant or weak, where we need more evidence and where we might need to rethink something. In the process we get closer to the truth and a more complete understanding.

> Writing is a form of thinking – the most difficult, yet most effective, form.

Nevertheless, this doesn't mean just any form of writing. As you can see, it involves being open about our ideas, so that we can all understand our arguments and where they need to be improved. In other words, it is a discussion, rather than a debate, where the aim is to win an argument by whatever means, such as exaggerating points, making claims where you have little evidence, even hiding parts of your case that you feel are weak. In a debate you are like a slick salesman: your only aim is to persuade someone of something, sacrificing logic, balance and evidence, if these get in the way.

Socrates   EXAMPLE

Over 2400 years ago the ancient Greek philosopher Socrates taught his students to be aware of this, to avoid the oversimplifications of traditional debate and rhetoric.

- **Critical thinking**
  Today we follow in Socrates' footsteps: universities around the world accept the importance of developing critical thinking skills, so that students can learn to

identify the fallacies, the suppressed evidence and the poorly developed arguments that conceal more than they reveal. All of this is aimed at countering those whose main concern is to persuade you by whatever means – to sell their point of view, rather than tackle the evidence squarely in order to get closer to the truth.

- **Essays should not be just one-sided**
  Unlike a debate, in a discussion we recognise that most problems have many sides to them; we cannot afford to present just one side, because we may miss something that is vital to getting at the truth. Scientists consider all the objections to their theories openly. To ensure that they have discovered a sound foundation on which they and others can build, they will not suppress anything that conflicts with their beliefs.

Charles Darwin, *On the Origin of Species*   **EXAMPLE**

Rather than ignore or suppress the objections to his theory of descent, Darwin meticulously collected them and then devoted an entire chapter to them in *On the Origin of Species*.

- **Co-operative, not competitive**
  As you can see, by contributing to our understanding in this way, writing essays involves co-operating with others, sharing honestly what we know and believe. The philosopher John Passmore once said, 'Understanding, not victory, is the object of discussion; co-operation, not competition, its method.' Like a scientist, when we write essays we invite criticism as an important step so that those who come after can build on our work to get closer to the truth. As Sir Isaac Newton famously conceded, 'If I have seen further it is by standing on the shoulders of giants.'

- **Authority**
  All of this points to one clear message for you as an essay writer: that you have something uniquely valuable to contribute. Nothing can be proved conclusively, beyond statements that are true by definition or logic. None of us have all the facts; all we can do is make a personal judgement after assessing all the evidence available. As Arthur Koestler elegantly put it, 'The ultimate truth is penultimately always a falsehood': there is always an evidential gap between the facts and our convictions, which we bridge by making a value judgement, and yours is as reliable as anyone else's. What you see, the ideas you bring together, reveals your unique perspective on the problems we study.

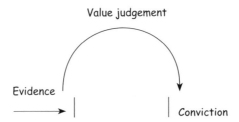

So, we must aim to do more than just recycle the opinions of those who are authorities in our subjects. We must put these to the test and critically evaluate them by revealing weaknesses where we find them in the consistency of their arguments, their use of language and in their evidence.

- **The ethics of essay writing**
  To help you put all this into practice, keep certain principles in mind:

  1 Suspend your judgement: keep an open mind and treat seriously different points of view.
  2 Tolerate uncertainty: there is no virtue in making your mind up quickly. Remember, arguments that lack sufficient thought and analysis are almost always worthless.
  3 Think naively: take nothing on trust; learn to question those things that seem obvious.
  4 Empathise with others: experience their thoughts and feelings, so you can develop a clear understanding of their point of view.
  5 Learn to present the other side of the argument as convincingly as your own; otherwise you will never completely understand it.
  6 Treat every argument, including your own, as a provisional hypothesis, which must be tested thoroughly before you accept it.
  7 Try to avoid:

     - being offended by criticism: it is not a personal attack;
     - defensiveness: accept with humility when you are wrong;
     - being aggressive with those who criticise your arguments;
     - impatience with those who are reluctant to accept your arguments;
     - intolerance with those who hold different views;
     - overconfidence: unwillingness to believe that there could be anything wrong with your argument.

Practical reasons

If you believe that all you must do in essays is accept and recycle what your authorities say, you cannot fulfil the second aim of academic work: to develop your higher cognitive abilities. Like any ability, you can only develop these by using them. If you want to develop your backhand in tennis, you must play the shot over and over again. Similarly, to develop your abilities to discuss issues, analyse concepts, synthesise ideas from different sources and critically evaluate arguments and evidence, you must use them. But to do this you must suspend your judgement. If you simply accept as true what your authorities say, there is nothing to discuss, so you cannot develop these abilities.

- **Essays give you the opportunity to develop your higher cognitive abilities**
  So, even though you are inclined to believe the arguments of your authorities, suspend your judgement as you write your essay, entertain the possibility that there are alternative explanations, so that you can discuss the issues and, in so doing, develop your higher cognitive abilities.

- **Essays force you to organise your thinking and develop your ideas on the issues**
  In one sense writing is *the* crucial step in the process of learning a subject, in that it helps you to get to grips with the new ideas. It is the most difficult form of thinking. It places you at the heart of your ideas, forcing you to pin down your ideas clearly and argue consistently. Without this, it is difficult, if not impossible, to know clearly just how well you've understood the subject.

- **Feedback**

  In the same way, it also provides you with the opportunity to get feedback from your tutor, not just on how well you've understood the subject, but on how well you've communicated this, and where your strengths and weaknesses are, so you can concentrate your energies more effectively. Numerous studies have shown that feedback on essays is more strongly and consistently related to academic achievement than any other form of teacher intervention. Therefore, in Chapter 41 you will learn what you need to do to make the most of your tutor's feedback.

- **Revision material**

  If you've planned the essay well, so that it's got a clear structure, you'll find, when it comes to preparing for the final exam, that the plan itself is just about the most important revision material you have. It shows you how you've come to understand the topic, and how you've organised the ideas. As such, it is the one thing that you will be able to recall and use most effectively under timed conditions. In fact, many students who plan well use just these clearly organised thought patterns as their only revision material. In Chapters 21 and 22 you will learn how to organise your revision and exam technique to improve your performance under timed conditions by using your essays and their plans effectively.

Writing an essay, then, is a valuable opportunity for learning, which ought to be approached positively. If you hide behind the text, just paraphrasing or copying what you've read, without processing those ideas and making them your own, your tutor will rarely see you, your abilities or your problems, and you will never glimpse the extent of your abilities, or just how much you understand.

The Stages

This book is not just about the actual writing of essays; it's also about the various stages you need to go through to produce a good essay, and about the ways in which this can improve your learning. Once you've worked your way through it, you will find you have an invaluable guide that you can keep by your side as you write your essays, to give you answers to problems as they arise.

The five stages

For any essay to achieve high marks it's essential to go through five distinct stages:

1 Interpretation of the question
2 Research
3 Planning
4 Writing
5 Revision

If you omit any of these or just rush them, certain familiar problems will emerge in your writing: irrelevance, weak structure, insufficient evidence and examples to support your arguments, lack of fluency between paragraphs, inconsistent arguments, and many others.

It's also as important to separate each stage, so that you leave, say, at least a day between each of them. Of course, it may not always be possible for you to do this. You may have a number of competing obligations that leave you only a few days to complete the essay. On these occasions the skills you'll learn in this book and on the companion website (www.howtowritebetteressays.com) to manage your time will help you cope more effectively.

They will also help you organise your time so that with most pieces of work you can in fact find sufficient time between each stage. Not only does this allow you to return to your ideas fresh, so that you're able to see which of them needs to be edited out, but you will also find that your ideas and arguments have developed in the meantime.

Separating the stages allows your ideas to develop.

Ideas are organic. Hardly ever are they the complete and finished article the moment you grasp them, like products on a supermarket shelf. They grow and develop over time. So, for example, returning to your plan after a day or two, you will almost inevitably discover new ideas, new evidence and new ways of developing your arguments. You are also likely to see a more sensible and logical way of ordering your ideas.

And the same goes for all the other stages. Each time you return to your work after leaving it to lie unattended for a while, you will find your subconscious has worked on the ideas, restructuring them, answering questions that you weren't sure of, and critically evaluating the arguments you've read in your texts.

But, be reassured, this is not an endless, confusing process, in which your ideas are thrown up in the air each time you return to your work. Within a short time, after revising your plan a couple of times, you will realise that it's ready and you can begin writing. The same is true of your interpretation of the question, your research and the revision of your work. You will know when enough is enough. It may take three or four essays before you feel confident about your judgement, and during these you will have to rely on your tutor's judgement, but it will come.

Interpretation of the Question

Introduction

Often, and for the best of motives, our problems in essay writing begin the very moment we are given the question. Anxious to get on with the work and not fall behind, we skip the interpretation stage and launch straight into our research. As a result, we read sources and take notes without a clear idea of what's relevant, beyond some very general idea of the subject of the essay. Then finally, after hours of toil, tired and frustrated, and no clearer about what we're doing, we're left with a pile of irrelevant, unusable notes.

Yet just an hour or two spent interpreting the question would not only have saved us this wasted time, but would have given us a clear idea of what the question is getting at and a better understanding of what our tutors are looking for in our work. And even more, it would have given us the opportunity to get our own ideas and insights involved at an early stage. Without this, our work can seem routine and predictable: at best just the recycling of the ideas that dominate the subject.

So, what should you be looking for when you interpret a question? All essay questions tell you two things: the **structure** your essay should adopt for you to deal relevantly with all the issues it raises; and the **range of abilities** tutors are expecting to see you use in answering the question.

Interpreting the question

1 Saves us wasted time.
2 Gives us a clear idea of what the question is getting at.
3 Tells us what tutors are looking for.
4 Gets our own ideas involved so that our work is not so predictable and routine.

Structure

Take the first of these: the structure. In the following chapters you will learn how to unwrap the meaning and implications of the question, so that, before you go off to do your research, you will have prepared for yourself a clear structure of the issues that the question raises, so you know what you're looking for. In many questions this will develop out of your analysis of the key concepts in the question. Most of us struggle to do this well, but the skills involved can be easily learnt. You will be shown a simple three-step technique for analysing the most difficult concepts.

Then you will be shown how to brainstorm the question. Again, this is not a time-consuming task, but it will help you to use more of your own ideas and avoid wasting time in your research. Once you've learnt to do this, you will be able to make two important things clear to yourself before you start your research: what *you* know about the issues the essay question raises, and the questions you want your sources to answer. Without this the authors of the texts you read are likely to dictate to you and you'll find it difficult to distinguish between what's relevant and what's not.

Two things become clear:

1 What you know about the issues.
2 The questions you want your sources to answer.

Range of abilities

Then, once you've brainstormed your ideas and know what questions you want your sources to answer, there's just one more thing you need to be sure about before you begin your research. You must be clear about the range of abilities your tutors want to see you use. Otherwise you may find yourself tackling the essay in a way that doesn't answer the question, and noting information that is irrelevant.

Revealing the Structure

In this chapter you will learn:

- how to avoid irrelevance in your essay by carefully interpreting the meaning and implications of the question;
- how to reveal from the question the structure your essay should adopt;
- how to make sure your essay qualifies for the highest marks on offer.

Obviously it's important to realise that you're not embarking on a piece of open-ended research. You're answering a particular question that raises particular sharply focused issues. You must, therefore, be rigorously selective in collecting your material in the research stage, and in planning and writing the essay. You should use only material that is relevant to answering *this* question.

There are times in the research of every essay when you find yourself collecting material that is interesting and so closely argued that you find it difficult not to take notes from all of it, particularly when it's relevant to the wider implications of the topic. But if it's not relevant to the problems raised in *this* essay, ditch it! File it away for other essays, by all means, but don't let it tempt you in this essay. Otherwise your writing will lose focus and the reader will fail to understand what you're doing and why.

Analyse the key concepts

With these warnings in mind, it's essential to pin down two things: how many parts there are to the question and what weight you will need to give to each part. With many questions these structural problems can be solved by analysing the key concepts used in the question. Indeed, in most, if you fail to do this, the examiners will deduct marks: they will expect to see you show that you can analyse difficult abstract concepts and allow this to influence, if not determine, the structure of the essay.

Concepts reveal:

1. How many parts there are to the question.
2. What weight you should give to each one.

For example, markers for the University of London are told to award the highest marks (70–100 per cent) to those students who 'note subtlety, complexity and possible disagreements, [which they] will discuss', while only average marks (40–60 per cent) are to be awarded to the student who adopts a 'More relaxed application' of the question, and who 'follows [an] obvious line [and] uncritically accepts the terms of the question'.[1]

Similarly, in the Department of Sociology at Harvard University students are told:

Papers will be graded on the basis of the completeness and clarity of your analysis and the persuasiveness of your recommendations. As always, we will be appreciative of well-organized and well-written papers.[2]

The same emphasis can be found at the University of Oxford, where examiners look for a good analytical ability to distinguish first class and upper-second class scripts from the rest. In the marking criteria it's only in these two grades that any mention is made of analytical ability, with those failing to display it more likely to end up with lower-seconds and below. A first class script should show:

analytical and argumentative power, a good command of facts, evidence or arguments relevant to the questions, and an ability to organise the answer with clarity, insight and sensitivity.[3]

An upper-second class script also displays these qualities, but 'less consistently' or 'to a lesser degree' than a first class script.

Questions

To give you an idea of what this means in terms of actual questions, listed below is a selection of essay questions from different departments at different universities around the world. You will see that the answer to each of them hinges upon the same 'clarity, insight and sensitivity' that we can bring to the analysis of the key concepts in the question.

Some of them, as you can see, incorporate the concept in an assertion or opinion, which is not always obvious. Others present it in a statement of incontrovertible fact, which you must analyse before you can evaluate it to see whether it is consistent with the facts or just a subjective opinion.

Alternatively the concept could be presented in the form of a generalisation.

Concept

Indeed this is, in fact, exactly what concepts are: they are general classifications that we develop from our observation of individual instances of something. When we 'conceptualise' from our experience we abstract the general concept from a group of things that all share particular characteristics. All occupations that share particular characteristics are grouped together and classified under the concept 'profession'.

So it is important to identify the opinion, the statement or the generalisation and let the markers of your essay know that you have done so. The first thing they will look for is evidence that you have interpreted the question with 'clarity, insight and sensitivity' – that you have seen the point of it. In the following questions I have underlined the key concepts.

- Do the narrators of *Pride and Prejudice* and *Great Expectations* speak with the same kind of <u>irony</u>? (The English Novel, Harvard University)

- Discuss the management of health <u>needs</u> within a population group in the Primary Care setting. (Nursing and Applied Clinical Studies, Canterbury Christ Church University)
- What is <u>bribery</u> and can it be justified as an acceptable business practice? (Business and Administration, University of Newcastle, Australia)
- How do culture, race and ethnicity intersect in social work practice in a <u>multicultural society</u>? (Social Work, University of British Columbia, Canada)
- '<u>Geomorphology</u> is a branch of <u>geology</u> rather than of <u>geography</u>.' Discuss. (Geography, University of Oxford)
- 'Mill has made as naïve and artless a use of the naturalistic fallacy as anybody could desire. "<u>Good</u>", he tells us, means "<u>desirable</u>", and you can only find out what is desirable by seeking to find out what is actually desired. The fact is that "desirable" does not mean "able to be desired" as "visible" means "able to be seen".' G. E. Moore. Discuss. (Philosophy, University of Kent)
- '<u>Authority</u> amounts to no more than the possession of <u>power</u>.' Discuss. (Philosophy, University of Maryland)
- In the light of a number of recent high profile complaints about invasion of <u>privacy</u>, critically assess whether the press should continue to be self-regulating. (Journalism, University of Newcastle, Australia)
- Is <u>democracy</u> always compatible with individual <u>freedom</u>? (Politics, University of York)
- Are concepts of <u>anomie</u> and <u>subculture</u> still of value in the explanation of <u>criminality</u>? (Sociology, University of Oxford)
- What are the assumptions of the <u>revealed preference approach</u> to life valuation? (Biology, Stanford University)
- 'Free Trade leads to a <u>Paretian Optimum</u>.' 'Free Trade leads to <u>unacceptable inequalities</u>.' Discuss. (Economics, University of Oxford)

Key concepts

As you can see, no matter what the subject, the analysis of the important concepts is the main focus when we come to interpret questions like these. They may be couched subtly in everyday language, like 'unacceptable inequalities', 'needs' or 'bribery', or they may stand out like beacons warning us not to ignore them, like 'Paretian Optimum' and 'anomie and subculture'. So ask yourself, as you read the question, 'Are there words or expressions here which different writers use in different ways?' If there are, the different ways need to be analysed. There is a concept here which is up for interpretation.

Are there words or phrases used differently? If so, there is a concept which is up for interpretation.

Many of them, as you can see, are non-specialist words and phrases, which we use every day without much deliberation. Historians, for example, are fond of using concepts like 'revolution' and 'crisis' – seemingly inoffensive and untroubling words. But then, look at the British Industrial Revolution and you find yourself wondering, was this a revolution or just accelerated evolution? Indeed, what is a revolution and what's the difference between a revolt and a revolution? Does a revolution always involve violence? Is it all a question of the speed of change? If this is the case, the Industrial Revolution was more an evolution than a revolution, spread as it was over 70 to 100 years. Or is it more to do with the scale of change? If this is true, then there's little doubt that it was a revolution, what with the mechanisation of labour, factory production, the growth of cities and the development of mechanised transport.

What makes something a 'revolution'?

1 Is it the speed of change?
2 Or the scale of change?
3 Does it always involve violence?
4 What is the difference between a revolution and a revolt?

Much the same could be argued for a concept like 'bribe'. Again it appears to be inoffensive and untroubling – until you ask yourself, what do we really mean by the word? Whatever your answer, if you find you use the concept in more than one way, you have a structure emerging: each way in which you use it needs to be explored and its implications unwrapped.

Alternatively, you may be able to draw a key distinction between the concept and something very similar; this then provides your structure. You may find that the way we use the word 'bribe' suggests that we draw a distinction between it and commissions, gifts, tips and incentive bonuses and that this distinction is based on our belief that one is private, the other public. It might show that we regard bribes as private and secretive: that they are used to sidestep the ethical norms of the market to gain an undeserved advantage over competitors. In contrast, commissions, gifts, tips and incentive bonuses are public: wherever we work we know about them and we all have an equal chance to benefit from them. They are incentives for working harder and more efficiently.

Creating an essay structure by analysing a concept

1 Either from the different ways in which we use it.
2 Or by drawing a distinction between it and something similar.

The same analysis of concepts and arguments can be found in just about every subject. In politics there are concepts like freedom, ideology, equality, authority, power, political obligation, influence, legitimacy, democracy and many more. Do we really harbour not a single fear of ambiguity when we use such a large and important concept as freedom, or was Donovan Leitch right when he admitted in the 1960s that 'Freedom is a word I rarely use without thinking'? What do we mean by legitimacy and how does it differ from legality? And when we use the word 'democracy' do we mean direct or indirect democracy, representative or responsible, totalitarian or liberal, Third World or communist?

In literature, what do we mean by concepts like tragedy, comedy, irony and satire? Indeed, it's not unusual to find university departments devoting complete courses to unravelling the implications of these and others like them: concepts like class, political obligation, punishment, revolution, authority and so on. In the following course outline the concepts of punishment and obligation, and the distinction between law and morality, are central concerns that run throughout the course. Entitled 'Moral Reasoning – Reasoning In and About the Law', the course is part of the programme at Harvard University:

> How is law related to morality? How is it distinct? Do we have an obligation to obey the law? What, if anything, justifies the imposition of legal punishment? These issues, and related issues dealing with the analysis and justification of legal practices, will be examined using the writings of philosophers, judges, and legal theorists.[4]

Take just about any course at any university and you will see the same: that many of the challenges we face are questions about concepts. For example, the Philosophy Department of the University of Southampton describes its Philosophy of Science course in the following terms:

> This course examines concepts of evidence, justification, probability and truth, in relation to scientific explanation, causality, laws of nature, theory and fact; the distinctions between science and pseudo-science, as well as between science and metaphor, are among the topics explored. Examples illustrating the philosophical argument will be drawn from the histories of the physical, biological and social sciences.[5]

Most subjects have concepts like these about which we can ask, 'But what do we mean by X?' In nursing there are concepts like 'abuse', 'care' and 'dignity', and in social work 'inequality', 'discrimination', 'race' and 'racism'.

Analysing a concepts starts with the question, 'But what do we mean by X?'

But then, in contrast, we also come across concepts about which there is not this doubt about their core meaning, so it seems we can't question them in quite the same way: concepts like 'globalisation' and 'diversification' in business; 'membranes', 'dimensions', 'strings', even 'dark matter', in physics; 'vectors' and 'chromosomes' in genetics; 'entropy' and 'negentropy' in engineering; and 'neurosis' and 'psychosis' in psychology. These have a definite core meaning about which there may be little dispute.

But still, by analysing them in essay questions we reveal for ourselves not only the organisational structure for our essay, but their implications, which in many cases raise questions of emphasis and interpretation that will need to be discussed. We all know what is meant by 'globalisation', but there is considerable debate about its implications, the effects it's likely to have on us. There may be no doubt about what is meant by 'membrane theory' and 'multi-dimensional universes', but there are many questions we can ask about their implications for our understanding of the universe.

PRACTICE EXERCISE

Concepts

In your own subject, list as many as you can of the key concepts which are important to your understanding of the topics you are studying and which need to be analysed carefully. It should be possible for you to list at least ten.

Qualifying for the highest marks on offer

Syllabuses like these indicate the importance of key concepts both in the courses you're studying and in the essays you're expected to write. By analysing them you not only give your essay a relevant structure, but, equally important, you qualify for the highest marks on offer.

If, at this stage, you don't acknowledge the significance of these concepts by analysing their implications, you will almost certainly fail to analyse them in your essay. This will indicate not only that you haven't seen the point of the question, but, more seriously, that you haven't yet developed that thoughtful, reflective ability to question some of the most important assumptions we make when we use language. It is as if you're saying to the tutor marking your essay that you can see no reason why these concepts should raise any particular problem and, therefore, they deserve no special treatment.

Summary

1 Make sure you are rigorously selective in collecting material for your essay.
2 Analysing concepts is important to pin down how many parts there are to a question and what weight to give to each part.
3 Markers give most marks to those who demonstrate analytical ability.
4 Key concepts can be found in every subject.

In the next chapter

In the next chapter we will look at a particular concept and show how you can prise it open to reveal its implications. In so doing you'll see how you can capture more of your own ideas and insights.

Notes

1   *General Marking Instructions* (London: University of London, 1987).
2   Peter V. Marsden, *Sociology, 25: Introduction to the Sociology of Organizations* (Cambridge, MA: Harvard University, 2000).
3   *Greats Handbook* (Oxford: University of Oxford, 2000), p. 46.
4   Michael Blake, *Moral Reasoning, 62: Reasoning in and about the Law* (Cambridge, MA: Harvard University, 2000).
5   *What is Philosophy?* (Southampton: Department of Philosophy, University of Southampton, 1986), p. 16.

A Practical Example

In this chapter you will learn:

- how to distinguish between closed and open concepts: those that can be left to a dictionary, and those whose meaning is not so easy to find;
- how to prise open the structure of a concept by looking at the way we use it in everyday language and examples;
- how to capture your ideas and follow your train of thoughts in a clear structure of notes, while you analyse a concept.

Despite what we said in the previous chapter, there will still be those who ask, 'But why can't we just look up the meaning of these words in a dictionary, rather than go through the process of analysis?' And, of course, they're right: with some words this is all you need to do.

Open and closed concepts

What you might describe as 'closed concepts' usually have an unchanging, unambiguous meaning. Words like 'bicycle', 'bachelor' and 'triangle' each have a structure to their meaning, which is bound by logical necessity. We all agree to abide by certain conventions that rule the meaning of these words. So, if you were to say 'this is a bicycle with one wheel', or 'this triangle has four sides', no one would be in any doubt that you had made a logical mistake. When we use these words according to their conventions we are, in effect, allowing our understanding of the world to be structured in a particular way.

But with 'open concepts' it tends to be the reverse: our experience of the world shapes our concepts. As a result, such words cannot be pinned down just by looking them up in a dictionary. Their meaning responds to and reflects our changing experience: they change through time and from one culture to another. A dictionary definition, then, can only ever be a single snapshot taken in a constantly moving reel of images.

Open and closed concepts

1 Closed concept: unchanging meaning bound by logical necessity.
2 Open concept: meaning changes in response to different experience.

Aunt

If you take concepts like 'aunt' and 'democracy', you can see that in some societies and at some times they have a fairly unambiguous, unchanging meaning. The concept of 'aunt', for example, in some societies has a narrow definition exclusively grounded in relations by blood and marriage. But in other societies it is more open, encompassing not just relatives in the strict sense, but also older, long-standing friends of the family. This is likely to be a reflection of the social practices prevalent in different societies and at different stages in their development. A predominantly rural society with limited social mobility might use 'aunt' in the narrow sense. In contrast, in a society undergoing rapid industrialisation, with greater social mobility and less permanent communities, the concept is likely to be applied more loosely to close friends of the parents of a child. A young couple, having recently moved to a city some distance from their parents' homes, may seek to reconstruct the security of an extended family by including close friends as aunts and uncles to their children.

Democracy

Much the same can be said for a concept like 'democracy'. We might all agree that it implies government in accordance with the popular will, but beyond this principle everything is open. Western liberal democracies, believing that democracy implies one-person-one-vote, regular elections, secret ballots, multi-party politics and freedom of expression, are just one adaptation of the principle, serving the needs of a particular type of society: a liberal society with its emphasis on the importance of individualism, competition, free trade and consumer sovereignty.

In other societies, under different cultural influences, democracy has taken on different forms where accountability, participation, multi-party politics and even regular elections and voter sovereignty are much less important. More significant is the progress that is being made towards achieving democratic goals, like the eradication of epidemic diseases, alleviation of poverty, improvement in literacy and even industrialisation. The achievement of these goals, rather than voter approval at elections, is seen as evidence of the democratic nature of government.

Start with the way we use them

As you can see from this, if any of the concepts in essay questions are up for grabs in this way, if there is any doubt about the way we use them, then we need to analyse them. In most cases this means we start with words we use in everyday speech, in some cases sharpening and tightening them, in others just unpacking their ambiguities. In the process, this will more often than not give us the structure of our essay, in terms of the arguments we need to explore and develop.

Questions

1 How do I use the concept?
2 Do I use it in more than one way?

So, start by asking yourself, 'How do I use the concept – do I use it in more than one way?' Take the concept of freedom. We tend to talk about being free *from* things, like repression, constraints and restrictions of one form or another. I might say with some relief that I am finally free from pain having taken tablets for pain relief, or that a political prisoner has at last been freed from imprisonment. In both cases we're using the word in a negative way, in that something is being taken away, the pain or the imprisonment.

In contrast, we also tend to use the word in what we might describe as a positive way. In this sense the preposition changes from being free *from* something to being free *to* do something. We may say that because a friend has unexpectedly won a large amount of money she is now free to do what she has always wanted to do – to go back to college or to buy her own home. Governments, too, use the concept in this way, arguing that the money they are investing in education will free more people to get better, more satisfying jobs and to fulfil more of their dreams.

Exercise

Try it for yourself. Take the following question, which uses the concepts of authority and power. As you tackle the exercise below, think about how you use a concept like authority. If you find you use it in more than one way, then you have a structure emerging: each way in which you use it needs to be explored and its implications unwrapped.

Consider the question below and complete the exercise that follows:

'Authority amounts to no more than the possession of power.' *Discuss.*

Interpreting the question – 1   PRACTICE EXERCISE

Underline what you consider to be the key concepts and then analyse what you think are the main implications of the question.

This can be done in the form of sentences, but a more useful way is a short structure of notes that allows you to capture your ideas effectively and follow your train of thoughts quickly. Something like the structure shown on p. 13 would be a useful way of outlining the central implications of the question, which you can then follow up in your research and, later, in the essay. If you find any of the abbreviations in these notes mystifying, you can find the meaning of them in Chapter 14.

Answer

How do we use the concepts 'power' and 'authority'?

Clearly in this question the key concepts that have to be examined are 'power' and 'authority', and the relationship between them. Start, then, by asking yourself how you use these words. For this you need to summon up a few examples of situations in which both of these concepts might come up. These might involve figures of authority, like police officers, teachers, parents and other people who have the power and influence to get you to do what you might not otherwise want to do.

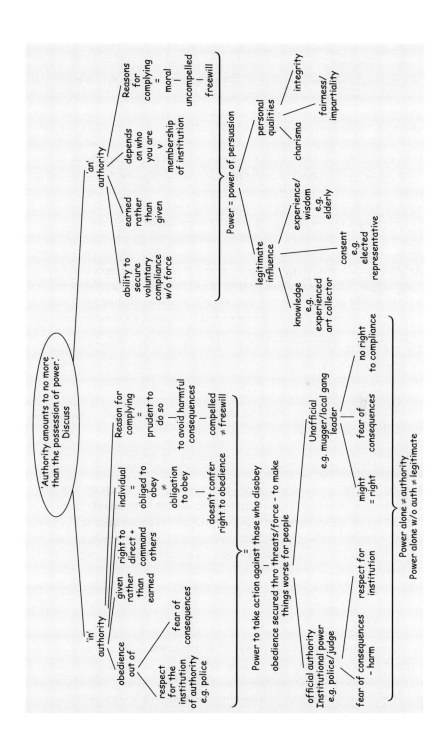

Power

From these examples you might conclude that the most obvious way in which we use the word 'power' is to describe somebody as having force, the capacity to compel us to do something against our wishes. A police officer has this sort of power, or a mugger, if he possesses a weapon with which to threaten us. But we also use it in the phrase 'the power of persuasion', in which the force involved is the force of an argument or the ability to persuade us to do something we would not otherwise do, by giving us good and persuasive reasons for doing it.

Authority

If the concept of power breaks down in this sort of way, then that of authority probably does too.

1 In authority

We talk about somebody being 'in' authority, somebody like a police officer or a judge. In this case we might not respect the person or the reasons they may give us for doing as they demand, but we might respect the institution they represent, or we might just comply with their orders because we fear the consequences of not doing so. Police officers have powers at their disposal that can seriously affect us, even denying us our liberty.

And, of course, there are others, like a mugger or a local gang leader, who can also compel us to do things, through force or threats of force, but who have no authority, although they still have this sort of power. This leads us to the conclusion that authority doesn't simply amount to the possession of power alone: the gang leader has no authority, in the usual sense, to command us to do anything, unlike the police officer, who has been appointed by representatives in parliament or the local council, whom we have elected. In this sense, then, the representatives and, in turn, their officially appointed officers, are said to have democratic legitimacy.

2 An authority

This seems to suggest that the word 'authority' has an alternative meaning – something similar to the sense we mean when we describe somebody as being 'an' authority. It may be that someone is an experienced art collector, so we are right to be persuaded by the arguments she presents because she knows what she's talking about. No force or compulsion is needed here, beyond, that is, the force of her arguments, her power of persuasion. She has the ability to secure voluntary compliance to her way of seeing things without the use of threats or force, because she has earned her authority.

We could say she has a **'right'** to her authority, although it's a different sense of 'right' from that exercised by the police officer; it's the right that has been earned rather than given. It's also different from the authority of the elected representative, although they can both be described as being 'an' authority. The difference is that the art collector's authority has been earned as a result of her study and devotion to her work, whereas the elected representative's authority has been earned as a result of putting himself up for election and campaigning for votes. Both have authority and exercise **'legitimate influence'** because of the **'respect'** they have earned.

Of course, others fit into this category of legitimate influence, too, even though they have earned their authority in different ways. The elderly in our communities have earned respect as a result of their years of experience and the wisdom this has brought.

Others have certain personal qualities that have given them a reputation for integrity and honesty – people we might go to for advice and support.

We could say that we have good **'moral' reasons** for complying with this sort of authority: that is, we have reasons that convince us to act in this way as a matter of our own free will; whereas when we comply with orders of those who are 'in' authority we do so not necessarily because we have any moral reason, that we respect them as individuals, but because we know that it would be prudent to do so. Otherwise we might suffer in one way or another as a result of the sanctions they can bring upon us. This threat is likely to force us, against our will, to comply with their orders.

In this sense we may be **'obliged'** to obey, if the local gang leader or the mugger is threatening to harm us, but we have no **'obligation'** to obey, because such threats are not backed by any right to make such orders; whereas the art collector has earned the right through many years of study, and police officers, while not having earned the same respect for themselves as a person, have been given the 'rightful', legitimate authority by our elected representatives.

This reveals the structure of the essay

The important thing to realise from analysing concepts in this way is how this opens up a question, revealing a clear structure that you can use in your essay. With this question you might have wondered, as most students do, 'Where do I start?' Now, having analysed 'authority' and revealed how it relates to 'power', you can see that there is a two-part structure to this essay.

The first part examines the relation between power and authority, when we talk about someone being 'in' authority, which leads us to support the assertion made in the question that authority does, indeed, amount to just the possession of power. But then, in the second half of the question, when we talk about someone being 'an' authority, we can argue that in fact there are more subtle and complex arguments that lead to the conclusion that 'authority' amounts to much more than this.

Some people find this sort of exercise easy to do. If, however, you've found it particularly difficult, don't despair. It is a lot simpler than it appears, as you'll see over the next four chapters.

Summary

1 A closed concept has an unchanging meaning.
2 An open concept changes to reflect different times and cultures.
3 To analyse an open concept, first ask yourself, 'How many different ways do I use it?'

In the next chapter

Over the next four chapters you will learn a simple three-step technique for analysing the most difficult of concepts.

Learning to Analyse

In this chapter you will learn:

- that of all the thinking skills, analysis is probably the most useful in opening up rich sources of ideas for you to use in an essay;
- how to free yourself from your own preconceptions, so that you can think more freely and see more of the implications of questions;
- how techniques, like the three-step technique, are the starting point for some of our best work.

Of course, not all the questions you tackle will offer up their concepts so easily as the authority/power question. In many of them the concept will hide, lurking behind the most innocent word. And in some questions it will be difficult to decide whether it's worth analysing the concept at all – it may not be central to the issues the question raises, taking you in a direction that's irrelevant. In these cases you just have to take the concept and analyse it carefully to see what's there. In most questions you'll find that by doing this you will open up a treasure house of all sorts of ideas you can use. The question just seems to unfold before your eyes and you know exactly the arguments to pursue and the research you need to do.

> Analysing a concept will open up a treasure house of ideas.

But, obviously, the key to this is to learn to analyse the concepts well. Of all the thinking skills we use this is the most neglected, even though it's probably the most useful. Without it we have no means of seeing a problem clearly, so that we can use our creative abilities to fashion a solution. Similarly, we have no means of seeing what it is about an argument that we dislike, so we can go on to criticise and improve it. In fact almost every intellectual activity begins with some form of analysis to make it clear what we're trying to tackle. It gives direction and purpose to our work. Without it we're likely to be at a complete loss as to how to set about the question.

Analytical ability

1 It helps us see the problem clearly.
2 It helps us criticise and improve arguments.
3 Almost every intellectual activity begins with it.
4 It gives direction and purpose to our work.

Unfortunately, we all seem to assume that everyone knows how to analyse, so there's no need to teach it. This, however, is far from the case. Most of us do it poorly because, rather than it being a natural thing to do, something we do almost by second nature, it seems to most of us to be the most *unnatural* thing. We have to force ourselves to ask the most deliberate questions about things that appear obvious. This seems to be unwarranted: it seems forced and unnecessary. I often ask students that most annoying and awkward of all questions, which begins, 'But what do you mean by … ?' Usually their response is to gasp in amazement that anyone, particularly one bearing the heavy responsibility for their education, could have any difficulty understanding a concept or the meaning of a word they use every day of their lives. Their usual response is, 'But everyone knows what that means!'

But then, once they've begun thinking about the word and arguing about what they all understand by it, they begin to realise that there is anything but consensus over its meaning. And, to their delight, as they analyse the implications of the concept they uncover for themselves rich sources of ideas they never knew they had, and the most perceptive observations that surprise even themselves.

We can be blinded by our preconceptions

In fact, the more awkward and deliberate this process feels the better the results are likely to be. In this lies the strength of the analytical method. We all carry around with us patterns of ideas through which we're able to structure unfamiliar experience and give it meaning. But, while this can be useful in giving us emotional safety, particularly in times of rapid change, it can be quite deceptive: we see what we want to see, even when it's perfectly obvious that we've got it wrong.

We've all heard police officers explain that if they have, say, 12 eyewitnesses to a crime, they will more than likely have 12 different accounts of what happened. We all carry certain preconceptions that prepare our minds to see what they want to see. For example, read the phrases in each of the triangles below.

Most people read them as 'Paris in the spring', 'Once in a lifetime', 'Bird in the hand'. But when they're urged to look a little closer, sooner or later they see the extra words, which their minds have selectively ignored because they were already prepared to see the familiar expressions. There are other examples, too, illustrating the same point: our preconceptions prepare our minds to see what they want to see.

A simple technique

To escape from these preconceptions and write essays that will be awarded the highest marks we must analyse the key concepts in the question. We all have the abilities to do this, if only we can develop the skills to use them. What follows is a simple technique that you can learn quickly.

But first, consider the question below and complete the exercise that follows:

'Advertisers seek only to ensure consumers make informed choices.' *Discuss.*

Interpreting the question – 2

PRACTICE
EXERCISE

Do what you did with the previous practice exercise and underline what you consider to be the key words. Then write a statement about the meaning and implications of the question.

Most students underline words like 'informed' and 'choices'. Some underline 'consumers', even 'advertisers'. But only those who feel confident about their analytical skills underline the word 'only'. Yet it not only alerts the reader to the suspicion that this may be a question largely about concepts, but also reveals the structure of the question.

Without it the statement is much weaker and the questions that are raised are much less contentious. The claim that advertisers try to inform the public is one that most of us would concede, albeit with certain reservations. But to claim that this is *all* they do is far more contentious and throws light on what we mean by the concept of 'advertisement'. Without it we might have been willing to accept the concept as if it raised no particular problem. Of course, it still might raise no particular problem, but you have to be sure.

Summary

1 The concept we need to analyse may be expressed in the most commonplace words.
2 Analysis is probably the most useful, although the most neglected, thinking skill.
3 It seems the most unnatural thing to do; yet if it seems awkward it is likely to produce the best results.
4 We are easily blinded by our unchallenged preconceptions.

In the next chapter

Given this, then, we have to work our way deliberately through three simple steps to analyse the concept. Once you've done this a few times and begin to feel confident about what you're doing, you'll be surprised at just how quickly you develop your skills. You'll be able to identify subtle distinctions and shades of meaning, and you'll bring to your analysis the sort of perceptive insight that you might never have suspected you possessed.

The Three-Step Technique – Steps 1 and 2

In this chapter you will learn:

- how we create our own concepts, even when we start out knowing nothing about the subject;
- how to start with your own examples and identify the common pattern of characteristics that underlies each one;
- how to analyse concepts into their essential characteristics.

In Step 1 of the three-step technique for analysing concepts we gather the evidence: the examples of the concept we want to analyse. Then, in Step 2, we analyse these examples to extract a common pattern of characteristics.

Step 1: Gather your typical examples

First, spend some time gathering the evidence. With the idea of 'advertisement' clearly in your mind, list what you think might be five or six of the most typical examples. Try to make them as different as possible. Avoid those for the same type of product or service, the same producer, and the same medium through which they are advertised. In this way you'll be able to strip away their differences to reveal more clearly their essential similarities.

Step 2: Analyse your examples

Now, using these examples, create your concept. In other words, analyse the common characteristics in each of your examples, isolating them so that you can then put them together to form the concept. This is one of those things we all know how to do, but most of us would be hard pressed to explain just how we do it. In effect it's simple pattern recognition. By recognising the common pattern of characteristics that each example possesses, we visualise what the concept might look like that underlies all the examples.

- Isolate the main characteristics common to each example.
- Using these, visualise what the concept might look like.
- This is simple pattern recognition.

It's always surprising how many people are willing to argue that they don't know how to do this, and that they've never done it in their lives, even though it's something they do every day, almost without thinking. When it comes to the advertising question there are always a sizeable number of students who claim they know nothing about advertising – certainly not enough to analyse the concept into its essential characteristics.

But we all know much more than we let on. Even with the briefest of acquaintances with a concept, after confronting just four or five examples of it for the first time, most people are quite clear about its core characteristics. Indeed, they can be surprisingly dogmatic in a discussion with others as to what is and what is not an example of it just minutes after declaring they knew nothing about it and had no idea how to analyse it.

EXAMPLE

For example, in the following case the concept is represented by a number of unfamiliar abstract patterns. As a result we're freed from all those preconceptions that might otherwise have forced our thinking down pre-programmed routes. Nothing has been said about the concept to lead us to believe that those who are authorities in these sorts of matters think the concept has certain definite characteristics. The concept is ours to form without assistance from anyone else.

PRACTICE EXERCISE

Analysing the concept

Examine in turn each of the figures on pp. 22–23. As you do this you will see a concept emerge. For want of a better name, let's call it an 'olic'.

Not all of the figures are olics, so you will have to form your idea of the concept and then use it to distinguish between the olics and the non-olics.

Once you've looked at all the figures, answer the following:

1 Which of the figures are olics?
2 Analyse the concept of an olic and list three of the essential characteristics common to all.

1

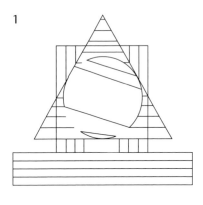

2

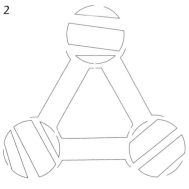

3

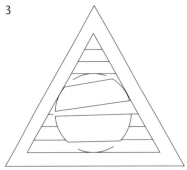

4

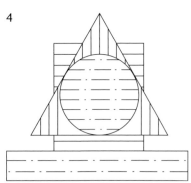

5

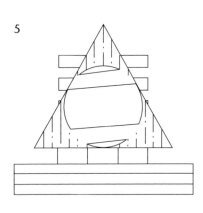

6

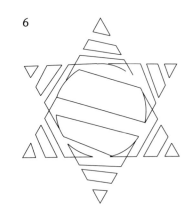

7

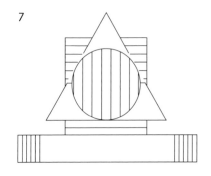

8

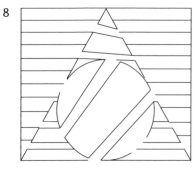

9

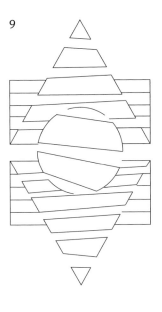

10

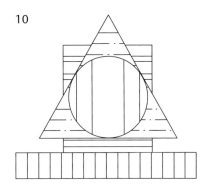

11

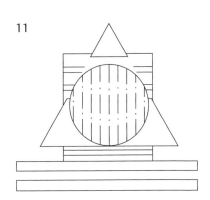

12

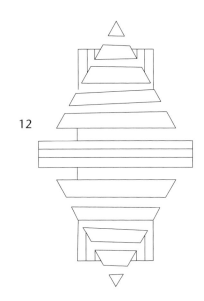

Answers

1 These figures are olics: 1, 4, 5, 7, 10, 11.

2 You could have chosen your three characteristics from any of the following:

- a long rectangular base
- a circle at the centre
- a triangle surrounding the circle
- a rectangle surrounding the circle and intersecting the triangle.

As you can see from this, even though you haven't come across an olic before, the concept emerges, leaving you in no doubt about its essential characteristics.

Analysing the concept of 'advertising'

PRACTICE
EXERCISE

Now consider the advertising question again:

'Advertisers seek only to ensure consumers make informed choices.'
Discuss.

Go through the first two steps, one at a time, deliberately and carefully. Don't rush them; they're important. If you need to, look back at the way we analysed the concepts of authority and power; you're doing exactly the same. It also helps if you can use a note-taking strategy, like the pattern notes we used with the authority/power question. This will allow you to capture your ideas effectively and follow your train of thoughts quickly.

Step 1: Gather your typical examples

First choose, say, five or six examples of advertisements that you may have seen on the television, the internet or in magazines.

Step 2: Analyse your examples

Now do the same with the concept of advertising as you've just done with the concept of olic. Using the question as your guide, ask yourself if there are certain essential characteristics that are always present, without which it would be wrong to describe something as an advertisement.

From your examples it will no doubt be clear that all advertisements are trying to persuade you in various ways. Yet, at the same time, it might be just as reasonable to conclude that they are also trying to inform you. In some cases this might not amount to much, but in most advertisements it's likely to be more than just the name of the product.

Can an advertisement be just informative?

In the light of this and the implications of the question that you revealed earlier, you should be asking yourself if an advertisement is always persuasive, or can it be just informative without attempting to get you to choose or act in one way or another?

You might conclude that almost all advertisements are informative, but that's not all they do. This analysis suggests there are two kinds of advertisement: those that seem largely preoccupied with passing on information, yet in fact are covertly manipulative; and those that are overtly manipulative, in that their intention is obvious – to persuade us as consumers to buy their product. Now you have a simple structure for the concept, which you can develop in the light of your examples in the same way we did for the olic and for the authority/power question.

Advertisements – 2 kinds:

1 Covertly manipulative – appear to be just informing.
2 Overtly manipulative – obviously seek to persuade us.

Covertly manipulative advertisements

Now, first take one side, then the other. Some advertisements that appear to be covertly manipulative, like those concerned with **public information**, say about a new tax or changes in regulations, or government health warnings about smoking or the use of fire alarms, seem to be entirely concerned with informing us. However, that's not to say there isn't a message hidden in the information. The government no doubt would like to persuade you not to continue to smoke, or to organise yourself so that you pay your taxes promptly.

Other advertisements clearly are intent on promoting the sales of their products. But, nevertheless, they do this through a strategy that disseminates **product information** in order to raise awareness of new products, new designs and new technology. New computer games, smartphones and technology, like tablet computers, are all promoted, at least in the initial stages, by advertisements that are designed to inform and to promote awareness of the new type of product or design that's on the market.

- Public information – for example, government health warnings.
- Product information.

Overtly manipulative advertisements

In the same way, the overtly manipulative advertisements can be broken down into their types. At the very least they attempt to manipulate the consumer by **using information selectively** to emphasise what's good about their product and to omit what's bad. Others will use comments and information **taken out of context** to promote their product, even though these may be taken from reports and reviews that are highly critical of it. An unfavourable report from a consumer association might contain just a single sentence of praise, yet it will be this that finds its way into the advertisement.

Equally effective are advertisers who appeal to a convincing, though **distorted, picture** of what is taken for **common sense or accepted values** in our societies. Archetypal characters and scenarios are created to evoke predictable responses that advertisers believe we will all share. Those promoting slimming products try to convince us that everyone wants to be slim, that it's associated with success, and that if you're overweight this is a sign of social failure and self-indulgence.

But perhaps the most common strategy is for advertisers to sell their products by **associating them with our strongest feelings, desires and prejudices**. In this way they can bypass our reason, thereby short-circuiting our ability to make conscious choices. As our understanding of the psychology of the individual has grown, so too has the advertiser's capacity to tap into our deepest motivations and develop more effective means of manipulation by exploiting the sex, status and prejudices of the consumer. Indeed, the most effective means of doing this, subliminal advertising, is now banned or regulated by many governments.

- Uses information selectively.
- Distorts comments and information by taking them out of context.
- Appeals to common sense or accepted values.
- Associates the product with our feelings, desires and prejudices.

Answer

Once you've done this, look at the analysis in the structure on p. 26. It's unlikely that yours will be a lot different. You may use different examples and you may have seen things that I haven't, but the final structure is likely to be quite similar. If you

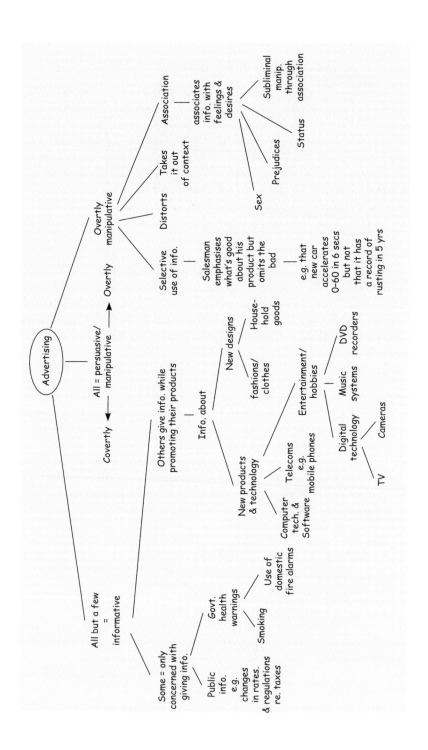

think you haven't gone far enough in your analysis, or you haven't seen enough, don't worry too much. You will get better at this with practice. And you've still got Step 3 to come.

If you would like to develop your skills by doing similar exercises, you can find more on the companion website. In fact, there is also a transcript of one of my tutorials with a student, in which we work through each of the stages. This reveals very clearly what we considered and the way we argued as we analysed the concept.

Summary

1 List five or six examples that are as different from each other as possible.
2 Note those characteristics that are common to each one.
3 This is the concept: the pattern of core characteristics.

In the next chapter

Although we have now seen how we analyse a concept, it might still be difficult to see exactly how we think up examples and use them to create a concept. In the next chapter we will do just this, working through each of these stages so you can see clearly how you do it.

Creating Your Own Concept

In this chapter you will learn:

- simple techniques to generate the examples you need to create your own concept;
- how to create your concept by identifying the common, core characteristics in all of these examples;
- how you can use the dissimilarities between some of these examples to test your concept in Step 3 of the three-step technique.

Most students have no difficulty creating the concept of an 'olic' as we did in the previous chapter, yet when they come to create a concept in their academic work it seems altogether more difficult and technical, requiring skills that only a few possess. This is simply not the case. So, before we move on to Step 3 in the three-step technique, let's examine exactly what we do to gather our typical examples and then analyse their common characteristics to create the concept. You should then be able to use the same process confidently in your academic work.

Gathering your typical examples

Imagine meeting up with a friend for coffee. She arrives late looking quite flustered, so you ask her what's wrong. She tells you that a tragedy has just occurred: she has broken the heel on one of her new shoes. To put this into some perspective you might argue that, if she thinks about it carefully, she'll find it's hardly a 'tragedy'. You might then define what you think a tragedy is by thinking up examples and pointing out their common characteristics.

We do exactly the same in our academic work. In fact the concept of 'tragedy' itself could arise in essay questions in a range of disciplines from English literature, history and philosophy to psychology, social work, economics and politics:

- History: Discuss the claim that 'The tragedy for the German people in the inter-war years was the failure of the Weimar Constitution to produce stable governments'.
- English literature: 'To what extent does Iago contribute to the tragedy of Othello?'
- Social psychology: 'How can we live with integrity in the face of temptation or tragedy?'

As we've already seen, the key to questions like these is to analyse the implications of the concept and for this we need to think of examples in the same way. So, how do we think of examples? If you find this difficult, start by asking yourself three questions.

1 How do I use the concept?

When we analysed the concept of authority we started by asking ourselves: 'How do I use the concept – do I use it in more than one way?' If you find it difficult to think of the different ways you use the concept, work through the following stages, asking yourself how you use it in:

- *Your own experience: events in your own life or conversations you have had.*
  You might remember a conversation with a friend in which she told you the tragic story of an emergency worker who rushed to the scene of an accident only to find that his own family were among the dead.
- *Your subjects: that you are studying.*
  You might be studying English literature, so you can probably recall examples of Shakespearean tragedies:

  Othello:
    Although he loves her, Othello murders Desdemona after Iago has convinced him she has been unfaithful. When he realises that she was not, he commits suicide.

  Romeo and Juliet:
    Juliet secretly marries Romeo, but her parents organise her marriage to Paris against her will. So she takes a sleeping potion to bring on the semblance of death. Romeo, believing she is dead, drinks poison at her tomb. When she awakes a few moments later to find him dead, she stabs herself to death.

  Macbeth:
    Driven on by his lust for power and his wife's ambitions, Macbeth destroys everything he loves: his best friend, his wife and finally himself.

- *Other subjects: you might have studied or read about.*

  Oedipus:
    Although warned by the Delphic oracle that he would kill his father and marry his mother, Oedipus unknowingly does just that, despite all his efforts to avoid it.

  Van Gogh:
    Despite his enormous talent and influence on modern art, he only painted for a few brief years. After spending some months in a mental institution, he took his own life at the age of just 37.

- *Reading outside your studies: novels you have read, papers, magazines, articles.*
  You might have come across stories like the following:

    After years of searching, a man finally discovers the whereabouts of his father, whom he has never seen. He takes a flight to meet him, but as the plane lands he suffers a heart attack and dies.
    A man backs his car out of his garage, but he runs over and kills his young son who, unknown to him, was playing in the drive behind the car.

- *Media reports: TV, radio and internet stories.*
  These are well-known events like the following:

    In the early 1990s, the chapel at Assisi, which contained many irreplaceable works of art, was destroyed by an earthquake, along with all its contents.

When terrorists destroyed the twin towers of the World Trade Center in New York on September 11, 2001, by flying two passenger aircraft into them, many on board the planes made last-minute calls on their mobile phones to say goodbye to their loved ones.

2 What sort of thing am I referring to?

If this doesn't help, ask yourself a second question: 'What sort of thing am I referring to when I use the concept?' This means recalling simple everyday situations in which you *might* find yourself talking about a 'tragedy', even if you don't actually use the word. This is different from the first question in that these are not situations in which you have *actually* used the concept. You are just imagining a situation in which you think you might use it.

3 How does it differ from similar things?

To help you with this question it is often useful to ask a third: 'How does it differ from similar things?' When I use the word 'bribe', how does it differ from other things, like commissions, gifts, tips and incentive bonuses? When I use the word 'authority', how does it differ from things like power, force, legitimacy and influence? So, when I use the word 'tragedy', how does it differ from similar things, like 'misfortune', 'accident', 'disaster' and 'catastrophe'?

Questions

1 How do I use the concept? Do I use it in more than one way?
2 What sort of thing am I referring to?
3 How does it differ from similar things?

Thinking of examples   PRACTICE
                                                              EXERCISE
Take the following essay question and think of six or seven examples of the concept of
'need' by working through the questions above:

'The most serious challenge that all health services face is how to divide the available
resources among those who need it.' *Discuss.*

Analyse your examples and create your concept

Now, using the examples of 'tragedy', we need to abstract the general from the specific. In other words, we identify the common characteristics in each example and then put them together to form the general concept. The obvious way to do this is to search first for similarities and then for dissimilarities.

Similarities

Some similarities will be obvious, but once you've noted these, if you start to struggle, ask yourself some simple, routine questions. Depending on whether the concept refers to types of people, things or events, you will discover that the same questions reappear each time you create a concept. For example, with the concept of 'tragedy' we are talking about a type of event, so ask yourself the following questions:

1   What actions were involved?
2   What were the results?
3   Who was responsible?
4   What were their motives and intentions?
5   What were the effects on others?

Not all of your answers to these questions will indicate common characteristics, but usually you will find that two or three of them do. And you may not find these characteristics in all of your examples: only four or five examples may have them. We will come back to this later. If you look at the examples of 'tragedy' that we have listed, you will probably conclude from these questions that our concept has the following characteristics:

1   These are events that involve some form of death, killing or destruction.
2   They involve the loss of something irreplaceable.
3   Those caught up in them cannot be held morally responsible for their actions, because they are driven by powerful emotions or they are unaware of important facts or they involve circumstances which are beyond their control.
4   Despite their intentions, which are in many cases good, they suffer the loss of those things they value most.

Dissimilarities

Having found similarities, now start looking for dissimilarities. These can often be quite subtle nuances in each example that seem to distinguish them from the rest. From the examples we are using you might find that only some have the following characteristics:

1   They involved people acting without knowing all the facts, which were hidden or undisclosed. There is an element of 'tragic irony' here, in that those involved were driven by a strong, overpowering desire that obscured the likely outcome of choosing to act as they did, while to the rest of us who looked on it was perfectly clear.
2   Some tragedies, like those of Macbeth and Oedipus, are prophetic: they involve a prediction that comes about despite the person involved knowing it and despite all his attempts to avoid it.
3   Some, like the Assisi tragedy and the works of art Van Gogh might have painted, involve not just people, but things that are irreplaceable.

Corralling

As you can see from these dissimilarities, you will often have, say, seven examples, four of which have the same core characteristics, while the other three fail to match them in all respects. That's OK; in fact it's ideal. Now we need to corral the four similar examples, using these to create our concept, and then use the remaining three to test it in Step 3 of the three-step technique. So, although we might begin with a simple concept, as we work through Step 3 we develop this by adding subtle nuances that often result in a complex, fascinating concept that provides the basis of an equally fascinating and subtle essay.

Summary

1   Analysing examples to create a concept does not involve special skills, but just those you use every day.
2   By asking yourself a series of simple questions you can routinely think of relevant examples in your own academic work.
3   Similarly, once you have your examples there are simple questions you can routinely ask to create your concepts.
4   The key to this lies in identifying the similarities and dissimilarities between your examples.
5   By corralling all those that are similar you can create your concept, while leaving those that are dissimilar for Step 3 of the three-step technique.

In the next chapter

Now that you've mapped out the concept, the next step is to test it in much the same way you did when you compared an olic with a non-olic. In this way you will sharpen and tighten up the concept, and in the process you will begin to see the best way of tackling the essay in terms of the structure you should adopt.

Step 3 – Test Your Concept

In this chapter you will learn:

- how to distinguish between those characteristics that are essential to the concept and those that are merely accidental;
- how to create a clear structure for the concept, which you can then use to catch the relevant ideas and evidence as you research the topic;
- how to test and refine your original analysis of the concept to uncover subtle distinctions and shades of meaning, for which you will earn high marks.

Now that you have your concept clearly analysed in a structure, it's time to test it. You may have the overall structure broadly right, but there may be details that are wrong, or subtle distinctions you haven't seen. By testing your concept you will shake out those characteristics that are essential and ditch those that are only accidental to it. In the process you will have sharpened up your understanding of the core characteristics. As a result you will have a fairly well-defined structure to catch the relevant ideas and evidence as you research the topic, and for most questions you will probably find that you already have the broad structure on which you will be able to build the plan of your essay.

- Testing your concept reveals subtle distinctions you may have missed.
- You will separate the essential from the accidental characteristics.
- This gives you a structure to guide your research.
- In many cases it forms the plan of the essay.

To test your concept of advertising in this way you need only take some simple, but quite deliberate, steps. Using the structure below you can follow what we are doing in each of these tests as we work through them.

1 Borderline cases

First, with the structure of your concept in front of you try to think of a borderline case, an example of advertising that doesn't fit comfortably within it, because either it doesn't have features that are in your structure, or it has others that are absent from it. Our objective is to identify all those features in our structure that are merely accidental. In the previous chapter we found that a number of our examples could be corralled so that we could abstract the concept from them. This left others that were not such a good fit. In these you are likely to find the examples you need for borderline, contrasting and doubtful cases.

Structure The three-step technique	
Activity	**Objective**
Step 1: Examples List five or six of the most typical examples that are as different as possible.	To get material that will illustrate similarities and differences.
Step 2: Analyse Pattern recognition – identify the common characteristics and their interrelations.	To form the prototype concept.
Step 3: Test **1 Borderline cases** Compare our concept with an example that either lacks features that are in our structure, or has others that are absent from it.	To identify all those features in our structure that are merely accidental.
2 Contrasting cases Compare our concept with an example that doesn't share one or more of the core characteristics of our structure.	To identify the core characteristics and their interrelations.
3 Doubtful cases Test the core characteristics by examining a case in which it would be difficult to accept their consequences.	To refine the distinctions in our analysis to get a clearer, sharper understanding of the core characteristics and their interrelations.

Once you've thought of a borderline case, analyse its characteristics to see if, in fact, it does fit after all. You may find there's more to this form of advertising than you first thought and that it does, in fact, fit within the structure. Alternatively, after thinking through all the possibilities it may become clear that it doesn't fit and you will have to adjust your structure to take account of it.

A bus or railway timetable   EXAMPLE

For example, take a form of advertising that appears to be wholly informative, say a bus or railway timetable. This is just a list of routes with times for arrivals and departures. There may be no enticing message at the top inducing you to 'Come to sunny Bognor, children travel free!' There may be no catchy jingles encouraging you to 'Let the train take the strain!' It might be just a simple notice containing travel information, erected in a prominent position in a bus or train station.

So, the question we have to ask is, does this suggest that advertisements can be just informative after all, or are we right in assuming that behind all of this information lies the covert message that we ought to travel by train or bus because it's more convenient and easier, and therefore less stressful than the alternatives? We could argue that in putting out this sort of information, the intentions of the managers of the bus and train companies are not just to give us information, but to so impress us with their efficiency and the convenience of travelling this way that we will use their services more frequently.

Tragedy   EXAMPLE

With our concept of 'tragedy' that we worked on in the previous chapter, we could take as our borderline example Oedipus or Macbeth, both of which have a characteristic the others don't: they predict that the tragic events will come to pass. Now we have to decide whether we believe this to be just an accidental characteristic or whether we need to revise our concept.

2 Contrasting cases

Once we've made our decision we can move to the second stage and test our analysis again, this time by imagining an example that is the complete contrast to this – one that doesn't share one or more of the core characteristics of our structure. Our objective is to identify the core characteristics and their interrelations. In this case you could choose an example that is composed of nothing but factual information, where the intention of the advertiser seems to amount to nothing more than to inform the public. So, the core characteristic that is missing seems to be the intention to persuade consumers.

A village sign   EXAMPLE

You might be travelling through the countryside one summer afternoon, and you come into a small village. At the centre of the village is a small green, dominated by a huge tree. On this tree someone has attached a small handwritten sign with the words:

August 31st
The Annual Village Fête.
On the Village Green.
Starting 3 p.m.

There is no enticing message with promises of gifts and untold wealth for the lucky person who wins the fête raffle, not even the simple appeal 'Come to the village fête!' There is nothing but information.

In this example, if we are still to assume that it is the *intentions* of those who put out the information that define a notice as an advertisement, then they are more deeply hidden here than those of the people who framed the bus and railway timetables. Nevertheless, we might still be justified in arguing that the writer of the sign had one unmistakable intention in putting it up: to encourage more people to attend and participate. This would no doubt mean more money for the local appeal to restore the church bells or to build an extension to the old people's day centre.

Tragedy   EXAMPLE

Our concept of tragedy seems to involve exclusively people. So, if we take as our contrasting example the Assisi tragedy, which involves no people, only things, we will be able to clarify one of our core characteristics that this involves not just the deaths of people, but the destruction of all things that are irreplaceable.

3 Doubtful cases

In both cases we seem to have reached a stage where we have shaken out a core characteristic that was not sufficiently clear in our original analysis. In the advertising case we seem to be saying that even though an announcement is concerned with imparting information, with advertisements this is only surface appearance. What matters above all are the intentions of those who frame the notice. In an advertisement they are suggesting or attempting to persuade us to adopt a certain course of action; whereas with a simple statement of information there are no ulterior motives: they are just presenting information and leaving it there.

Given this, we must move to the next stage and test the consequences of adopting this distinction in the context of our essay question. We need to imagine cases in which it would be difficult for us to accept these consequences. Our objective is to get a clearer understanding of the core characteristics and their interrelations. Clearly, if we're right in thinking the way we have been, then any announcement or statement of fact that suggests a possible course of action is an advertisement.

Health statements   EXAMPLE

For example, a factual statement made in a television programme that smoking cigarettes is responsible for over 80 per cent of cases of lung cancer, or a report by a health authority that a diet containing large quantities of salt is likely to lead to high blood pressure, are both suggestive of a course of action. But it would be odd to describe either of these two statements as an advertisement.

If this is right, then we have reached a point where we can refine another of the distinctions that was in our original analysis. Each time we do this we inject more subtle shades of meaning for which we will earn high marks from a tutor who reads the arguments we've developed so far. You might consider arguing that these are not advertisements in the normal sense, by virtue of their subject matter. They are concerned with contentious political and social issues, not commercial products and services that businesses or local communities are trying to sell.

Indeed, those who suspect the intentions of the people making this type of statement might describe it as propaganda. This could include tobacco companies, who at one stage might have criticised governments for warning people about the dangers of smoking cigarettes. If this is right, we might conclude that advertising and propaganda, in so far as they share the same intention of trying to get people to choose and act in a particular way, are of the same family, only distinguishable by their different subject matter.

Now, if we take the general structure we started with at the beginning of this chapter and apply it to the advertising question, you can see clearly what we have achieved in each stage.

Structure   The three-step technique: advertising question

Activity	Objective
Step 1: Examples List five or six of the most typical examples that are as different as possible.	To get material that will illustrate similarities and differences.
Step 2: Analyse Pattern recognition – identify the common characteristics and their interrelations.	To form the hypothesis: the prototype concept, which you can see on the pattern note structure.
Step 3: Test **1 Borderline cases** Bus or railway timetable – no promotional messages, just information about arrivals, departures and routes.	 Advertisements = not just informative – covert message beneath. In this case it is the efficiency and convenience of the trains and buses.
2 Contrasting cases Village fête sign – no covert message beneath the information.	Core characteristic = the intention of those who put out the information that defines it as an advertisement.
3 Doubtful cases Factual statements about the effects of smoking and salt consumption. The intention = to change habits, but they are not advertisements in the normal sense.	Difference might be subject matter. Persuasive intentions involving contentious political and social issues might be better described as propaganda.

If you are uncertain about any of this, go to the companion website (www.howto writebetteressays.com) and look at the transcript of one of my tutorials. This very detailed account will give you a clear idea of what you need to be doing and the questions you need to be asking as you test your concept in each of these three ways.

As you can see, as we have worked our way through each of these stages we have deliberately asked awkward questions to test and refine the distinctions we made in our original analysis. By doing so we've not only revealed some important subtle shades of meaning, for which a tutor will award us high marks, but in effect we have rehearsed some of the more complex arguments we'll develop when we come to write the essay.

Analysing concepts

IN YOUR OWN WORK

- Choose an essay question from one of the subjects you are studying. As you've already done in the practice exercises, underline the key words and write a short statement outlining the meaning and implications of the question. This will help you clarify the key concept in the question, which you will need to analyse.
- Now analyse the concept deliberately, step by step. First, think up three or four <u>typical examples</u> that reflect the way the concept is used in the question. Then <u>analyse</u> the core characteristics, those that are common to each of your examples. This will take a little thought,

but remember the 'olic': your mind will have a fairly clear idea of the concept. You've just got to bring it in front of your mind's eye so that you can list the core characteristics. You may only come up with three or four, but that's fine.

- Then, <u>test it</u>. Think up a <u>**borderline case**</u>, one that doesn't easily fit. This will lead you to refine your original concept. Other characteristics may appear that are far more important, or you may adjust one or two of those you've listed. Once this is done, test your new refined concept by imagining a <u>**contrasting case**</u> that seems to conflict with it. This might lead you to adjust your concept again – either that, or you will realise that there's more to your example and it does fit within your concept after all. Either way, after you've done this you will no doubt feel that you've mapped out the concept: you've got all the core characteristics sharply in focus.
- Armed with this, you can now go back and reveal more of the implications of the question by imagining a <u>**doubtful case**</u>. This will throw a sharper light on the consequences of using the concept in the way it was used in the question. At the end of this, as a result of your careful analysis, you're quite likely to have in front of you, in your notes, the structure that will form the basis of the final essay.

Now that you've analysed the concepts and unwrapped the implications of the question, you're in a better position to research the essay. You should have a clear structure of the key issues raised. In a great many questions these will develop out of your analysis of the key concepts in the question. In others they will come from your initial attempt to describe what you believe to be its meaning and implications. Either way, you cannot begin your research without arming yourself with a clear idea of what the question is getting at and what you should be looking for when you begin to read and take notes.

Summary

1. Testing your concept is important to identify the core characteristics and to ditch those that are only accidental to it.
2. This will give you a structure through which you will catch more relevant ideas as you research your essay.
3. It is likely that it will also give the broad outline of the plan of the essay.

In the next chapter

In the next chapter we will look at the best way of getting your own ideas down, so that when you begin your research you know what questions you want answered and you're less likely to be dictated to by the texts you read.

Brainstorming

In this chapter you will learn:

- how to use more of your own ideas through effective brainstorming;
- why it is important to separate analysis from brainstorming;
- how to get clear answers from the texts you use;
- how to avoid being dictated to by the authors you read.

Over the previous six chapters we have seen how important it is to interpret carefully the meaning and implications of questions. Learning to do this well means we're better able to see the structure our essays should adopt in order to produce a full and relevant answer to the question. What's more, we're less likely to overlook the significant, though subtle, issues that might be hidden in the question. Almost inevitably, when we overlook the importance of doing this well, we end up with essays that not only are confusing and poorly organised, but miss the point.

In this lies the importance of the three-step technique. It develops those skills you need in order to use your analytical abilities effectively. Once you've used it two or three times, you'll be confident that you can interpret any question whose meaning and implications depend upon a perceptive analysis of its concepts. But, as we saw, there are other reasons why these skills and abilities are so important. If we overlook them we're likely to disqualify ourselves from the highest marks on offer. Those who mark our essays are likely to assume that we simply haven't developed that thoughtful, reflective ability to question the assumptions we make when we use language.

Analysis and brainstorming: two different things

What all this amounts to is the importance of 'staking your claim' as early as possible, indeed as soon as you get the question. This involves two things: first, as we've seen, thinking through *your* analysis of the concepts and implications of the question, and second, writing down *your own* ideas on the question.

Staking your claim

1 Think through *your* analysis of the concepts and the implications of the question.
2 Write down *your own* ideas on the question.

It's now time to turn to the second of these: brainstorming your own ideas. This means that you empty out your mind on the subject, without the aid of books. As quickly as possible you track the flow of your ideas as you note what you know about the subject and what you think might be relevant to the question.

Brainstorming

1 Empty out your mind on the subject without the aid of books.
2 Track the flow of your ideas as you note what you know about the subject.
3 Note everything you think might be relevant to the question.

You might be tempted to think this sounds strikingly similar to what we've just done – so much so that you're tempted to assume that brainstorming is just a part of the process of analysis. After all, they both involve your own ideas, which you get down on paper as quickly as you can without the aid of books. But they are, in fact, quite different, and if you allow yourself to merge the two, skimping on one, you will almost certainly have problems.

In *analysis* you're unwrapping what's already there. It may be buried deep, but by a process of introspection, through which you examine the different ways you use a concept such as 'authority' or 'advertisement', you come to see more clearly the contours of the concept, its essential characteristics.

In contrast, with *brainstorming* you are going beyond the concept: this is synthesis, rather than analysis. You are pulling together ideas, arguments and evidence that you think may have a bearing on the question's implications that you have already revealed through your analysis. So, whereas analysis is a convergent activity, brainstorming is divergent, synthesising material from different sources. Confuse the two and you'll do neither well.

- Analysis is *convergent*: you unwrap what's already there.
- Brainstorming is *divergent*: you pull together different ideas, arguments and evidence.

The importance of brainstorming

If you overlook this distinction and merge the two activities, you're likely to struggle with two problems. First, if you abandon analysis too soon and embark on brainstorming your focus will shift away from the implications of the question and the concepts it contains. Consequently, you're likely to find that you don't have the guidelines to direct your brainstorming into profitable areas. You will find a lot less material and much of what you do unearth you will no doubt discover later that you cannot use because it's irrelevant.

On the other hand, if you analyse without brainstorming you'll fail to arm yourself with *your* ideas and what *you know* about the topic. As a result, almost certainly two things will happen:

1 **The authors you read for your research will dictate to you**
   Without your own ideas to protect you, it will be difficult, at times impossible, for you to resist the pull of their ideas and the persuasiveness of their arguments. As a result you'll find yourself accepting the case they develop and the judgements they

make without evaluating them sufficiently, even copying large sections of the text into your own notes.

2 **And, equally serious, you will find it difficult to avoid including a great mass of material that is quite irrelevant to your purposes**

All of this material may have been relevant to the authors' purposes when they wrote the book, but *their* purposes are rarely identical with *yours*. Nevertheless, having spent days amassing this large quantity of notes, it's most unlikely that you're going to find the detachment somewhere to decide that most of these notes are irrelevant to your essay and you've got to ditch them. You're more likely to convince yourself that they can 'be made' relevant, and you end up including them in a long, discursive, shapeless essay, in which the reader frequently feels lost in a mass of irrelevant material.

So, brainstorming should be seen as distinct from analysis. It needs to be done straight after you've completed your analysis, which in turn needs to be done as soon as you have decided upon the question you are going to tackle. This will give your subconscious time to go away and sort through your data banks for what it needs before you begin to set about your research.

> If you don't make clear *your own* ideas and *your* interpretation of the implications of the question, your thinking is likely to be hijacked by authors and their intentions. If you don't ask your authors clear questions you are not likely to get the clear, relevant answers you want.

Empty out your mind

Now that you've analysed the implications, use this to empty out your mind on the question. Most of us are all too eager to convince ourselves that we know nothing about a subject and, therefore, we have no choice but to skip this stage and go straight into the books. But no matter what the subject, I have never found a group of students, despite all their declarations of ignorance and all their howls of protest, who were not able to put together a useful structure of ideas that would help them to decide as they read what's relevant to the essay and what's not.

Once we tap into our own knowledge and experience, we can all come up with ideas and a standard by which to judge the author's point of view, which will liberate us from being poor helpless victims of what we read. We all have ideas and experience that allow us to negotiate with texts, evaluating the author's opinions, while we select what we want to use and discard the rest.

- We all know something about the subject before we reach for our books.
- We all have ideas and experience to evaluate the author's opinions and select what we want.

Throughout this stage, although you're constantly checking your ideas for relevance, don't worry if your mind flows to unexpected areas and topics as the ideas come tumbling out. The important point is to get the ideas onto the page and to let the mind's natural creativity and self-organisation run its course, until you've emptied out your mind. Later you can edit the ideas, discarding those that are not strictly relevant to the question.

**PRACTICE
EXERCISE**

Empty out your mind

Taking the advertising question, empty out your mind on the subject, using the analysis you've already created as your basic structure, but not restricting yourself to that if you think there are other ideas that are connected.

The most important point to remember is not to put unnecessary brakes on your mind; allow it to run freely over the issues, making connections, analysing issues and arguments, and pulling ideas and evidence together. Therefore, don't worry too much about relevance at this stage.

Although it is bound to be different, the structure that results from brainstorming is likely to be similar to the structure outlined on pp. 43–46. You might use different examples, different evidence, and you might have thought of different points, but the overall structure, based on the principal issues the question raises, will be broadly the same.

Of course, not everything in these notes will find its way into your final essay: they simply may not be strictly relevant. Brainstorming depends upon your ability to follow your ideas and record them quickly without close attention to relevance. Your internal editor will exert his or her influence later. For now, the key is to allow your mind to make all the connections, contrasts and extensions of ideas without slowing it up with concerns about relevance.

Brainstorming: preparing your mind to catch ideas

One last point worth making: ideas come from many different sources, and they only come to the mind that is prepared to receive them. Almost everyone has had the experience of looking up an unfamiliar word in a dictionary, and then, in the days and weeks that follow, seeing and hearing the word everywhere – on advertising hoardings, in newspapers and magazines, on the radio and television, even from friends. But this is not because it is simply being used more frequently by people; it's just that we've prepared our minds to notice it.

The same applies to ideas: once we have prepared our minds we begin to pick up, from a range of different sources, ideas and evidence that we can then use in our writing. This explains why it's so important to carry a notebook with you, so you can record the ideas whenever they come, from whatever source, rather than allow them to disappear for good.

Ideas only come to minds that are prepared to receive them.

In this context it's worth re-emphasising that ideas are organic: they grow and develop through time. If at an early stage you have allowed these ideas to come tumbling out onto the page, the subconscious will go away to sort through your data banks for more ideas and evidence, making connections and analysing your arguments and concepts in ways that you just hadn't suspected when you set out to think about the issues. As a result, when you next come to look at your ideas, you'll be surprised by just how far they have developed.

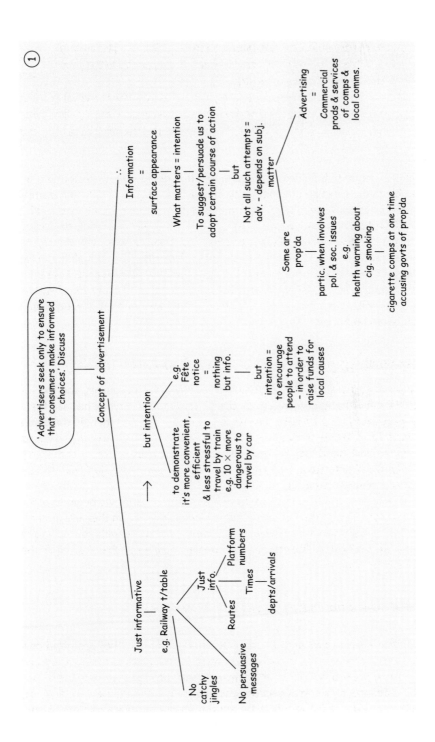

①

'Advertisers seek only to ensure that consumers make informed choices.' Discuss

Concept of advertisement

Just informative

e.g. Railway t/table

Just info.
— Platform numbers
— Times
— Routes
— depts/arrivals

No catchy jingles

No persuasive messages

but intention

to demonstrate it's more convenient, efficient & less stressful to travel by train e.g. 10 × more dangerous to travel by car

e.g. Fête notice = nothing but info.

but intention = to encourage people to attend – in order to raise funds for local causes

∴ Information = surface appearance

What matters = intention

To suggest/persuade us to adopt certain course of action

but

Not all such attempts = adv. – depends on subj. matter

Advertising = Commercial prods & services of comps & local comms.

Some are prop'da

partic. when involves pol. & soc. issues

e.g. health warning about cig. smoking

cigarette comps at one time accusing govts of prop'da

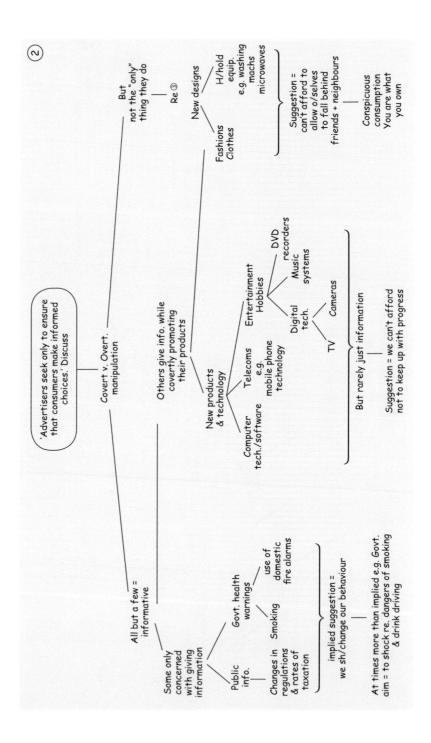

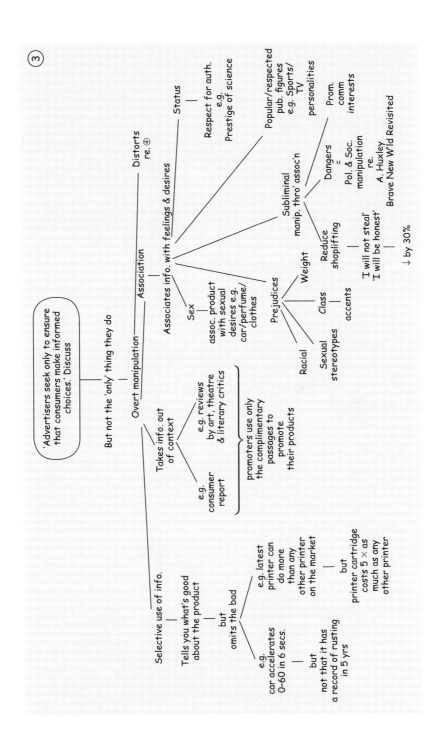

③

'Advertisers seek only to ensure that consumers make informed choices.' Discuss

But not the 'only' thing they do

Overt manipulation — Association — Distorts re.④

Associates info. with feelings & desires

Status
|
Respect for auth.
e.g.
Prestige of science

Popular/respected pub. figures
e.g. Sports/ TV personalities

Prom. comm interests

Subliminal manip. thro' assoc'n

Dangers
=
Pol. & Soc. manipulation
re.
A. Huxley
Brave New W'ld Revisited

Reduce shoplifting

'I will not steal'
'I will be honest'

↓ by 30%

Weight

Sex
|
assoc. product with sexual desires e.g. car/perfume/ clothes

Prejudices

Class
|
accents

Racial

Sexual stereotypes

Takes info. out of context

e.g. reviews by art, theatre & literary critics

e.g. consumer report

promoters use only the complimentary passages to promote their products

Selective use of info.
|
Tells you what's good about the product
|
but
omits the bad

e.g. latest printer can do more than any other printer on the market

but
printer cartridge costs 5 × as much as any other printer

e.g.
car accelerates 0–60 in 6 secs.
|
but
not that it has a record of rusting in 5 yrs

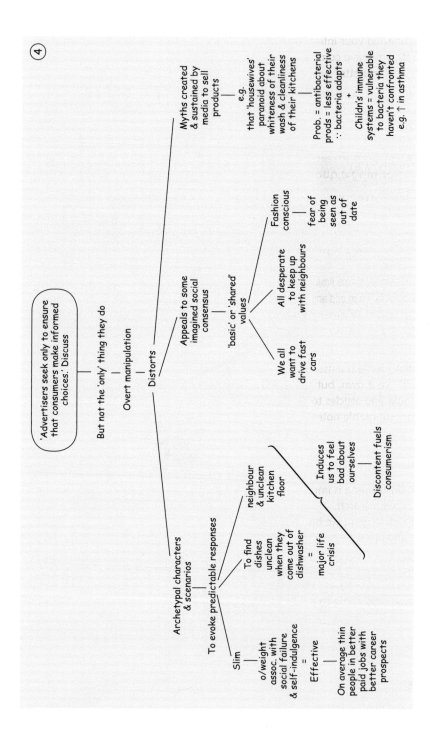

And each time you work on them you set the mind a new set of problems to go away and solve, which develops your ideas still further. Consequently, by the time you've finished your interpretation, research and planning, and you begin to write the first draft, you have come a very long way indeed. Your ideas are more developed, subtler and far better supported by evidence than they were when you first started out.

- To catch our best ideas we must prepare our mind to receive them.
- Ideas grow and develop though time.
- Each time we set our mind new problems it develops our ideas still further.

Brainstorming a question   IN YOUR OWN WORK

Take the question that you selected from your own work that you started to work on in the previous chapter. You've already underlined the key words and concepts in the question and you've analysed what you think are its main implications. Now brainstorm the question, getting all your ideas down as quickly as possible in pattern-note form as we have in this chapter.

Give yourself a time limit, say 30 minutes, to get it all down. Then put it aside. After a day or so, come back to it and add any ideas you've come up with since. Some ideas may push themselves into your conscious mind before that, so note them, don't lose them.

Now that you've brainstormed the question you've not only tapped into ideas that are genuinely your own, but by clarifying what you know and what questions you want your books and articles to answer, you are less likely to waste time taking mounds of irrelevant, unusable notes.

Summary

1 Brainstorming is important to stake our claim: to get *our* ideas down before we do our research.
2 It is divergent: we bring ideas together from different sources.
3 It arms us with our own ideas and experience to evaluate what we read.
4 We must avoid being dictated to by the authors we read.
5 Brainstorming is also important to prevent us noting and including in our essays a mass of irrelevant material.
6 Ideas only come to a mind prepared to see them.

In the next chapter

Nevertheless, there is still one last thing you need to be sure about before you launch into your research. You must be clear about the range of abilities the tutor who marks your essay wants to see you use.

Using the Right Ability: Instructional Verbs

In this chapter you will learn:

- how to make sure we answer the question using the abilities that tutors want to assess;
- how to interpret accurately the 'instructional verbs' in questions.

So far we have seen how important it is to interpret the question carefully, because it tells us the structure our essay should adopt for us to deal relevantly with all the issues it raises. With this clear in our mind we can avoid taking masses of irrelevant notes, which are likely to find their way into our essays, making them irrelevant, shapeless and confusing.

But we also made it clear in Stage 1 'Interpretation of the Question' (pp. 1–2) that there is one other thing that the question tells us: the range of abilities tutors want to see us use in answering the question. This is normally made clear through what are known as 'instructional verbs'. Given below is a list of short definitions of those most frequently found in questions, which should help you avoid the common problems that arise when you overlook or misinterpret them.

Instructional verbs

Analyse	Separate an argument, a theory or a claim into its elements or component parts; to trace the causes of a particular event; to reveal the general principles underlying phenomena.
Compare	Look for similarities and differences between two or more things, problems or arguments. Perhaps, although not always, reach a conclusion about which you think is preferable.
Contrast	Set in opposition to each other two or more things, problems or arguments in order to identify clearly their differences and their individual characteristics.
Criticise	Identify the weaknesses of certain theories, opinions or claims, and give your judgement about their merit. Support your judgements with a discussion of the evidence and the reasoning involved.
Define	Outline the precise meaning of a word or phrase. In some cases it may be necessary or desirable to examine different possible, or often used, definitions.

Describe	Give a detailed or graphic account, keeping to the facts or to the impressions that an event had upon you. In history this entails giving a narrative account of the events in the time sequence in which they occurred.
Discuss	Investigate or examine by argument; sift through the arguments and the evidence used to support them, giving reasons for and against both sides; examine the implications. It means playing devil's advocate by arguing not just for the side of the argument that you support, but for the side with which you may have little sympathy.
Evaluate	Make an appraisal of the worth of something, an argument or a set of beliefs, in the light of their truth or usefulness. This does involve making your own value judgements, but not just naked opinion: they must be backed up by argument and justification.
Explain	Make plain; interpret and account for the occurrence of a particular event by giving the causes. Unlike the verb 'to describe', this does not mean that it is sufficient to describe what happened by giving a narrative of the events. To explain an event is to give the reasons why it occurred, usually involving an analysis of the causes.
Illustrate	Explain or clarify something by the use of diagrams, figures or concrete examples.
Interpret	Reveal what you believe to be the meaning or significance of something; to make sense of something that might otherwise be unclear, or about which there may be more than one opinion. So usually this involves giving your own judgement.
Justify	Show adequate grounds for a decision or a conclusion by supporting it with sufficient evidence and argument; answer the main objections that are likely to be made to it.
Outline	Give the main features or the general principles of a subject, omitting minor details and emphasising its structure and arrangement.
Relate	This usually means one of two things. In some questions it means narrate a sequence of events – outline the story of a particular incident. Alternatively, it can mean show how certain things are connected or affect each other, or show to what extent they are alike.
Review	Examine closely a subject or a case that has been put forward for a certain proposal or argument. Usually, although not always, this means concluding with your own judgement as to the strength of the case. However, if it involves examining just a subject or a topic, and not an argument or a proposal, it will mean just examining in some detail all the aspects of the topic.
State	Outline briefly and clearly the facts of the situation or a side of an argument. This doesn't call for argument or discussion, just the presentation of the facts or the arguments. Equally, it doesn't call for a judgement from you, just reportage.

Summarise	Give a clear and concise account of the principal points of a problem or an argument, omitting the details, evidence and examples that may have been given to support the argument or illustrate the problem.
Trace	Outline the stages in the development of a particular issue or the history of a topic.

Direct or interrogative questions

However, although we can pin down fairly clearly what each instructional verb means in terms of what we must do in response to the question, there are still some questions that have no obvious instructional verb in them at all. These are the direct or interrogative type of questions, which might ask, 'Do you agree that …', 'To what extent is it true to say that …', 'How significant is the claim that …' or 'Comment on the view that …' Clearly these questions are not just asking for a statement of our opinions or comments: they are asking us to discuss the issues and to analyse the different positions that are held on them.

You will probably have noticed in those questions you've already tackled in your work that each one asks us to discuss different types of evaluation. One might ask us to consider the 'extent' to which something is true, implying that we must discuss the limits to which it can be relied upon. Another might ask us to consider the 'significance' of a claim, which means we must examine how well it answers a problem – whether it deals only with a part of it or with all of it – and whether there are better solutions. Some questions that ask us just to 'comment', or ask us whether we 'agree' with a claim, leave open the sort of evaluation involved, so we must interpret the question in the way we've done in the previous chapters to find out what type of evaluation we ought to be discussing.

Instructional verbs   PRACTICE
                                                                 EXERCISE

Gather together as many past examination papers for your course as you can, at least enough to give you a representative sample.

For each paper, list the questions in three columns: those that ask for a descriptive and factual answer (the 'what', 'how' and 'describe' type of question); those that ask for an analytical answer (the 'outline', 'analyse', 'compare' and 'contrast' type of question); and those that ask you for a discussion of the issues (the 'criticise', 'evaluate' and 'discuss' type of question).

Once you've done this, calculate the percentage of each type of question on each paper.

Summary

1 Instructional verbs are important indications of the range of abilities tutors want us to use.
2 If we overlook or misinterpret them we can lose valuable marks by using an ability that was not asked for in the question.
3 But some questions have no obvious instructional verb. For these we must rely on our interpretation of the rest of the question.

In the next chapter

On the face of it this should be the end of a simple story: get the instructional verbs right and we won't make the mistake of answering the question in the wrong way. However, although this is right, it doesn't go far enough. Unless we acknowledge the difference in the assumptions about the nature of education at this level, in sharp contrast with what has gone before, we're unlikely to change the way we work. Instead, we'll just tack a few new techniques and skills onto our existing pattern of study and then quietly abandon them when we realise they don't fit within the way we work. In turn, this will deprive us of those skills we need to access and develop the abilities that are assessed at this level.

The Abilities Essays Assess

In this chapter you will learn:

- that university education is less preoccupied with learning and recalling the facts than with developing the skills and abilities that are crucial to your subject;
- the importance of adjusting to a different style of learning at university;
- about the range of abilities essays are designed to assess.

It's at this point that most of our problems in studying begin. Although we will talk about this again later when we come to the writing stage, it's worth confronting it twice, so important is the problem.

Most students at university are handicapped in one form or another by the restricted notion of education they bring with them. Unfortunately, we spend most of our time in schools believing that education is largely about 'knowing things' – that studying a subject involves just learning the facts dispensed by authorities, such as teachers and textbooks. A clever person, we're led to believe, is one who can remember a vast number of isolated facts.

This perception of education is reinforced not just by the syllabuses we study, the examinations we take and the teaching styles of some of our teachers, but by a whole range of social and cultural conventions, not least the ever popular TV quiz show, in which contestants are asked to recall isolated items of information.

A passive style of learning

The result is that we all assume a passive style of learning. We sit silently in class absorbing the truths, the right answers that we come to believe should be our paramount concern. The teacher dictates while we silently note. The best students, then, are those who are quiet, who patiently and uncritically record word for word all that the teacher says. They are not there to question, to discuss or to challenge, but to absorb the teacher's statements, to imitate authority and to reproduce it accurately without alteration. They believe their success depends upon how effectively they can trade the facts for marks. And that's all there is to it.

But if that were the case, the last thing we would be setting as a form of assessment would be essays, because they are notoriously unreliable. They assess a wide range of abilities – to analyse, to criticise, to discuss, to synthesise ideas, to construct consistent arguments, to use evidence, to evaluate, as well as to remember the facts.

- Learning at university does not involve just the accurate reproduction of facts.
- It involves a wide range of abilities.
- Essays are designed to assess these.

The more abilities you try to assess, the less reliable that form of assessment is for any one ability alone. And, despite all our attempts to reduce the subjective element in marking, most markers would acknowledge that it's impossible to remove it entirely from essay marking.

Essays are not the most reliable means of assessing what we know.

Other forms of assessment, that target just one ability, have a much better record. The most reliable, the multiple choice question paper, boasts 100 per cent reliability. Using this we are guaranteed that each student's paper will be assessed with absolute objectivity, on exactly the same criteria. Indeed, the human element can be removed entirely with computerised answer sheets.

It follows, then, that if we were really assessing our ability to recall the facts, as so many of us have come to believe, the essay would be the very last form of assessment we would use. Far better to use the reliable, though restricted, multiple choice question paper. Here we know we have absolute objectivity, albeit at the cost of assessing only a restricted range of abilities.

Challenging authority

As most of us come to realise, however, we're not just assessing our ability to recall what we've heard in class or read in our books. After years of believing that our main task is to learn the facts and reproduce uncritically what the authorities say, we reach university where we're suddenly expected to challenge the opinions we hear, to analyse, discuss and come to opinions of our own.

Not surprisingly, most students find it difficult to make sense of this. They have learnt that if they use their study skills in a particular way it will bring success. After all, that's exactly what has happened so far in their education. Therefore, understandably, they continue to back what they believe to be a winner: they continue to take notes in the same way, to read in the same way and to write essays in the same way.

At university, with different syllabuses and exams, we need to change our pattern of study.

However, they face different examinations, with different assumptions about the nature of learning, requiring a different pattern of study. Unless this is explained, they will continue to get poor marks for their essays. And they will have no idea why, when all they're doing is just what they've done successfully in all their work before. Confused and dispirited, many will go through the whole course believing that while they might have been up to taking the examinations at school, they're just not up to these at university. Whereas, in fact, it is not that they lack the abilities, the motivation or even the capacity to understand, but just the right skills to unlock their potential.

- At university we are asked to challenge, not just reproduce, the opinions of authorities.

- Syllabuses and exams are based on different assumptions, so we need to adopt a different pattern of study from the one we used in school.
- Otherwise, even though we have the abilities, motivation and capacity to understand, we are still likely to get poor marks.

The range of abilities

It should be clear, then, that by setting essays as a mode of assessment our aim is to assess not just the limited ability to understand and recall, but a much broader range of abilities. All syllabuses are written in the context of six 'cognitive domains' – six intellectual abilities. Listed from the simplest to the most complex, they are as follows:

1 Recall
2 Comprehension
3 Application
4 Analysis
5 Synthesis
6 Evaluation

While many of us find it difficult to shake off the belief that essays and exams are set exclusively to assess our recall and understanding (abilities 1 and 2), most syllabuses at universities are designed largely to assess abilities 4, 5 and 6. The questions set use instructional verbs such as 'Discuss', 'Criticise', 'Analyse' and 'Evaluate', to assess our abilities to analyse difficult concepts and arguments, to synthesise ideas and evidence drawn from a range of different sources, to construct consistent arguments, and to discuss and evaluate the ideas and arguments of others.

These are not the 'What', 'How' and 'Describe' questions used to assess our ability to recall information. This would assume that there are right answers, whereas in fact there are none at this level. As one tutor at the University of Oxford makes clear in the guidance he gives to his students,

> It is never a question of coming to the 'right' answer (though you can expect a tutor to defend his or her position if it differs from yours) but rather of demonstrating that you understand what the issue is about and that you can produce a well-reasoned, balanced and critical argument concerning it.[1]

Syllabus objectives

PRACTICE
EXERCISE

Get a copy of the syllabus for each of the courses you're taking. Then, underline the passages that describe the syllabus objectives. For this exercise ignore the description of the course content, the topics the course will be covering. You're interested just in the abilities that the course sets out to develop, which will be assessed during the course or in the examination at the end.

See if you can work out what proportion of the marks will be awarded for the recall of knowledge and for the other abilities. Some syllabuses will give the actual percentages; others are not so helpful. If this is the case, ask your tutor. Ultimately, of course, the best guide is the type of essay question that is set. So, again, look at past papers and assignments from previous years.

Even so, we still have to show that we understand and can recall the facts, the core knowledge at the heart of the subject. But for most syllabuses that employ essays as a mode of assessment this comprises as little as 30–40 per cent of the mark. So try to avoid too much description. It's not so much what we know, but what we do with it that our tutors are interested in.

> A good thinker is judged not on how much she can recall, but on what she can do with what she knows.

Tutors want to see us use our abilities, so even though we may come to a conclusion that they disagree with, this should not affect our mark, because we're not working with a syllabus that assumes there are indisputable right answers that have to be traded for marks. Tutors should be more concerned with the way we have analysed the issues, discussed them, played devil's advocate, used evidence to support our arguments and come to a measured evaluation that's backed up by our discussion.

EXAMPLE

In the Sociology Department at Harvard University students on one first-year course are left in no doubt that the course's main objective is to develop a particular range of abilities and skills that are central to sociology as a discipline:

> This course is intended to help students to develop an understanding of and ability to do social science analysis – to appreciate what a research problem is, how to pose it, what alternative answers might be, how to evaluate relevant evidence, and generally to understand the logic of establishing knowledge about how society works. ... The emphasis in the course is on developing writing skills, the ability to formulate and design research projects, and the ability to critically evaluate empirical work in the social sciences.[2]

As this shows, most university departments now realise that you don't learn how to think like a scientist or a historian by simply learning scientific or historical facts. In literature courses recognition of this has led universities to allow students to take their set texts into the examination room. This has largely done away with that horrifying, yet futile, annual spectacle of thousands of candidates frantically memorising huge tracts of text for the exam, all of which they will certainly forget within three weeks of taking it.

Summary

1 Learning is not passive – just recalling the right answers in exchange for marks.
2 It is active – we use and develop the higher cognitive abilities.
3 Essays are designed to assess these.
4 Only 30–40 per cent of marks are awarded for our ability to recall knowledge.

The next stage

Now you should be clearer about what the question is getting at and what you want from the texts you're about to read. You will also know the range of abilities tutors want to see you use when you come to answer the question. As you move into the research stage this should be reflected in your pattern of study – in the way you use your skills, like reading and note-taking.

In the next stage you will learn how to use these skills to ensure you do more than just recall what you've read and imitate your authors. You will be shown how to use your skills to process ideas in more complex and sophisticated ways. You will learn how to analyse a passage and extract the structure from what you read, and how to criticise and discuss the ideas and opinions of authors, rather than just reproduce them accurately. You will also learn how you can release and develop your creative abilities to use more of your own ideas in your essays. As a result you will be better equipped to produce essays that are genuinely your own, rather than just recycle the ideas of others.

Notes

1   Eric Eve, *A Guide for Perplexed Students, 4: Tutorial Essays* (Oxford: University of Oxford, 2000), pp. 3–4. Available at: www.hmc.ox.ac.uk/

2   Mary Waters, *Sociology, 128: Paradigms of Social Inquiry* (Cambridge, MA: Harvard University, 2000).

Research

Introduction

We have now reached the point where we can confidently set about our research. We've interpreted the meaning and implications of the question, in the course of which we've analysed the key concepts involved. From there we've brainstormed the question using our interpretation as our key structure. As a result, we now know two things: what questions we want answered from our research; and what we already know about the topic. The latter is important if we are to graft the ideas we come across onto our own understanding and make them our own. Only in this way will we be able to use these ideas skilfully and persuasively when we come to write.

Now we know:

1 What questions we want our research to answer.
2 What we already know.

Lastly, we've identified the range of abilities our tutors want to see us use and on which we will be assessed. Otherwise, as we saw, there is a danger that we will simply assume the question is about demonstrating that we understand and can recall the facts about the topic in the question, rather than showing that we can use our higher cognitive abilities to analyse its implications, synthesise arguments and evidence from different sources, discuss and argue consistently, and criticise and evaluate the ideas we use.

This means that we must reorganise our pattern of study. Otherwise we will continue to use our skills, like note-taking and reading, in the way we have always used them: to meet the demands of questions that test the lower cognitive abilities. In effect, if we don't reorganise it, we will be preparing ourselves for the wrong exams: for those we have already taken, rather than for those we are about to take. In this stage, therefore, we will examine the key skills in research, showing how we can reorganise our pattern of study to meet the newer demands of the higher cognitive abilities.

The range of abilities the essay assesses will determine the most effective pattern of study, i.e. the way we read, take notes and organise our work.

Reading

In our reading we will see that to use these skills effectively it's important to read purposefully: to be clear about why we're reading a particular passage so that we can select the most effective reading strategy. Many of us get into the habit of reading every passage word for word, regardless of our purpose in reading it, when in fact it might be more efficient to skim or scan it. Adopting a more flexible approach to our reading in this way frees up more of our time, so that we can read around our subject and take on board more ideas and information.

It also gives us more time to process the ideas. We will see how important this is if we are to avoid becoming just 'surface-level processors', reading passively without analysing and structuring what we read, or criticising and evaluating the arguments presented. We will examine the techniques involved in analysing a passage to extract its structure, so that we can recall the arguments, ideas and evidence more effectively. We will also learn the different ways we can improve our ability to criticise and evaluate the arguments we read. In this way we can become 'deep-level processors', actively processing what we read and generating more of our own ideas.

- Read purposefully.
- Be more flexible – skim and scan as well as read word for word.

Note-taking

Many of the same issues resurface when we consider note-taking. As with reading, we will see that it's important not to tie ourselves to one strategy of note-taking, irrespective of the job we have to do. We will see that for different forms of processing there are the most appropriate strategies of note-taking: linear notes for analysis and structure, and pattern notes for criticism and evaluation, and for creative thinking as we generate our own ideas. Cultivating flexibility in our pattern of study helps us choose the most effective strategy and, as a result, get the most out of our intellectual abilities.

> To develop our higher cognitive abilities we must learn to be flexible in our use of the different note-taking strategies.

But our problems in note-taking don't end there. The best notes help us structure our own thoughts, so we can recall and use them quickly and accurately, particularly under timed conditions. In this lie many of the most common problems in note-taking, particularly the habit of taking too many notes that obscure the structure, making it difficult to recall.

We will examine ways of avoiding this by creating clear, uncluttered notes that help us recall even the most complex structures accurately. Given this, and the simple techniques of consolidating notes, we will see how revision for the exam can become a more manageable, less daunting task. On the companion website (www.howtowrite betteressays.com) you will find other things you can do and strategies you can adopt to create clear structures that will help you recall your ideas more effectively.

Finally, if our notes are going to help us recall the ideas, arguments and evidence we read, as well as help us to criticise and evaluate an author's arguments, they must be a reflection of our own thinking. We will examine the reasons why many students find it difficult to have ideas of their own, when they read and take notes from their sources, and how this affects their concentration while they work.

- For each of the different ways we process ideas there is the appropriate strategy for taking notes.
- Clear, uncluttered notes make exam revision far less daunting.
- Good notes must be a reflection of our own thinking.
- The right strategy helps our concentration.

Organisation

Needless to say, if we are to make all these changes successfully, we will have to make sure we organise our work in the most effective way. In Chapter 18 we will look at how to reorganise our retrieval system to tap into our own ideas and to pick up material wherever and whenever it appears. On the companion website we also examine the way we organise our time and the problems that can arise if we fail to do it effectively. Indeed, if we ignore either of these, we make it difficult for ourselves to get the most out of our abilities and to process our ideas well. Even though most of us routinely ignore it, organisation is the one aspect of our pattern of study that can produce almost immediate improvements in our work.

- To make these changes we need to reorganise our retrieval system.
- And we need to reorganise our time.
- Both can produce immediate improvements in our work.

10

Using our Study Skills Effectively

In this chapter you will learn:

- about the causes of many of our most common study skills problems;
- about the need to change the way we study.

In the previous chapter we examined the assumptions we need to adopt about the purpose of learning tasks like essay writing. In the light of these, it should be obvious that we now need a new pattern of study – we need to use our study skills differently, in a more effective way for the tasks we're set. If we don't, if we retain the assumption that education is exclusively about 'knowing things', then certain things will follow. When we start to research an essay, we will be cursed with the sort of problems of which most of us are all too aware.

Common problems

Note-taking

In our note-taking we will continue to argue, quite reasonably on these misplaced assumptions, that when we take notes in tutorials, seminars and lectures, or from the source material we use for research, we cannot leave anything out, because these are the facts, the right answers, and if we omit them we will not have all the facts we need to pass the examination. As a result we take vast quantities of verbatim notes. Even worse, they're unstructured, because all we're doing is recording them accurately – we're not processing them in any way for fear of getting them wrong.

Consequently, we're left with masses of unusable notes, most of them irrelevant to the essays we are set and the questions we're going to have to answer in the examination. This presents us with the most daunting of problems when we come to revise for the exam, which leaves even the most resourceful with little idea where to start.

- Masses of unusable notes.
- Verbatim notes.
- Unstructured notes.

Reading

But now consider the impact of these assumptions on other areas of our pattern of study. Quite reasonably, we argue that when we come to read books and articles we cannot exercise any flexibility by adopting different, more effective reading strategies, such as skimming and scanning, for the different types of passages and texts. We argue that the text must be read word for word, otherwise we might miss something vital.

Remember, under these assumptions we believe that these are the facts in the passage before us. If we fail to read it carefully we are likely to miss a vital fact that we will need to trade for marks in the exam. Reading, then, becomes a slow, time-consuming activity. Along with note-taking it takes up nearly all of our study time. Consequently, we never have sufficient time to read around our subject, to make comparisons with what others are saying and to explore our understanding.

- No flexibility.
- Slow reading.
- No time left to read around our subject.

Writing

Much the same goes for our essay writing. No matter how many times we might be told by our tutor that we must try to put things in our own words, this makes no sense if we accept the assumption that education is dominated by authorities, and our job is just to understand and recall the facts.

We argue, again quite reasonably, that here is the text, the authority, the source of right answers, so if we were to spend time putting it into our own words, rather than copy passages from it accurately, we would be changing what is already right. We would be making it less right; in effect we would be getting it wrong. So, far better to plagiarise the text and put large chunks directly into our own work. And no matter how many times students are told not to plagiarise, because this is literary theft, a form of cheating that constitutes just about the most serious offence in academic writing, they still continue to do it, because they are convinced that these are the facts and their role is to trade them for marks, if they are to succeed.

- We fail to put things in our own words.
- We plagiarise.

Plagiarism

In fact plagiarism illustrates perfectly the point we've been making in this chapter. As we've seen, one of the causes of it is this belief that we get high marks as a result of giving right answers. But, unfortunately, all too often the solution to plagiarism reflects the same assumption, thereby compounding the original problem. We argue that the only way to avoid plagiarism is to give a reference for every idea quoted, paraphrased or borrowed in any way. In other words, students come to realise that to get high marks they must continue to trade for marks as many right answers as possible, only now in the form of references.

Students trade references for marks in the belief that they are the right answers.

Worse still, they are given the impression that there is nothing new in education. It reduces academic work to the far less significant exercise of just recycling received opinion. There is no room for originality, or at least you are not required to produce it. All that's asked is that you show evidence of hard work by breaking up every paragraph with five or six references. The only challenge this presents for most students is how they can throw in as many references as possible at minimum cost. Inevitably they gather the impression that education is more concerned with *what* they think than *how* they think.

EXAMPLE

One mature student explains the problem in his student magazine:

In my opinion the most important purpose of higher education is to teach the student how to think in a sophisticated manner. Sadly … universities … cannot resist the temptation to teach the student what to think as well – not the best way to produce enquiring and innovative minds.

There seems to be a tradition … that an opinion is somehow more valid if someone has said it before: I can see a justification for this, in that if an opinion has been in the public domain it has been subject to public scrutiny, but I suspect that the motivation has more to do with the 'hero-innovator' notion: if the person who has said it is important enough it must be right.

When I write essays I am required not only to give facts and ideas, but to quote exactly where I found them: if I simply thought of them myself does that mean they are not valid? Generally, I feel a strong pressure to reflect back the opinions and prejudices of the course team: maybe this is not justified, but that's how it feels. I am reminded of what Henry Beeching wrote in the 19th century concerning the Master of Balliol:

'I am Master of this College: What I don't know isn't knowledge.'[1]

Of course, most students know that they should be rejecting this assumption that their paramount concern is to impress the tutor marking their essay by exchanging facts, in the form of references, for marks. But plagiarism seems vague and all-encompassing: like the medieval crime of witchcraft, just about anything seems to qualify. Inevitably, then, they play it safe and give a reference for anything that might seem to deserve it: out of fear they are driven into this regressive, primitive form of learning. In Chapter 35 we will look at the problem of plagiarism and how you can avoid it without just becoming a recycler of what others have said.

Creating a new pattern of study

In this stage we will set about creating a new, more flexible pattern of study that will equip you to tackle the different challenges presented by essay writing at university. But the success of this will depend upon how much you're willing to accept the need to change.

We only ever really learn when we have a genuine need. If we retain the assumption that education is exclusively about knowing things, there will be no need to change. The new flexibility and skills in reading, note-taking and writing will only be tacked on to our present pattern of study as we go about studying in the way we've always studied. And in time, of course, they will be silently dropped, because in the light of our unchanged assumptions, they are irrelevant.

We only ever really learn when we have a genuine need.

It's worth reminding ourselves that the real joy and challenge of education lies not in how much we can remember, but in what we learn to do with our minds. Out of this come students who can genuinely think for themselves, capable of real innovation that pushes back the frontiers of knowledge. As B. F. Skinner describes it, 'Education is what survives when what has been learnt has been forgotten'.[2]

Planning your research   IN YOUR OWN WORK

- When you were given the essay question you are working on you were no doubt also given a reading list by your tutor, composed of books and journal articles. You won't have to read every text on the list, so before you begin your research you will need to prioritise them. First, categorise them into those whose approach is general and those that are specific. Then consider, in each of these categories, which appears to be the most useful. Some may appear too general, others too specific. In some cases you will need to skim and scan the texts before you're sure. In this stage you will be shown how to do this.
- Now that you know the meaning and implications of the question, you will know what you're looking for. Generally tutors try to indicate the pages you will find most helpful, but this is not always possible. For most questions it helps to begin with the more general text and move to the specific, but this will depend upon your prior knowledge of the topic. Either way, you will still have to narrow down the specific sections you need to read. In the next chapter you will be shown ways of doing this.
- The same applies to the journal articles. Your interpretation and brainstorming of the question will have given you a much clearer idea of the specific issues raised and where you need to devote more of your time. In most cases, of course, we're not lucky enough to find that the author of an article is examining exactly the issue we need to think about. So, again, you will have to prioritise and be selective about the sections that are most useful.

Summary

1 Unless we change our assumptions about learning we will experience common learning problems in note-taking, in reading and in essay writing.
2 Despite our best intentions it will be difficult to resist the need to plagiarise.
3 We will be left with the impression that there is nothing new in education and all we must do is recycle received opinion.
4 We can only develop a new, more flexible, pattern of study if we have a need to – we only really learn when we have a genuine need.

In the next chapter

In this stage, to help you use your skills more effectively to unlock your abilities, we will examine each skill in turn. In the next chapter we will learn how we can waste less time by reading more efficiently with more flexible techniques.

Notes

1   Lem Ibbotson, 'Teach us how, not what, to think', *Sesame*, August/September 2000 (Open University).
2   B. F. Skinner, 'Education in 1984', *New Scientist*, 21 May 1964, p. 484.

Reading Purposefully

In this chapter you will learn:

- how to use your time more effectively by reading only what you need to read;
- about the importance of being clear about your purpose in reading the text in order to select the right reading strategy;
- how to read more efficiently with more flexible techniques.

Having got our own ideas down on paper, the concepts analysed and a clear idea of what we're looking for, we are now in a position to begin our research, confident that we can identify what's relevant and what's not.

Locating relevant material

But before you hit the books, a warning! It's all too easy to pick up a pile of books that appear vaguely useful and browse among them. This might be enjoyable, and you might learn something, but it will hardly help you get your essay written. Now that you've interpreted the question and brainstormed the issues, you have a number of questions and topics you want to pursue. You are now in a position to ask clear questions as you read the books and the other materials you've decided to use in your research.

Nevertheless, before you begin you need to pin down exactly the sections of each book that are relevant to your research. Very few of the books you use will you read from cover to cover. With this in mind, you need to consult the contents and index pages in order to locate those pages that deal with the questions and issues you're interested in.

Avoid the temptation to browse aimlessly. Ask clear questions and you'll get clear answers.

For most books this is all you will need to do. However, there are those books that have very misleading chapter titles, which tell you little about the content of each chapter. The same books may also have a short and unhelpful index. In this case you'll find it helpful to read the first paragraph of each chapter, where the authors explain what they will be doing in this chapter, and then the last paragraph, where they explain how they've done it.

Failing this, and this will be rare indeed, you can *skim* each page, picking up a general impression of the contents of each chapter. Alternatively, if you know the specific problem you want the book to address, you can *scan* each page swiftly, looking for those key words through which you can find the answers. It's surprising just how effective both of these strategies can be, but they will only work well if you've already pinned down the issues clearly in the interpretation stage.

In a nutshell

Check:

- the contents page;
- the index;
- chapter headings;
- the first and last chapters;
- summaries at the end of the chapters and at the end of the book;
- the first and last paragraphs in each chapter.
- Skim the text for a general impression of the contents, key ideas and structure.
- Scan for key words.

Through this process you should be able to answer a number of important questions which will determine exactly how you use the text:

1 Is it relevant?
2 If so, what sections?
3 What approach does it take?
   – Is it too difficult?
   – Or too technical?

This underlines again the importance of flexibility in the way we approach our work. We have three different reading strategies to choose from, each one appropriate to a different type of job.

1 We can read carefully **word for word** when we're reading a text or a passage we know is of central importance to our work, from which we want to extract in our notes the detailed structure of the main points and subsections.
2 In contrast, when we just want to pick up the general impression of the contents, the key ideas and the broad structure of a text or an article, then we would do better to **skim** it.
3 And, if we're just looking for an answer to a specific question, say a date, a name, a set of figures, or what the writer says about a certain subject, then we need to **scan** it.

The key is flexibility and, in turn, the key to this is to read with a clear purpose in mind, so you can choose the most effective strategy.

Reading purposefully

PRACTICE
EXERCISE

10

Faced with the following situations, decide which reading strategy would best suit your purpose.

1 You're given a 50-page report the night before a conference you're attending. Do you skim, scan or read word for word?
2 You're attending a press conference held by the head of state of a country which has a very poor record on human rights. To prepare yourself you refer to a detailed report on the country's judicial

system compiled by Amnesty International. In particular you want to know how many political prisoners are at present detained without trial and the length of time they've been in custody. Do you skim, scan or read word for word?

3   You've been asked to take over the job of secretary at your local golf club, because of the sudden illness of the current secretary. You've got to compile an agenda for the next meeting by reading the minutes of the last meeting. Do you skim, scan or read word for word?

4   After ordering it some months ago you receive a copy of the latest novel by your favourite author. You start reading it on the train going to work. Do you skim, scan or read word for word?

5   You're studying at a university on a scholarship grant. But the terms of the grant are changing next year, which might mean you no longer qualify. You've just received a copy of the new regulations. Do you skim, scan or read word for word?

Now compare your answers with those below.

Answers

1   Skim to get the general impression of the contents.
2   Scan to see what Amnesty says about political prisoners and their detention.
3   Skim to identify those things that were discussed at the last meeting and were to be raised again at this meeting.
4   Not wanting to miss anything, you read word for word.
5   You read them carefully word for word, like you would a legal document, until you are completely clear one way or the other whether you qualify.

Summary

1   Pin down exactly those sections of each source that are relevant to your research.
2   Choose the most effective reading strategy that will best suit your purpose: reading word for word, skimming or scanning.

In the next chapter

We can all see the common sense of scanning the telephone directory in search of the number for a mechanic when our car has broken down; but in our academic work it seems much more difficult to use the same common-sense judgement. With many of us, as we've already seen, the most likely reason is that we still harbour the belief that to pass an exam we must accumulate as many right answers as possible, and the only way of doing this is to use just one reading strategy: read every passage word for word. This, in turn, affects the quality and depth at which we process the ideas we read, as we'll see in the next chapter.

Processing the Ideas

In this chapter you will learn:

- about the different ways we process ideas as we read;
- how to improve your recall of what you read;
- how to read analytically, to take the structure out of a passage.

Ultimately, the quality of the work we produce will depend upon the quality of our internal processing of the ideas we read. There are 'surface-level processors', who read passively, that is without actively analysing and structuring what they read, and without criticising and evaluating the arguments, evidence and ideas the author presents.
In most cases this sort of student will have poor recall of what they read, and in general they will be restricted to just 'describing' the ideas.

If the question asks them to 'evaluate' or 'assess critically' a certain claim, they will, more often than not, find themselves answering the question irrelevantly, employing the lower ability range, in which they merely 'describe' an argument or 'outline' a particular case. As we have seen, this is a mistake that derives from overlooking the importance of the instructional verbs. But more often than not it has its origin in a reading habit that drives students into the lower ability range, when they least want to be there.

Surface-level processing

1   Reading without analysing and structuring the ideas.
2   Reading without criticising and evaluating what we read.
3   It develops from ignoring instructional verbs.
4   And from reading habits that drive us into the lower ability range.

Multiple readings

To avoid this problem, and to ensure that you're able to do 'deep-level processing', it may be necessary to accept that you need to do two or three readings of the text, particularly if it is technical and closely argued.

Reading for comprehension

In your first reading you might aim just for the lower ability range, for comprehension, just to understand the author's arguments. It may be a subject you've never read about before, or it may include a number of unfamiliar technical terms that you need to think about carefully each time they are used.

Reading for analysis and structure

In the next reading you should be able to analyse the passage into sections and subsections, so that you can see how you're going to organise it in your notes.

If the text is not too difficult you may be able to accomplish both of these tasks (comprehension and analysis) in one reading, but always err on the cautious side, don't rush it. Remember, now that you've identified just those few pages that you have to read, rather than the whole book, you can spend more time processing the ideas well.

Reading for criticism and evaluation

The third reading involves criticising and evaluating your authors' arguments. It's clear that in this and the second reading our processing is a lot more active. While in the second we're analysing the passage to take out the structure, in this, the third, we're maintaining a dialogue with the authors, through which we're able to criticise and evaluate their arguments. In Chapter 16 you can find all the typical problems that you need to look for as you read an author's arguments critically.

Give yourself breathing space

One last caution – don't rush into this. You will have to give yourself some breathing space between the second reading and this final evaluative reading. Your mind will need sufficient time to process all the material, preferably overnight, in order for you to see the issues clearly and objectively. If you were to attempt to criticise and evaluate the author's ideas straight after reading them for the structure, your own ideas would be so assimilated into the author's that you would be left with no room to criticise and assess them. You would probably find very little to disagree with the author about.

Reading for analysis and structure

PRACTICE EXERCISE

11

Read the following passage, first for comprehension, and then for analysis and structure. Leave it for a few hours, even a day or so, then go back to it to take out the structure in normal linear notes. If you're unsure about how to do this, read the first part of Chapter 13.

But remember, your aim is to take out the hierarchy of points, the main sections and the way they break down into subsections. Cut out as much unnecessary detail as you can. Where there are examples or explanations, and you think you might need reminding of them, briefly note them in one or two words to act as a trigger for your memory, and nothing more. Choose words or succinct phrases that you know will make the connections to the information you want.

Keep in mind that the most important part of this exercise is to have a clear, uncluttered model of the passage. You will not achieve this if you allow yourself to be tempted into noting unnecessary detail. Your mind will have self-organised in the interval between reading and noting, producing a very clear structure of the passage in your subconscious, so you must develop the skills to tap into this to get an accurate picture of it clearly and simply on paper.

You won't do this if you continually tell yourself that you must note this and this and this otherwise you're bound to forget them. Don't make it difficult for your mind by doubting its capacity to remember details that don't need to be noted.

Passage

Ethics in business

Over recent years we have seen an unprecedented growth in the numbers of students around the world taking courses in professional and business ethics. Research suggests that in the USA, the UK and Canada alone there are at least 3 million students engaged in philosophy modules as part of their professional degree courses, most of which are in ethics.

More than half of the leading international business schools now feature courses dealing with ethics and corporate responsibility as part of their compulsory syllabuses, according to recent research by the World Resources Institute and the Aspen Institute. In their 'Beyond Grey Pinstripes', a biennial ranking of international business schools, the 91 accredited schools featured in their 2005 report offer 1074 such courses. And the number of schools requiring students to take them as part of their individual programmes rose from 34 per cent in 2001 to 54 per cent in 2005. Indeed, the top ten schools worldwide each offer around 50 courses.

At the London Business School, ranked by the *Financial Times* as the best in Europe, all MBA students are required to take a course in business ethics and social responsibility. De Montfort University in Leicester has recently set up an MSc in International Business and Corporate Social Responsibility. The Saïd Business School at the University of Oxford and the Achilles Group have recently announced the creation of 'The Oxford–Achilles Working Group on Corporate Social Responsibility', an initiative designed to bring intelligent debate and practical recommendations to what they describe as an important but underdeveloped field of corporate life.

In the USA a number of business schools have set up specialist centres to meet the increasing demand for ethics-related courses. Georgetown University, for example, established a Business Ethics Institute in the year 2000 to stimulate empirical and applied research into the issues involved. Boston College has established five distinct institutes, with themes ranging from corporate citizenship and responsible investment to work–life balance and ethical leadership.

There are several reasons for this rapid increase. Perhaps the most obvious is that the recent corporate scandals have made professionals and corporate executives more aware of the damage that unethical practices could do to their professional lives and businesses. Even so there is probably more to it than this. In the USA the growth of these courses has been fuelled by consumer pressure groups demanding more ethical corporate management and improved environmental performance, as well as accountability to stakeholder groups other than just shareholders. Public outrage, particularly over the dramatic increases in the incidents of business crime, corruption, irresponsibility and environmental degradation, has also led to growing interest in business ethics over the last few years. And in Europe similar forces are working to raise awareness of the importance of good ethical practices as European integration brings with it increasingly stringent sets of standards.

But for many businesses the key motivating factor is self-interest. As the business environment changes they are beginning to realise that good ethics is good business. A good business ethics policy is the key to building a good reputation, which is likely to bring more business in the future, prevent fraud and motivate employees, who tend to be more productive when they can trust the ethical standards of their employer.

Self-interest works in another way, too. Aside from their concerns about developing a good reputation, more and more businesses in the USA are also beginning to realise that a good business ethics policy is the first and most important line of defence against unethical or illegal activities. Under US federal sentencing guidelines, companies whose employees break the law can be fined a maximum sum based on the amount of money involved in illegal acts, plus legal and court costs; the total is then multiplied by four. But companies with an effective ethics programme pay a maximum 20 per cent of that total. Unethical acts cost North American businesses over $100 billion a year.

With the changes in government and public attitudes it seems ethics is at last beginning to pay its way.

Answer

Ethics in business

1 Increasing numbers taking ethics courses:
   - approx. 3m in USA, UK and Canada

   (a) Compulsory courses:

   'Beyond Grey Pinstripes' (World Resources Institute & Aspen Inst) research on international business schools

   (i) More than half have compulsory courses
   (ii) 2005 report – 91 schools offer 1074 courses
   (iii) Number with compulsory courses:
   2001 – 34%
   2005 – 54%
   (iv) Top 10 schools worldwide each offer around 50 courses

   (b) Business schools:

   (i) London Business School – all MBA students
   (ii) De Montfort Univ., Leicester – MSc in International Business and Corporate Social Resp.
   (iii) Saïd Business School + Achilles group – 'The Oxford–Achilles Working Group on Corporate Social Resp.'
   (iv) Georgetown Univ – Business Ethics Institute estab. 2000
   (v) Boston College – 5 distinct institutes

2 Reasons:

   (a) Recent corporate scandals:
   - realisation of the damage they cause

   (b) Consumer pressure groups:
   - demands:
   (i) More ethical corporate management
   (ii) Improved environmental performance
   (iii) Accountability to all stakeholders

   (c) Public outrage:
   - about increase in

(i)   Business crime
(ii) Corruption
(iii) Irresponsibility
(iv) Environmental degradation

(d) European integration:
    – increasingly stringent standards

(e) Self-interest:

(i) Good reputation –
     I.   More business
     II. Less fraud
     III. Motivated employees – trust

(ii) Defence against unethical & illegal activities –
     Total annual cost to North American businesses = \$100bn

     e.g. US fine = (sum involved + legal/court costs) × 4
     $$v$$
     Effective ethics prog = 20%

Your notes may not contain as much detail as there is in these, but you shouldn't be discouraged by that. Your primary aim in this exercise was to create notes that reflect your understanding of the main structure of the passage as clearly as possible. Therefore, if you've been able to extract the main reasons for the increase in numbers studying ethics along with some of the hierarchy of subpoints, then you've done well.

As you know now, this is not an easy exercise. It will take a few more attempts at different passages to get it right, but you will see quite dramatic improvements in a short time as long as you remain clear about what you're trying to achieve. While you were reading the passage, your mind self-organised to produce a structure out of what you read. Your main goal, then, is to reproduce this in your notes.

Summary

1 To avoid surface-level processing, some sources may have to be read more than once.
2 For the most difficult passages it helps to read first for comprehension, second for analysis and structure, and third for criticism and evaluation.
3 Give yourself a breathing space between each reading so that you can see the issues clearly and objectively.

In the next chapter

Having done this, you should then be able to recall the structure accurately as long as the main points are triggered off by memorable key words. In the next chapter we will examine ways to improve this and other aspects of our note-taking.

Note-taking for Analysis and Structure

In this chapter you will learn:

- how to increase your flexibility in note-taking to make better use of all your intellectual abilities;
- how to choose the most effective strategy for the different levels at which we process ideas: comprehension, analysis and criticism;
- how to use linear notes to produce clear, uncluttered structures of the passages you read.

Choosing the right note-taking strategy

By now, no doubt, you will have realised that for each of these different levels of processing (analysis/structure, and criticism/evaluation) there is the most effective note-taking strategy.

Of course, this should come as no surprise. It endorses what we've said a number of times already, that flexibility and choosing the most effective strategy is the key to good essay writing. For most of the jobs we have to do, the choice is clear: linear notes (see pp. 77–78) for analysis and structure; and pattern notes (see pp. 13, 26 and 43–46) for criticism and evaluation.

Nevertheless, there will always be a text or an article which seems to fall between the two strategies, neither of which alone seems to do the job we want to do. On these occasions I find myself taking the highly structured linear notes first, and then creating a set of pattern notes to give me a broad overview of the issues involved. In this way you can get around the problem of seeing nothing but detail – of not being able to see the wood for the trees.

Note-taking for analysis and structure

As we've already discovered, our aim here is to identify and extract the hierarchy of ideas, a process which involves selecting and rejecting material according to its relevance and importance.

Although by now this sounds obvious, it's surprising how many students neglect it or just do it badly. As with most study skills, few of us are ever shown how best to structure our thoughts on paper. Yet there are simple systems we can all learn. Some students never get beyond the list of isolated points, devoid of all structure. Or, worse still, they rely on the endless sequence of descriptive paragraphs, in which a structure hides buried beneath a plethora of words.

> Our aim is to identify and extract a clear hierarchy of ideas.

This makes it difficult to process ideas even at the simplest level. Without clear structures we struggle to recall much more than unrelated scraps of information. As a result students do less well in exams than they could have expected, all because they haven't learnt the skills involved in organising and structuring their understanding. They sit down to revision with a near hopeless task facing them – mounds of notes, without a structure in sight, beyond the loose list of points.

- Extract the hierarchy of points.
- Select only relevant and important points.
- We all need clear structures in our notes to recall them accurately.

This could be described as the parable of two mental filing systems. One student uses a large brown box, into which she throws all her scraps of paper without any systematic order. Then, when she's confronted with a question in the exam, she plunges her hand deep into the box in the despairing hope that she might find something useful. Sadly, all that she's likely to come up with is something that, at best, is trivial or marginally relevant, but which she's forced to make the most of, because it's all she's got.

On the other hand there is the student who files all of her ideas systematically into a mental filing cabinet, knowing that, when she's presented with a question, she can retrieve from her mind a structure of interlinked relevant arguments backed by quotations and evidence, from which she can develop her ideas confidently. And most of us are quite capable of doing this with considerable skill, if only we know how to do it.

Note-taking structures

PRACTICE
EXERCISE

12

The question we need to ask ourselves is, where do we sit along the spectrum between these two points? How much structure is there to our notes? They may be full of paragraphs and long wordy descriptions that are difficult to recall, or they may be highly structured with key words triggering off all the ideas we want without a mistake.

Take a set of notes you have taken over the last two weeks and try to assess it as objectively as you can on the basis of three criteria:

1   whether there is a clear hierarchy of points with main sections, subsections and sub-subsections;
2   whether there are clear key words or phrases that trigger off each of these ideas;
3   and whether there is clear space between each section so that you can see at a glance the overall structure of the notes.

Give yourself marks out of ten for each of these.

If you've got a total in the range 24–30 you have little to worry about. If you've given yourself, say, 15–24 you still have work to do. You may need to make your structure clearer by selecting more memorable key words or by leaving more space between each section so you can see it clearly. If you have awarded yourself less than 15 then you're probably not making clear to yourself exactly why you're taking notes – what questions you want answered. As a result everything seems relevant and worth noting and the structure gets lost in a mass of words. The answer is to interpret the question more clearly, so you know exactly what's relevant and what's not. Alternatively, you may simply need to improve your basic note-taking skills and, as you'll see in what follows in this and the next two chapters, we can all benefit from this.

Of course, the acid test is whether we can recall the main structure of the notes we have taken, so, after you've given yourself marks, commit your notes to memory and then try to recall them. If, like most of us, you find this difficult you need to make changes to the way you take notes to make the structure clearer, so that you can recall them faultlessly.

Linear notes

This is, perhaps, the most familiar and widely used note-taking strategy, because it adapts well to most needs. As we've already seen, at university the exams we prepare ourselves for are designed to assess more than just our comprehension, so notes in the form of a series of short descriptive paragraphs, and even the list, are of little real value. Exams at this level are concerned with a wider range of abilities, including our abilities to discuss, criticise and synthesise arguments and ideas from a variety of sources, to draw connections and contrasts, to evaluate, and so on. To do all this requires a much more sophisticated and adaptable strategy that responds well to each new demand. It should promote our abilities, not stunt them by trapping us within a straitjacket.

A good note-taking strategy should promote our abilities, not stunt them.

Linear notes are particularly good at analytical tasks, recording the structure of arguments and passages. As you develop the structure, with each step or indentation you indicate a further breakdown of the argument into subsections. These in turn can be broken down into further sub-subsections. In this way you can represent even the most complex argument in a structure that's quite easy to understand. Equally important, with clearly defined key words, highlighted in capital letters or in different colours, it's easy to recall the clusters of ideas and information that these key words trigger off.

The set of linear notes below is taken from a course on genetics:

Genes

1 Definition:
   (a) Basic physical & functional units of heredity
   (b) Sequences of bases – encode instructions on how to make proteins
   (c) Carried on chromosomes

2 Disorders:
   (a) Changes in genes prevent proteins from carrying out normal functions
   (b) Proteins:
       (i) Perform most life functions
       (ii) Make up majority of cellular structures

3 Gene therapy:
   (a) Definition: technique for correcting defective genes responsible for disease
   (b) Methods:
       (i) Replacements –
            I.   Normal gene replaces non-functional gene
            II. Abnormal gene replaces normal gene thro homologous recombination
       (ii) Repairs – abnormal gene repaired – selective reverse mutation
       (iii) Regulation (i.e. degree to which regulation is turned on/off) altered

4 Common method = I:
   (a) Vector = carrier molecule delivers gene to target cells
   (b) Virus = most common vector:
       (i)   Evolved to infect cells
       (ii) Replace disease-carrying genes with therapeutic genes
       (iii) Types:
             I.   Retroviruses
             II. Adenoviruses
             III. Adeno-associated viruses
             IV. Herpes simplex viruses
   (c) Non-viral delivery systems:
       (i)   Direct intro of therapeutic DNA into target cells
       (ii) Creation of a liposome – artificial liquid sphere with aqueous core – to pass DNA thro target cell's membrane
       (iii) Linking therapeutic DNA to a molecule that binds to special cell receptors
       (iv) Introduce 47th (artificial human) chromosome into target cells

5 Cells:
   (a) Germline (sperm cells, ova & their stem cell precursors) – modification = Controversial – affects future generations
   (b) Somatic (adult cells of people who have a disease):
       (i) ex vivo – cells modified outside the body & reinserted
       (ii) in vivo – genes changed in cells still in the body

As you can see, the structure is clear and concise. At a moment's glance you can pick out the main points and their supporting arguments and evidence, commit them to memory and then test yourself that you can recall the structure.

Summary

1 There are different note-taking strategies for different levels of processing.
2 Flexibility and choosing the right strategy are important.
3 We can all recall and use our ideas more effectively if we learn to structure them clearly.
4 Linear notes are good at recording the structure of arguments and passages.

In the next chapter

In the next chapter we will look at ways of organising your notes, so that you can make this structure as clear as possible and retrieve your ideas accurately and quickly whenever you need them.

14

Remembering Your Notes

In this chapter you will learn:

- the techniques for producing clear notes that you can recall accurately;
- how to avoid the most common problems in note-taking;
- how to organise and consolidate your notes.

The key to good note-taking is to make the structure clear. The mind remembers structures, not lists or paragraphs of continuous prose. So, keep it free and uncluttered. Don't convince yourself that unless you include this one fact you'll never remember it. You will. The structure will act as a net bringing to the surface of your mind more than you ever thought you could remember. But it has to be a good net – well constructed, with clear logical connections and free of all unnecessary material.

- The mind remembers structures, not lists or paragraphs.
- Keep your notes free of all clutter.
- A good structure will act as a net, bringing to the surface more than you thought you could remember.

Creating a clear structure

Here are a number of things you can do to make sure your structure works:

1 **Key words** Choose sharp, memorable words to key off the points in your structure. In the notes above on genes the five main points are not difficult to remember, particularly with key words, like 'Definition', 'Disorders', 'Therapy', 'Common method' and 'Cells'. But you need other words to key off the subsections, although you don't need them for every step and every subsection in the notes. Keying off the main points and the principal subsections will trigger off the rest. Don't doubt yourself on this; it will – try it.

     So just choose sharp, memorable words for the principal subsections, words like 'Vector', 'Virus', 'Germline', 'Somatic' and the alliteration of 'Replacements', 'Repairs' and 'Regulation'. They don't have to be snappy and bright, just memorable.

2 **Capitalisation** Once you have chosen your key words they must stand out, so you can see at a glance the structure of your notes. It's no good having a structure if it can't be seen beneath the undergrowth of words. Some people choose to put all their key words into capitals.

3 **Colour** If you don't think this is sufficiently prominent, put your key words in different colours. This doesn't have to be too fussy – you're not creating a piece of modern art – but it's not too much of a bureaucratic task to get into the habit of

working with two pens of different colours, one for picking out the key words and the other for the rest. You will be surprised at just how well this works. It's not unusual to come across people who can still visualise accurately in their mind's eye pages of notes they took when they were studying for their school exams many years ago.

4   **Gaps**   If the structure is to stand out, your notes must not appear too crowded. To avoid this, leave plenty of gaps between your points. This also gives you the opportunity to add other related things as you come across them in your reading, although you need to do this in such a way as to avoid overcrowding.

5   **Abbreviations**   Most of us use these; indeed, we tend to create our own personalised abbreviations for those words we seem to use most often. Even so, it's still surprising how many students look with open-mouthed astonishment when you list the standard abbreviations, like the following:

Therefore	$\therefore$
Because	$\because$
Leads to	$\rightarrow$
Increase/decrease	$\uparrow\downarrow$
Greater than/smaller than	$><$
Would/should	wld/shld
Would be, should be	w/be, sh/be
Equivalent	$=$
Not	$\neq$
Parallel	llel

Nevertheless, as your tutors have no doubt told you, although these abbreviations are indispensable in compiling clear, concise notes, they shouldn't find their way into the final draft of your essay.

Being brief

If you've left sufficient time between reading the text the first time for comprehension, and then reading it for structure, you're more likely to have a clear, uncluttered set of notes free from all unnecessary material. You'll certainly be free of that most time-consuming of activities, taking notes on notes, which many of us are forced to do because our notes are not concise enough in the first place.

Unfortunately, there are many students, even at university, who convince themselves that this is a valuable thing to do; that it's a way of learning their notes if they rewrite them more concisely. They seem to believe that by committing their notes to paper they're committing them to their minds, whereas, in fact, they're doing anything but that.

Taking notes on notes is time-consuming and a relaxing substitute for real thinking.

Taking notes can be a pleasant substitute for thinking. It's something we can do on autopilot. In fact it can be one of the most relaxing parts of our pattern of study. While we are placing few demands on our mind, it can go off to consider more pleasant things, like the plans for the weekend, or reminiscences about last year's holiday.

This underlines the main problem in note-taking: most of us find it difficult to be brief. While we have our minds on autopilot we're able to convince ourselves that almost every point, however insignificant, is vitally important to our future understanding. Not surprisingly, then, we end up omitting very little, obscuring the structure so that when we come to revision we have to start taking notes on our own notes.

- Give yourself time between reading for comprehension and reading for structure.
- This will help you produce clear, uncluttered notes.
- Don't convince yourself you must record almost every insignificant point.
- Be brief.

Notes must be a record of our understanding

But there's another reason that's more difficult to tackle. Most of us, at times, doubt our ability to remember details, so we allow ourselves to be seduced into recording things that 'might' be useful in the future. Inevitably, this results in masses of notes that obscure the main structure, which, as we've seen, is the only means by which we can recall them in the first place.

To avoid this we need to remind ourselves constantly of two things: first, that almost certainly we have better memories than we think; and second, that we're not producing encyclopaedic accounts of the subject, in which we record every known fact. To be of any use notes should be an accurate record of *our* understanding, of *our* thinking, not someone else's.

Remind yourself:

1 You have a better memory than you think.
2 You're not producing an encyclopaedic account.

We can easily lose sight of this when we try to take notes while we're reading the text for the first time or straight after we've read it. We lose our objectivity: all we can see is the author's ideas and opinions, not our own. We need to give our minds time to digest the ideas and self-organise. You will find that if you leave time between reading and noting, your mind will have created its own structures out of the ideas it has taken from the text.

Then, after we've allowed our minds sufficient time to do this, we need to organise ourselves to tap into it, to get our own understanding down on paper without using the text. Otherwise the author will hijack our thinking and we'll simply copy from the text without thought. Remember, you can always go back to check on details afterwards.

- Don't record things which just 'might' be useful in the future.
- Leave time to allow your mind to organise the ideas.
- Don't let the author hijack your thinking.

Note-taking for analysis and structure

Take a chapter from one of the books you're using for the essay you've chosen to use in the 'In your own work' exercises. Read it through, first, for comprehension. Then, a day or so later, read it again, this time for analysis and structure. Leave it a few hours for your mind to self-organise. Then, take a blank sheet of paper and try writing the broad structure of what you can recall of the main points that interest you from the chapter.

Don't be tempted to go back to the text, even if it's just to check up on an isolated fact. And give yourself up to an hour trying to recall the structure. Normally you won't need this amount of time, but for this exercise give yourself plenty of time to do it thoroughly.

You will be pleasantly surprised by the complex structure of interconnected points you've been able to produce unaided. You will never again be entirely convinced when you try to tell yourself that you cannot trust your memory. You'll find that what your mind has given you is a clear, uncluttered structure around which you can build a fuller set of notes, if you need to.

But if you do decide to fill this out with more detail, always remind yourself not to clutter and obstruct your view of the structure with unnecessary detail. Remember, notes are of little use if they're not a record of your understanding of the subject.

Taking out the author's structure

In most passages it's quite easy to see the author's plan, the structure he or she has created, but not in all. In the most difficult cases you will need to interpret and translate what the author says into terms and structures that make sense for you. This will help you graft it onto your own thinking, making the ideas your own. At this point the ideas become universal; they are yours as well as the author's, leaving you in no danger of plagiarism. Just take the essence of the idea, stripped of all the phrases and sentences that are distinctive of the author.

- Choose your own words to give the notes a structure *you* can recall.
- Graft the ideas onto your own thinking.
- Ideas are universal – it's the way they are expressed and developed that is unique to the author.

However, even the most difficult and poorly organised author is likely to leave you a trail of literal symbols that indicate the structure he or she is following. We're all familiar with these, although we don't always pay as much heed to them as we should. The introductory and concluding sentences often indicate the main points of the passage. Here you're likely to find the memorable key word that will trigger off in your mind a whole cluster of ideas.

Once you get into the body of the text, words like 'first' and 'finally' act as pointers to the structure, indicating the number of points that are to be, or have been, made. Others, that introduce illustrative material, like 'for example' and 'for instance', indicate that you need not take close and detailed notes from what's to come. A word, a brief phrase or sentence should be enough to remind you of the example when you want it. And then there are the familiar 'logical indicators', which we will examine more closely in Stage 4 (see Chapters 29 and 32): words that indicate changes in direction ('In contrast', 'However') and extensions to the argument ('Further', 'Therefore', 'Thus').

Follow the trail of symbols

1 Introductory and concluding sentences.
2 Words that indicate:
   Structure: 'first', 'second', 'finally'
   Examples: 'for example', 'for instance'
   Changes in direction: 'in contrast', 'however'
   Extensions: 'further', 'therefore', 'thus'

Consolidating your notes

All of this means you're better able to take out a clear structure from what you read. But, if structure is one of the main features of good note-taking, then, as we've said before, flexibility is the other.

There are few things worse during revision than finding that your notes on a particular topic are spread throughout your file in different places, because each time you've taken notes your organisation hasn't allowed you to change or to add to those you already have. As a result you have different packets of notes on the same subject spread throughout your file, none of them related, and all of them taking a slightly different approach to the subject.

Notes are not fixed in stone: they evolve as you add to them and reshape them to reflect your changing understanding.

Few things can be more confusing and frustrating. At just that moment when you want to get down to some organised revision for the exam, you realise you've got to reorganise your notes. You have to take notes on all the notes you have, so that you end up with the one integrated package of notes you should have had in the first place.

It's worth reminding yourself that notes are only the raw material, they're not fixed in stone as soon as they're written. You add to them, adapt and reshape them as your ideas change, and as you read and see more. They must be able to adapt continually to the changes in your understanding of the subject. You must, then, have a note-taking strategy that is flexible enough to record these changes, while leaving you with one coherent set of notes.

Consolidating your notes

1 Loose-leaf file.
2 Index-card system.
3 Leave space between each section.
4 Write on just one side of the paper.

To create this flexibility in your note-taking use a loose-leaf file, so you can slip into your notes at the appropriate place new notes that expand or adapt what you already have. Use an index-card system or an electronic equivalent, such as Dropbox and Google Docs, organised into the topics on your course, to record isolated quotations, statistics and examples (see Chapter 18). Spread your notes out on the page, leaving enough space between each section, so you can add new material as it arises. And, for the same reason, write just on one side of the paper, so you always have a blank sheet opposite your notes on which you can enter new information.

Summary

1 Try to create clear uncluttered structures.

2 Trust yourself to remember those things you omit from your notes.

3 Leave a gap between reading and note-taking.

4 Make your notes a record of *your* understanding, using *your* words wherever possible.

5 Consolidate your notes on a subject in one place.

In the next chapter

With these techniques and the flexibility they bring to your study you can, with more confidence, note your own responses to the ideas and arguments you read, as we'll see in the next chapter.

15

Note-taking for Criticism and Evaluation

In this chapter you will learn:

- a four-step technique for criticising and evaluating arguments;
- how to take notes that allow you to record your own criticisms and evaluations of the passage;
- how to improve your concentration.

Obviously, our ability to discuss and criticise the implications of arguments depends first on the skills needed to lay bare their structure: to isolate clearly the points for and against, so that we can enter into the discussion more confidently. But we also need a note-taking strategy that will allow us to go one step further and record our own arguments and criticisms in the body of the notes.

Unfortunately, many of us never get to the stage of being able to criticise and evaluate an author's arguments, because we're handicapped by note-taking skills which condemn us to many hours of patient toil, taking irrelevant, verbatim notes. A large part of the reason for this lies in our willingness to omit the interpretation stage, and the pattern notes we should have made there in response to two questions:

1 What issues does the question raise that need to be researched and examined in the essay?
2 What do I know and think about the issues raised?

In effect, by ignoring these questions we've failed to preview any passage we're likely to read when we undertake our research. As a result we're going in blind. We have little idea of the important issues raised by the question and, consequently, we don't really know what we're looking for.

Having a standard by which to judge the author's ideas

Equally important, because we haven't declared what *we* know and think about the issues, we have no way of grafting onto our own understanding the ideas we're about to read and consider. Not surprisingly, then, they will always appear to be somebody else's. And, because of this, the most we'll be able to recall are mere scraps of what we've read without any consistent organisation to them. However, perhaps the most serious consequence is that we'll have nothing to judge the author's ideas against. We'll be in no position to criticise and evaluate the arguments.

Having read the passage we're likely to be so thoroughly convinced by the author's arguments that we find little to criticise. Then, when we go on to read another text by another author, who presents views conflicting with the first, we're likely to find we're equally convinced by these arguments. Lost between the two, we find it almost impossible to discuss the merits of either. Having failed to establish where we stand, we have nothing to argue with. Consequently, we're left just to imitate and reproduce uncritically what we read.

If we fail to interpret the question ...

1 We won't know what we're looking for.
2 We won't know what *we* think, so we won't be able to graft what we read onto our own understanding.
3 We will only be able to recall scraps of ideas and information without any organisation.
4 We will have nothing to judge the author's ideas against – we won't be able to criticise and evaluate them.
5 We will just imitate and reproduce uncritically what we read.

Poor concentration

This also goes a long way towards explaining why many of us find it so difficult to concentrate on our work for all but fairly short periods. Because we're asking the mind to do relatively simple things, just translating the words on the page and copying them into our notes, it's under-utilised, so it looks around for more interesting pursuits. It looks forward to the party at the weekend or back at last summer's holiday. It can do all this and still cope with the trivial tasks we set it. The only problem is that when we get to the bottom of the page, or after we've spent two hours taking notes, we struggle to recall a word of it. We've read it, but we haven't processed it beyond copying the words.

> If we cannot inject our own ideas into our notes, our minds are inclined to wander and we lose concentration.

There are, therefore, very good reasons why we should, at all times, attempt to escape this tendency towards passive, surface-level processing. Splitting up our reading and note-taking into the three levels of processing helps, but so does a more flexible note-taking strategy that will allow us to inject more of our own ideas and criticisms into the structure of the notes.

Therefore experiment, particularly with your pattern notes. If you still feel that linear notes are more appropriate for a particular piece of work, set time aside later to sit down with a blank sheet of paper and tap into your own ideas and criticisms, which will have been self-organising in your own mind since you finished reading. As you know, it won't take long. The ideas will come tumbling out and you will be surprised at just how good they are and how much you have to say about it.

> Set aside time to sit down with a blank piece of paper and write down *your* ideas about what you've just read.

Playing devil's advocate

Even so, there are many students who still believe they don't see as much to criticise in a passage as other students do. If this is your problem, the following four-step technique will help you think more critically about what you read. Then, in the next chapter, I have listed the most common weaknesses you should look for as you read. To help you use these more systematically, try working through the following steps.

Step 1: Are there exceptions?

When authors make claims that are important to their arguments, even though you might agree with them, play devil's advocate: ask yourself, are there exceptions to these?

For example, an author might argue that 'All criminals come from socially deprived backgrounds.' However, you can probably think of convicted criminals that you've read about in the newspapers, who, on the contrary, come from quite privileged backgrounds.

Step 2: If there are exceptions, are they general or specific?

2.1 Specific exceptions   If they are specific, then while an author can still retain his or her claim, you have found sufficient grounds to justify qualifying the claim in order to take account of the special cases you have uncovered.

To return to our example, if the exceptions were just limited to one or two individuals from privileged backgrounds, the author would have to qualify the original claim by arguing that 'Most criminals come from socially deprived backgrounds.'

2.2 General exceptions   However, if you have found a general category of exceptions, then you will have to move on to Steps 3 and 4.

Say you have discovered that most white-collar and computer crime is, in fact, committed by criminals with university degrees. In this case the objection cannot be dealt with so easily: you will have to ask the following questions.

Step 3: Is the claim too strong?

If you have found a general category of exceptions you must first ask yourself, does this make the original claim too strong: more than the evidence can support? If it does, then your author cannot maintain his or her claim. They must either rein it in, qualifying it in general terms, or abandon it altogether.

In our case the evidence can't support the claim, so, if the author wants to maintain it, she must qualify it by excluding all white-collar and computer crime, so that her argument then becomes: 'With the exception of white-collar and computer crime, all criminals come from socially deprived backgrounds.' However, this might weaken and restrict it so much that it might be wiser to abandon it altogether, particularly when it leads you to suspect that you could probably find other groups, too, if you looked hard enough.

Step 4: Does it account for only part of the case?

Alternatively, if it can't be qualified, and there is sufficient merit in the argument to warrant not abandoning it, then the only thing you can do is to extend the claim to cover the general category of cases that is currently excluded. However, if this is possible, it is quite likely to lead to conclusions your authors either didn't see in the first place or wouldn't agree with on the basis of their argument so far.

You might, for example, agree with the claim our author has made, although you question the notion that it is the 'socially' deprived that is the source of crime. You might argue that there are others responsible for crime, who are deprived in different ways. They may never have been socially deprived, but they may not have had a stable father figure in their lives: there may have been a family breakdown, or they may have been moved from one boarding school to another without ever being able to establish long-lasting paternal relations.

So, in this case the claim may be worth holding on to, but only in the extended form to cover this new category of deprivation. However, this may lead the author either to conclusions she didn't foresee or in a direction that doesn't serve the main purpose of her argument, which may have been to establish the claim that all crime can be identified with a particular social class.

Whichever is the outcome, whether you step off at Step 2, 3 or 4, you will have discovered for yourself that you have well-thought-out reasons for criticising and discussing the authors' arguments. Try it in the following exercise. To help you follow each step in this technique, keep a copy of the diagram below by your side as you work.

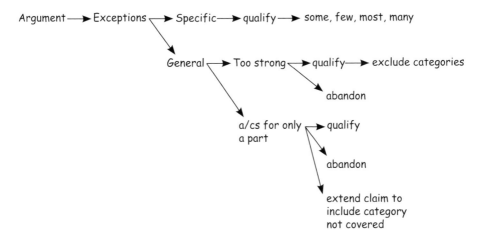

PRACTICE
EXERCISE

Note-taking for criticism and evaluation

Read the following passage carefully for comprehension. Then, after you've read it a second time, take the structure out of it in pattern notes. Now go through each of the steps above, asking yourself the questions about the principal claims made in the passage. You may not come up with much at this stage, but at least you've set your subconscious mind thinking about the issues. Then leave it for a day or two.

When you come back to it, go through the steps again, critically assessing the author's arguments. Your aim is to map out your reactions in pattern notes. So allow your mind to range free and fast over the issues. Remember, you're trying to tap into your mind's self-organised structures, so fluency and quick responses, as the ideas come flowing out, are important to get it all down in a structured form without losing any of it.

After you've completed this, compare it with the answer given below.

Passage

A Carnivore's Credo

This may be the age of enlightened sympathy for all animals, but certain facts are unassailable. We are at the end of a long evolutionary process that has produced a human society for whom meat-eating is natural. Indeed man's superiority is built on exploiting inferior species, who lack our intellectual and moral capabilities: they cannot think, make decisions or communicate.

The loudest and most successful critic of this view over recent years has been Peter Singer, whose book, *Animal Liberation,* has achieved cult status since its publication in 1975. Singer criticises meat-eating because he claims it is based on the arbitrary moral distinction of species: whereas we wouldn't condone eating humans, we do accept eating non-human animals. This, he argues, ranks alongside other arbitrary moral distinctions which we are only too ready to condemn, like sex or race. These, we believe, are irrelevant to moral judgements. We condemn racism and sexism, and any other form of discrimination, not based on relevant moral distinctions, like the practice of treating people differently because they have lower intelligence.

The only non-arbitrary moral distinction, he argues, is sentience, the capacity to suffer. This is a prerequisite for having interests. While there is no moral responsibility if we kick a stone, there is if we kick a mouse. So, anything that can suffer, that can experience enjoyment and happiness, has interests in avoiding pain and, therefore, deserves moral consideration.

However, as R. G. Frey points out in his article 'Pain, Interests, and Vegetarianism',[1] it is not the case that the capacity to suffer is a prerequisite of having interests – it is not, as this suggests, a necessary condition. In fact, he argues, we still speak of people having interests even when they can feel no pain at all.

His first example is of a soldier friend, who suffered extensive spinal, head and nervous injuries while serving in Vietnam. He is conscious, but cannot feel pain, yet still he has interests. Indeed his interests in being cared for are now greater because of his injuries. What's more, he has interests in the care of his wife and children, and in protecting his good name. These interests continue to exist even though he can feel no pain and even though he may not know his good name might be harmed.

His second example is that of Karen Quinlan, a comatose patient, who cannot feel pain, yet who, again, clearly has interests. For example, as Frey points out, if a photographer entered her room and photographed her, her interests in maintaining her privacy would have been invaded; whereas Singer would argue that because she can feel no pain, she has no interests. In fact, as individuals we all seem to have interests, like privacy, that have nothing to do with our capacity to feel pain.

Given these arguments, it would seem that humans are distinct from animals in non-arbitrary ways that may be difficult to pin down, but are no less real.

Answer

As we will see in the next chapter, usually our criticisms of arguments focus on one of three things:

1 the consistency of the argument;
2 the evidence used to support it;
3 the language used to develop it.

In this passage our criticisms are mostly to do with the language used. We're entitled to ask, 'Is this what we mean when we use the concept of pain, or do we mean more than this, or less?' Take Frey's criticism of Singer's argument and the cases that he raises to make his point.

Step 1: Are there exceptions?

When Frey uses the concept of 'pain', are there exceptions to this – types of pain that he doesn't include within his concept? In other words, is there just more to it than this? In the case of his friend, the Vietnam soldier, he appears to use 'pain' in a narrow sense, meaning just physical pain. Yet his friend is, of course, also capable of feeling emotional pain, anguish, insecurity and fear, for himself, his family and his good name. So, according to Singer's principle, he does have interests, because he can feel pain of this type.

Step 2: If there are exceptions, are they general or specific?

In this case they are general, not specific, so we cannot qualify Frey's case to acknowledge special cases. We are driven, then, to consider Step 3 or 4.

Step 4: Does it account for only part of the case?

It's not that the claim is too strong and can be reined in (as in Step 3), but that it's too narrow: it only accounts for a limited range of types of pain. If you were then to extend Frey's claim to cover the general category of cases that is currently excluded, this would amount to conceding the argument to Singer.

By the same process you can arrive at all the other criticisms in the answer on pp. 92–93. As you gain confidence with this technique, you will be able to adapt it to your needs and apply it to every question that asks you to criticise, discuss and evaluate arguments. For example, select one of the books you prioritised on your reading list for the essay you've chosen to use in the exercises 'In your own work' and complete the following exercise.

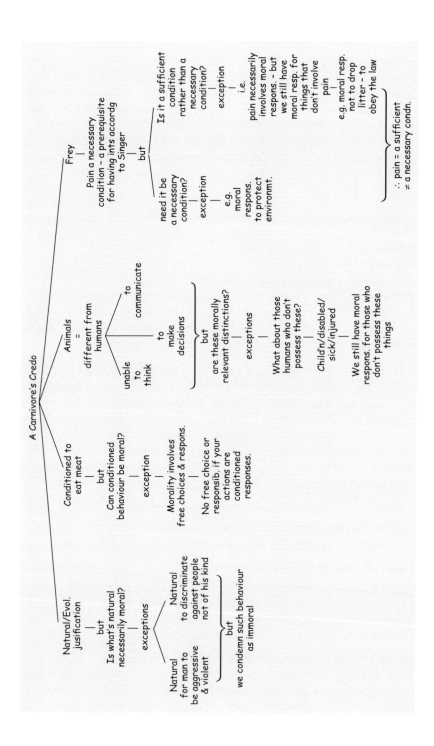

A Carnivore's Credo

Natural/Evol. jusification
but
Is what's natural necessarily moral?
|
exceptions
Natural to discriminate against people not of his kind
Natural for man to be aggressive & violent
but
we condemn such behaviour as immoral

Conditioned to eat meat
but
Can conditioned behaviour be moral?
|
exception
Morality involves free choices & respons.
No free choice or responsib. if your actions are conditioned responses.

Animals = different from humans
to communicate
to make decisions
unable to think
but
are these morally relevant distinctions?
|
exceptions
What about those humans who don't possess these?
Child'n/disabled/ sick/injured
We still have moral respons. for those who don't possess these things

Frey
Pain a necessary condition – a prerequisite for having int's accordg to Singer
need it be a necessary condition?
|
exception
e.g. moral respons. to protect environmt.
but
Is it a sufficient condition rather than a necessary condition?
|
exception
i.e.
pain necessarily involves moral respons. – but we still have moral resp. for things that don't involve pain
|
e.g. moral resp. not to drop litter – to obey the law

∴ pain = a sufficient ≠ a necessary condn.

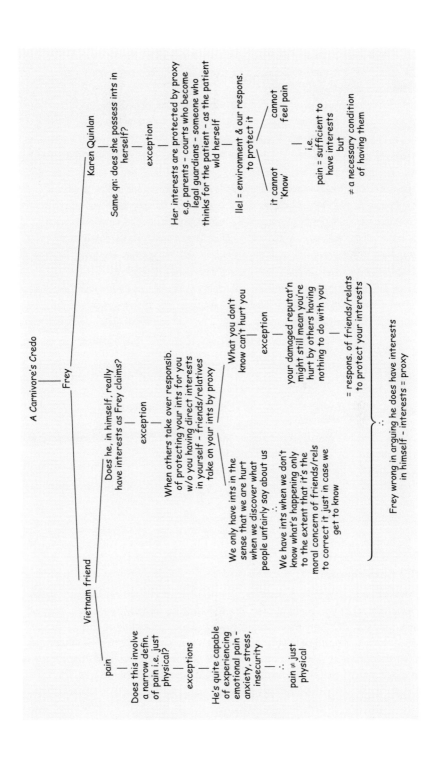

A Carnivore's Credo

Frey

Vietnam friend

Karen Quinlan

pain

Does he, in himself, really
have interests as Frey claims?

Same qn: does she possess ints in
herself?

Does this involve
a narrow defin.
of pain i.e. just
physical?

exception

exception

exceptions

When others take over responsib.
of protecting your ints for you
w/o you having direct interests
in yourself - friends/relatives
take on your ints by proxy

Her interests are protected by proxy
e.g. parents - courts who become
legal guardians - someone who
thinks for the patient - as the patient
wld herself

He's quite capable
of experiencing
emotional pain -
anxiety, stress,
insecurity

What you don't
know can't hurt you

llel = environment & our respons.
to protect it

∴
pain ≠ just
physical

We only have ints in the
sense that we are hurt
when we discover what
people unfairly say about us

exception

it cannot
'Know'

cannot
feel pain

∴
We have ints when we don't
know what's happening only
to the extent that it's the
moral concern of friends/rels
to correct it just in case we
get to know

your damaged reputat'n
might still mean you're
hurt by others having
nothing to do with you

i.e.
pain = sufficient to
have interests
but
≠ a necessary condition
of having them

= respons. of friends/relats
to protect your interests

∴
Frey wrong in arguing he does have interests
in himself - interests = proxy

Note-taking for criticism and evaluation

In this exercise select a chapter that you plan to read for your essay. Read it through first for comprehension. Then, after a day or so, take a blank sheet of paper and try to recall the broad structure of the chapter.

After you've done this, go over each point in the structure, critically assessing the argument in the way we have in this chapter. Map out your reactions in pattern notes, allowing yourself to explore quite freely your reactions to the arguments the author has made. If you appear to be going off the point at times, don't worry. Try to exhaust your ideas on an issue before you move on to another. But if an idea comes up out of place, note it, don't rely on picking it up later. Give yourself licence to analyse points thoroughly, to make contrasts, and to bring in other evidence you've come across elsewhere that you think has a bearing on the issues raised.

Remember, you are trying to get your mind's natural self-organisation down on paper. It's there, if only you can tap into it. To do that, you must allow it to pick up top speed. At this point it's more likely to make connections, to draw contrasts and comparisons, and to use items of information, evidence and examples, that you might never have thought of.

To help you identify the type of criticism that might be relevant, use those explained in the next chapter. Print off the checklist at the end of the chapter (pp. 105–6) and get into the habit of referring to it routinely before you read critically.

Summary

1 The right note-taking strategy can release our abilities to criticise and evaluate what we read.
2 Interpreting the question puts us in the position of being sufficiently detached from the author's arguments to criticise them.
3 It also helps improve our concentration.
4 Experiment with pattern notes to get your own ideas and criticisms down as quickly as they appear.
5 Use the four-step technique to reveal your criticisms.

In the next chapter

You should be pleasantly surprised by the number of interesting ideas, criticisms and examples that you were able to produce from your own resources. This will make your essay not only more interesting, but also more fluent and persuasive, because these are genuinely your own ideas. However, if you find it difficult to think of the different ways of criticising what you read, in the next chapter we will examine the most common mistakes and weaknesses you should look for.

Note

1   R. G. Frey, 'Pain, Interests, and Vegetarianism', in his *Interests and Rights: The Case Against Animals* (Oxford: Clarendon Press, 1980), ch. XI.

Thinking and Reading Critically

In this chapter you will learn:

- how to reveal the mistakes that authors make as they develop their arguments;
- how to assess whether an author has supported his arguments with sufficient relevant evidence and drawn reliable inferences from it;
- how to identify the most common mistakes authors make in their use of language.

We all make mistakes when we write, no matter who we are. We fail to apply elementary tests of logic to determine whether one idea does in fact lead to another. We rely on partial, untested evidence. And we use language in a misleading, inconsistent way without reflecting on its hidden implications. These three types of mistake cover virtually all of the points of criticism you need to identify as you read, so develop the habit of checking for them routinely.

Three types of mistake

1 **Arguments**
    1.1 Does the conclusion follow from the reasons the author gives?
    1.2 Are there hidden assumptions in the argument?
2 **Evidence**
    2.1 Does the author have enough reliable evidence?
    2.2 Does he represent the evidence accurately?
    2.3 Does he draw reliable inferences from it?
    2.4 Does he draw relevant inferences from it?
3 **Language**
    3.1 Is the author's meaning clear?
    3.2 Does she use words consistently?

1 Arguments

1.1 Does the conclusion follow from the reasons the author gives?

Check the qualifiers

Qualifiers are the words we use to indicate the strength of our claims, words like 'some', 'all', 'few', 'every' and 'never'. If an author claims that 'most' people agree about something, he cannot then conclude that 'all' people agree about it. In many cases the mistake is made more difficult to spot because authors hide their qualifiers.

A report on safe driving

An author might report that researchers have found that older drivers are safer than younger ones. He might then argue that because Philip is older than Mark he is a safer driver. But the researchers might have meant that it is only true in 'most' cases, whereas the author has argued that it is 'always' true and, therefore, it must be true in the cases of Philip and Mark.

Invalid conclusions: Distributing terms in an argument

Hidden qualifiers not only result in exaggerated conclusions, they also encourage authors to draw conclusions that are not supported by their argument. An author might assume that the terms of an argument are distributed, when they're not. To distribute a term means to refer to everything denoted by the term ('all drivers', not 'some drivers'). If an author argues that

'Businessmen treat their workers badly',

and then concludes,

'because John is a businessman, he treats his workers badly,'

she has assumed that the hidden qualifier is a universal, like 'all', when it may in fact only be a partial qualifier, like 'some'. If this is the case, the terms are not 'distributed' in the argument. As only 'some' businessmen treat their workers badly, John may be one of those who treat their workers well. So, get into the habit of asking the simple question, 'Is this a universal claim?'

Converting claims

When we convert our claims we interchange the *subject* of the sentence with the *complement*. So if I say

'No women (subject) are members of the football team (complement)',

I can also say

'No members of the football team are women.'

This works where there is *total exclusion* of one group from another, as you can see in the example. However, we cannot convert our claims when they involve *total inclusion*. We cannot say, for example, that 'All cats are animals', therefore 'All animals are cats'. So the two principles to keep in mind are:

Conversion – two principles

1 Total exclusion is convertible.
2 But total inclusion is not.

Affirming and denying

The *hypothetical* or *conditional* argument is easily recognisable by its familiar 'if … then' structure. You might argue,

> If an athlete is found to have taken performance-enhancing drugs, then he will be disqualified.

As you can see, it has two parts: the 'if' part, known as the *antecedent*, and the 'then' part, known as the *consequent*. So, in this case, it would be consistent to argue that,

> Stephen has been found to have taken performance-enhancing drugs, therefore, he will be disqualified.

In other words, it is consistent to **affirm the antecedent**. And, as you might expect, the opposite is also true: it is consistent to **deny the consequent**. So we can argue,

> Stephen has not been disqualified, therefore, he has not been taking performance-enhancing drugs.

As you can see, there are two quite simple rules. An argument is only valid if you *affirm the antecedent* or *deny the consequent*. Keep in mind the following simple table:

	Antecedent	Consequent
Valid	Affirm	Deny
Invalid	Deny	Affirm

Affirming and denying

PRACTICE EXERCISE

Explain in your own terms why the following arguments are invalid:

1   Stephen has not been found to have taken performance-enhancing drugs. Therefore, he will not be disqualified.
2   Stephen has been disqualified. Therefore, he has been found to have taken performance-enhancing drugs.

Answer

> In both cases he may have been, or may still be, disqualified for other reasons.

1.2 Are there hidden assumptions in the argument?

Not only are qualifiers often hidden, but assumptions too. Authors may be unaware they have made them or believe it's not worth making them clear, because we know and agree with them. Of course, the arguments may still be valid, but we won't know that until we have revealed the assumptions.

Hidden assumptions

EXAMPLE

You might read a claim like the following in your research: 'The significant increase in church attendance in recent years shows that we are becoming a much more religious society.'

As you can see, there is a hidden assumption here: that the only reason people attend is to celebrate their religion. In fact there may be many reasons. So ask yourself, 'Has the author made an unjustified assumption?'

2 Evidence

2.1 Does the author have enough reliable evidence?

Untypical examples and insufficient or weighted evidence

One of our most common problems is that we generalise on the basis of untypical examples, or on insufficient or weighted evidence. It results from three fairly common errors, which we can identify by asking three simple questions:

Three questions

1 Is the generalisation based on a sufficient number of instances?
2 Do these instances represent a fair sample?
   2.1 Are they typical?
   2.2 Are there special conditions prevailing?
   2.3 Are there any exceptions?
3 Does the probability that such a generalisation is true make it reasonable to believe it?

2.2 Does the author represent the evidence accurately?

Even when there is enough reliable evidence, some authors exaggerate or underestimate it. Identifying this is not difficult. Look at Chapter 33, where we discuss how to identify and avoid it in our own work.

Statistics

One way of avoiding it should be to use the precision of statistics, but these can be just as misleading. So when an author presents his evidence, get into the habit of asking three simple questions:

1 Are there **hidden factors** that need to be considered?
   – If the annual crime statistics show an increase in crime, is this because it is now easier to report certain types of crime that have previously gone unreported, rather than because there has been an increase in criminal behaviour?
2 Is there a **lack of uniformity** between different sets of statistics that are being compared?
3 Are **absolute figures** being used in an argument to establish a comparison?
   – If the annual crime figures show an increase, we also need to know how fast they have been growing in previous years and how fast the country's population has been increasing, otherwise we have no way of knowing how significant this is. A more reliable indicator is a comparative figure like the number of crimes per 100,000 people.

2.3 Does the author draw reliable inferences from it?

Analogies

The most natural way of drawing an inference from evidence is to find an analogy: a familiar thing that resembles in most respects what we are trying to explain, which we assume will continue to resemble it in some further respect and this gives us our inference.

> ### Sir Isaac Newton   EXAMPLE
>
> Sir Isaac Newton used the analogy of billiard balls to explain the behaviour of light as molecules or particles. As billiard balls bounce off the cushions of billiard tables at different angles, so molecules were thought to refract at different angles as they hit the sides of a prism.

However, beware of authors who commit the fallacy of analogy by ignoring the differences between the analogy and what they are explaining, or by pushing similarities beyond what is reasonable.

> ### A newspaper report   EXAMPLE
>
> A newspaper account of a speaker at a conference reported, 'He told the Conference that football hooliganism was exacerbated by press coverage. This was rather like blaming the Meteorological Office for bad weather.'

The other thing to remember is that although analogies are remarkably effective in clarifying ideas, they can only *suggest* an inference, they cannot *establish* one. We can only safely argue from the possession of one set of characteristics to another, if we can establish a causal connection between them and not just a vivid similarity. So, when authors use an analogy to draw inferences, check three things:

1 The **connection** between the analogy and the inference:
   1.1 When does the connection break down? They all tend to at some point.
   1.2 Is there a causal connection: does the evidence show that one thing really does cause another?
2 The **numbers** involved:
   2.1 The number of examples between which the analogy holds – the more we have, the more confident we can be.
   2.2 The number and variety of the characteristics shared by the analogy and what it is being used to explain.
3 The **relation** between the analogy and the inference drawn from it:
   3.1 Is it the right strength or does it exaggerate the extent of the similarity?
   3.2 How significant are the similarities and differences between the analogy and what is being explained?

Oversimplifying

1 **Stereotypes** All authors use stereotypes; some are justified, but many are not. So get used to questioning whether these are reliable generalisations about those who

make up the stereotypes. If they are not, then they are likely to be statements designed to get us to respond in a particular way by appealing to our prejudices, rather than thinking carefully about the argument. In this way they act as a short cut to avoid the difficult task of assessing the evidence thoughtfully.

Are these reliable generalisations or are they intended just to appeal to prejudice?

2   **The straw man** To strengthen their arguments some authors oversimplify their description of a situation or a proposition, either deliberately or accidentally, so that they can dismiss it as false.

Miracles   EXAMPLE

'It's absurd to argue that miracles never happen, after all we live in an age of miracles: the existence of the TV, computers, space travel, and medical treatment that can now save people from what would have been certain death just fifty years ago.'

In this argument the author has reinterpreted the claim that miracles never happen to mean that extraordinary inventions cannot take place. Of course, in this form it's not difficult to prove the claim to be false, but it's unlikely that this was the way in which those making the argument against the possibility of miracles meant it to be interpreted.

3   **Special pleading** Like the straw man, this, too, oversimplifies an argument, only this time by omitting those things that might weaken an author's argument, while emphasising those points that support it. Alternatively, an author might use an argument in one context, but refuse to use it in another where it would lead to an opposite conclusion.

If you suspect an author of either of these, test her claims:

1   **Compare** what she says with what she has said at other times.
2   Try to evaluate her **motivation** for making the argument. She might be paid to promote these opinions.
3   Ask her to **specify** what she means. For those arguments that omit relevant points and gloss over the omission using general, unspecific language, get into the habit of asking the author to be specific – the 'who', 'what', 'why' and 'how' questions:

    3.1   **Who** did the research? Who financed it?
    3.2   **What** does she mean by X? What numbers were involved in the study?
    3.3   **Why** should this be the only explanation? Why was the study undertaken?
    3.4   **How** was the research conducted?

4   **The fallacy of false dilemma** In this very common strategy the argument is oversimplified in such a way that favours the conclusion the author wants you to draw. He encourages you to accept that the problem has an either/or solution; that there are just two solutions, when in fact there may be several. It forces you to accept a solution out of fear for the less desirable alternative. Many of the most obvious examples can be identified by the use of the word 'only'. So, whenever you see the word used in an argument, ask yourself whether these are indeed the 'only' alternatives.

'Advertisers seek only to ensure that consumers make   EXAMPLE
informed choices.'

In our essay question on advertisers we did exactly this by asking whether this really was the 'only' intention of advertisers.

Invalid causal inferences

You will often find that authors infer one thing causes another, when there is good evidence to suggest that it might not. There are three ways in which this commonly occurs:

1   the *post hoc* fallacy;
2   cause/correlation;
3   multiple and underlying causes.

1   **The *post hoc* fallacy** More accurately, this is the *post hoc ergo propter hoc* ('After this, therefore because of this') fallacy. It is the mistake of assuming that just because an event follows another, it must be caused by it. When we see two things regularly occur together, one after the other, we're inclined to associate them as cause and effect.

Superstitions   EXAMPLE

In fact, so common is this mistake that, like analogies, it's the source of many of our most enduring superstitions. No doubt someone noticed often enough that walking under a ladder was followed by bad luck, so the superstition got started that the former was responsible for the latter.

2   **Cause/correlation** A similar mistake occurs when we confuse a cause with a correlation.

Heart disease   EXAMPLE

In our attempt to explain the rise of heart disease in Western societies, we might find that 80 per cent of sufferers are obese. Such a correlation is very persuasive, but is it any more than this? We might find that 80 per cent also watch daytime TV, but we're less likely to believe that this is the cause.

3   **Multiple and underlying causes** Situations are often more complex than we imagine. For most events there are almost certainly many interrelated causes and not just one: the causes of the outbreak of the Second World War or the reasons for the increase in antisocial behaviour. A single cause is confirmed only if it *alone* can produce the effect. By contrast, in some circumstances, where there appear to be multiple factors operating, there may in fact be a single underlying cause explaining them all. So ask yourself:

3.1   Could this alone cause the effect?
3.2   Is there one underlying cause that explains all these effects?

2.4 Does the author draw relevant inferences from the evidence?

Eager to defend their point of view, some authors shift attention away from weaknesses in their argument by proving another that is irrelevant. As you read, check for the following.

1 **Attacking the person** (The *ad hominem* argument) The weaknesses in the argument are sidestepped by discrediting the person who drew attention to them.

2 **Popularity** (The *ad populum* argument) Some bolster their argument by appealing to popular opinion on the assumption that whatever the crowd thinks must be right. So, beware of those who make these appeals by starting a sentence with phrases, like 'As we all know' or 'It's common knowledge that'.

3 **Authority** This diverts attention away from criticism by appealing to an authority. So get into the habit of asking these simple questions:

   3.1 Does the authority know what she's talking about?
   3.2 Are her views based on careful study or extensive experience?
   3.3 Does her position offer her greater authority than others?
   3.4 Has she shown herself to be a better observer and a shrewder judge than the rest of us?
   3.5 What are her motives? Is she promoting her own self-interest?

4 **Fear** Rather than show you that his argument can be trusted, an author might try to raise your fears about the consequences of accepting his opponent's argument.

5 **Compromise** Alternatively an author might get you to accept an argument on the basis that it is the most 'reasonable' compromise between two undesirable extremes. Almost any argument can be presented as a compromise between two others, so this alone doesn't mean there is good reason to accept it. And, of course, the truth is just as likely to lie on one of the extremes as in the middle.

3 Language

At the beginning of this book I said that writing is a form of thinking, the most difficult form. To think and write well we must be clear about our ideas and develop them consistently.

3.1 Is the author's meaning clear?

Jargon

There is no better way of revealing the confusion in our thinking than by writing down our ideas. The most effective way of concealing confusion is to resort to jargon. This is the language of specialists who have convinced themselves that their ideas cannot be expressed in any other way. As students we are all inducted into this way of expressing our ideas on the back of the assumption that if we are to be successful in our chosen field we must use this sort of language, even though it makes little sense and produces more confusion than clarity.

The most effective way of concealing confusion in our thinking is to resort to jargon.

Put simply, it is the language of people who are too busy to think seriously. When authors use jargon their aim is to import ideas into their writing without having to argue for them. The jargon evokes a clutch of indistinct ideas, all of which can be interpreted in numerous ways. But rather than reflect upon them, we are encouraged to move on, driven by our concern that we should know what this all means.

Don't be fooled into thinking this is your fault. Train yourself to be a jargon buster. Where you don't understand something, demand to know what this means precisely. As you read, convert the jargon into concrete words that ground the ideas in everyday reality. Nothing short of that will do. If this is not possible, then it is meaningless nonsense.

Jargon busting

PRACTICE
EXERCISE

Try your own jargon busting skills by translating the following into everyday language. Then compare your answer with the one below. However, I cannot guarantee that this answer is correct: there is plenty of room for doubt.

communication facilitation skills development intervention

Answer

a programme to help people communicate better

Loaded language

Many of the words we use and read are 'loaded'. It is not like jargon, that we don't understand the meaning of them, just that not all the meaning is being disclosed to us. They have an emotional content or a value judgement, which manipulates our thinking without us being conscious of it. In this way an author can encourage us to accept her argument without us looking at it too closely.

Words like 'democracy' and 'freedom' have positive associations, while those like 'hardliner' and 'extremist' are negative. So, without having to argue her case too strenuously, an author can just describe her points using these words and be confident that we will accept her conclusions. So, get into the habit of asking whether a word is loaded and, where you suspect that it is, translate it into neutral terms so you can see whether the argument is then so convincing.

Translate them into neutral terms. Is the argument still convincing?

Begging the question

The other way authors manipulate our thinking is by begging the question, which occurs when they accept as an assumption what they are arguing for as a conclusion: in other words, they smuggle into their assumptions the conclusion they are about to deduce.

> ### A politician   EXAMPLE
>
> A politician might argue, 'You must admit that too much help for single parents is a bad thing', or, 'You can't deny that giving students too much freedom in the classroom is not a good thing.'

And you cannot avoid agreeing, not because giving help to single parents or freedom to students is in principle a bad thing, but simply because of the phrase 'too much', which means 'a quantity so great that it is a bad thing'. We are presented with a mere tautology, nothing more significant than 'X is X', which is trivially true. Too much of anything is a bad thing, so the real point at issue is what do we mean by too much freedom or too much help?

3.2 Does the author use words consistently?

However, clarity on its own is not enough: once an author has made clear what he means by a word, he must stick to it. Often the most difficult errors to identify are the result of authors using words inconsistently.

The fallacy of equivocation

The most common form of this is known as the *fallacy of equivocation*, where an author uses a word to mean one thing in one part of the argument and something else in another part.

> ### Australian commercial   EXAMPLE
>
> An Australian commercial promoting concern for the environment has the presenter surrounded by people planting trees. He is clutching a handful of soil, which he allows to fall gradually through his fingers, while he tells us that those who fought for this (holding up the soil), their land, in the two world wars would be deeply disappointed by our generation, if we fail to protect it.

The aim of those who wrote the commercial was to exploit our inattention in not seeing that there is a difference between the 'Land' that was fought for, and the 'land' as in soil. By 'Land' we mean our culture, values and heritage, indeed our whole way of life, which might be threatened by an invader. This is quite different from the soil in which we plant crops. Clearly the persuasiveness of the argument rests on the equivocation of the concept 'land', which means different things at different stages in the argument.

> ### Advertising campaign   PRACTICE EXERCISE 16
>
> Read the following argument and see if you can identify what's wrong with it. Then compare your answer with mine below.
>
> As citizens we all have a patriotic duty to protect our country from attack from other countries. At this very moment we are under attack from foreign imports, so we have a duty to protect ourselves by buying home-produced products, like XXX, which is wholly owned by citizens of this country.

Answer

The persuasiveness of this argument rests on the equivocation of the concept 'attack'. In the first sense it refers to military attack and our patriotic duty to defend the country. But in the second sense it refers to economic competition, which we accept as a normal part of foreign trade.

Checklist

If you want to improve your skills in identifying these problems, go onto the companion website (www.howtowritebetteressays.com), where you'll find exercises to practise on. For most of us the problem is how to organise ourselves to check for these things routinely as we read. It will help if you can keep a copy of the following checklist by your side as you work.

1 Arguments	
1.1 Does the conclusion follow from the reasons given?	☐
Qualifiers	☐
Distributing terms	☐
Converting claims	☐
Affirming and denying	☐
1.2 Are there hidden assumptions in the argument?	☐
2 Evidence	
2.1 Does the author have enough reliable evidence?	☐
Untypical examples/insufficient or weighted evidence	☐
2.2 Does he represent the evidence accurately?	☐
Statistics	☐
2.3 Does he draw reliable inferences from it?	☐
Analogies	☐
Oversimplifying (Stereotypes, Straw man, Special pleading, False dilemma)	☐
Invalid causal inferences (*Post hoc* fallacy, Cause/correlation, Multiple and underlying causes)	☐
2.4 Does he draw relevant inferences from it?	☐
(Attacking the person, Popularity, Authority, Fear, Compromise)	☐

3 Language	
3.1 Is the author's meaning clear?	☐
Jargon	☐
Loaded language	☐
Begging the question	☐
3.2 Does she use words consistently?	☐
Equivocation	☐

This looks like a lot, so don't try to check for everything as you read. Just remind yourself of the checklist before you begin to read the text critically. Having done this two or three times, you will find more and more of it sticks and you won't need reminding. Then, after you've finished the passage, go through the list again and check with what you can recall of the text. These are the sorts of questions you will be asking in Stage 5 (Revision) about your own essay before you hand it in. So it's a good idea to develop your skills by practising on somebody else first.

Summary

1 By learning these simple mistakes we can identify virtually all of the most common points of criticism in what we read.
2 The most common mistakes are found in how authors develop their arguments, represent their evidence and draw inferences from it, and use language.
3 We can improve our ability to identify these by routinely referring to the checklist before we read and then again after we've finished.

In the next chapter

In the next chapter we will look at ways we can use our note-taking skills to catch our most creative ideas, so that we can generate more of our own ideas and insights, and use them more effectively.

Note-taking for Creativity

In this chapter you will learn:

- how to use your skills more flexibly to get the best out of your abilities;
- how to capture more of your most creative ideas;
- how to make better use of your mind's potential in your essays.

As we have seen, all of these different strategies for note-taking and reading are designed to get the best out of our abilities. Indeed, most of us have abilities we have barely used before. In order to get at these, you've probably experimented with different ways of note-taking and planning your essays to find a method that suits you. But, as we've seen, the key to it is to be flexible. Choose note-taking, planning and reading strategies that are the most effective for the job you have to do. This way you will find the right key that will unlock your abilities. Don't just stick to one strategy that you've always used even though you know it isn't always as much help as you would like it to be.

- To get the best out of your abilities, be flexible.
- Choose strategies that are effective for the job.

Pattern notes

This is particularly the case with creative tasks: when we generate our own ideas as in brainstorming and when we plan our essays. One of the most effective note-taking methods for creative work is the method known as 'pattern notes', as shown in the examples on pp. 13, 26 and 43–46. Rather than starting at the top of the page and working down in a linear form in sentences or lists, you start from the centre with the title of the essay and branch out with your analysis of concepts or other ideas as they form in your mind.

The advantages

The advantage of this method is that it leaves the mind as free as possible to analyse concepts, to make connections and contrasts, and to pursue trains of thought. As you're restricted to using just single words or simple phrases, you're not trapped in the unnecessary task of constructing complete sentences. Most of us are familiar with the frustration of trying to catch the wealth of ideas the mind throws up, while at the same time struggling to write down the sentences they're entangled in. As a result we see exciting ideas come and go without ever being able to record them quickly enough.

Pattern notes

Try it for yourself: take one of the following statements and list the pros and cons as quickly as the ideas come to you. Write the statement out on a blank sheet of paper and then draw two lines down from it, one to the right, the other to the left, representing the arguments for and against.

Then try to think of all the arguments that might be made in support of the statement. As each idea comes to you draw lines fanning out below the word 'pro' and use a word, or a simple phrase of two or three words at most, to represent it. If an idea breaks down into separate parts, or leads to different implications, draw lines down from it in the same fashion as you record each part or implication. Then move to the next idea.

Work fast, allowing yourself to record all the ideas as quickly as they come to you. When you've completed one side of the argument, move to the other and do the same. As you do each side you'll find that arguments supporting the other side will come to you. Note them; don't lose them. The secret is to let your mind run freely and keep pace with it in your notes.

Statements

1   A law should be passed preventing journalists from invading the privacy of individuals.
2   The suffering of animals used to test pharmaceutical products is worth it if it saves human lives.
3   Restricting the freedom of the individual to smoke in public places cannot be justified.

Generating ideas

Now that you've done this you'll be even more aware than maybe you were before that the mind can work so much faster producing ideas than we can find the words to write them down. So, we need a system that can catch all the ideas it can throw up, and give us the freedom to put them into whatever order or form appears to be right. The conventional linear strategy of taking notes restricts us in both these ways.

Not only does it tie us down to constructing complete sentences, or at least meaningful phrases, which means we lose the ideas as we struggle to find the words, but even more importantly, we're forced to deal with the ideas in sequence, in one particular order, so that if any ideas come to us out of that sequence, we must discard them and hope we can pick them up later. Unfortunately, all too often when we try to recall the ideas, we just can't.

Pattern note-taking

1   Allows us to be more creative.
2   We can catch ideas as they come to us without losing any.
3   We're not tied down to writing complete sentences.
4   We're not forced to deal with the ideas in one particular order.
5   It gives us the freedom to use more of our own ideas.
6   And to see more connections between them.
7   It is fast and flexible.

Creating our own connections between ideas

The same is true when we take linear notes from the books we read. Most of us find that once we've taken the notes we're trapped within the order in which the author has dealt with the ideas and we've noted them. It's not impossible, but it's difficult to escape from this. By contrast, pattern notes give us complete freedom over the final order of our ideas and the connections we want to make.

Asking for directions   EXAMPLE

It's probably best explained by comparing it to the instructions you might get from somebody if you were to ask them the way to a particular road. They would give you a linear list of instructions (e.g. 'First, go to the end of the road, then turn right. When you get to the traffic lights, …' and so on). This forces you to follow identically the route they would take themselves. If you don't, you're lost. By contrast, pattern notes are like a copy of a map or the *A to Z* of a large city: you can see clearly the various routes you can take, so you can make your own choices.

Coping with difficult situations and competing demands

Not only do they allow you to keep up with the ideas as they come at you rapidly from all angles without any apparent predictability, but they give you the tools to respond creatively to different challenges and situations. For example, using pattern notes we can work on several lines of discussion simultaneously, so we can catch all manner of ideas that we would otherwise be forced to let go while we worked on just one discussion. Then, once the pattern is completed, all the ideas are readily available and all we need to do is make a decision as to the final order in which to develop the arguments.

In the same way, they help us cope in unstructured situations, in which ideas can come to us without any obvious order or predictability. Linear notes work well in structured tasks, like taking notes from a book. But often we have to work in situations or at tasks that are unpredictable. For example, pattern notes are useful when we're trying to make notes from recall and the ideas come tumbling out thick and fast. The same is true of taking notes during a class discussion, where ideas might be thrown about quite rapidly and, unlike those in a book, you have no control over them. You can't go back to get something down you may have missed, as you can in your book by re-reading a difficult passage. Therefore you need a note-taking strategy that is fast and flexible.

- Pattern notes give us the tools to respond creatively to different challenges and situations.
- They work well in unstructured situations.
- They help us cope when we are presented with ideas in no obvious order or predictability.

Freeing the mind to work more imaginatively

Indeed, those who advocate pattern notes argue that the brain just doesn't work in a linear manner and that conventional ways of planning and taking notes are, therefore, not the most useful. They force the mind to operate in artificial ways, thereby releasing only a small fraction of its potential. If the brain works best within the clusters of key concepts in an interlinked and integrated manner in the way we've already seen, it makes sense to structure our notes and our word relations in the same way, rather than in the traditional linear manner.

> Conventional ways of taking notes force the mind to operate in artificial ways, thereby releasing only a small fraction of its potential.

This is borne out by those students who've adopted the method as an integral part of their pattern of study. In one study, undergraduates at the University of Oxford were able to complete their essays in a third of the time they usually took, while at the same time receiving higher marks. Moreover, for many students when they use this method it is the first time they realise that education can be an exciting business in which they have a valuable and significant role to play in producing their own insights and perceptions seen only by them in their own unique way.

By leaving them as free as possible to write down their own ideas it not only injects more creativity into their work, but it also gives their own ideas greater prominence. Consequently, when they come to research them they're better prepared to evaluate and select from what they read, rather than finding themselves just reproducing the ideas they read.

- The brain doesn't work in a linear manner.
- It works in clusters of interlinked ideas like pattern notes.
- You can use your own insights and perceptions in your own unique way.
- Therefore you're better prepared to evaluate and select from what you read.

Indeed, the flexibility of this strategy is almost unlimited. You can go on adding connections and new ideas as and when they occur to you. So, unlike many other systems, rather than stunting your abilities, it gives the mind the freedom to work more imaginatively, creating new analyses, seeing unexpected connections and contrasts, and synthesising ideas from different sources.

Pattern note-taking is better ...

1 for making notes from recall;
2 for creative tasks;
3 in class discussions.

Summary

1 To get the best out of your abilities, try to be more flexible.
2 Choose the right method for the right job.
3 Pattern note-taking is best for creative work and for those unstructured situations such as class discussions.
4 The mind works naturally, linking concepts and ideas in this way.
5 It helps us use more of our own ideas.

In the next chapter

In this chapter we have seen how we can use note-taking strategies that will help us catch and develop our most creative ideas. In this way we will make better use of our mind's potential. In the next chapter we will extend this by learning to use simple systems that will help us catch our best ideas. Without these our work will struggle to be more than a reproduction of the ideas of others. Indeed, with an effective retrieval system we will have access to ideas that will make our work unique.

18

Organising Your Retrieval System

In this chapter you will learn:

- how to create an effective retrieval system to catch more of your own ideas and insights, using a manual or electronic system;
- the importance of using a journal and a notebook;
- how to gather material by using a card-index and a project box.

If we are to generate and use more of our own ideas and insights, we will have to spend some time organising an effective research strategy. The key to this is to have a retrieval system that is sufficiently adaptable to catch the material *whenever* and *wherever* it shows itself, and then provide us with a means of accessing it easily whenever we want it.

Creating such a system isn't difficult, but it calls for a little imagination and, above all, flexibility. As we've already seen with our reading and note-taking, inflexibility can force us into surface-level processing, leaving us dependent on the ideas that our tutors and texts can give us.

> Without a good retrieval system we will lose many of our best ideas and our work will be predictable and imitative.

The same goes for our retrieval system. Unless we choose and organise its various components thoughtfully, we're likely to lose most of our best ideas, and produce work that is predictable and imitative of the ideas we've been given. To put it simply, our system should promote, not frustrate the quality of our work. This is not an unimportant part of our pattern of study, and its influence is never neutral. Get it right and we can find ourselves with an abundance of insightful ideas that are genuinely our own. Get it wrong and our work struggles to rise above the mundane and imitative.

Searching out your own sources

Most of us are used to using the obvious sources of material, such as the booklists and references provided by our tutors. But you can go further than this and uncover texts and articles of your own by checking the bibliographies of the recommended texts.

Certain texts will be common throughout each bibliography, which is often a good indication of those that are the most useful and respected in the field. But check the date of the publication. If you're looking at a text published in 1995 and its bibliography is recommending another text published in 1975, you might find that other texts have been published since that have superseded it. However, don't be surprised if this is not the case: there are still the classic, highly respected, indispensable texts in most subject areas.

Beyond bibliographies, probably the most under-used resources are libraries and their staff. Modern libraries are more than just a source of books: they collect and classify information from a wide range of sources. Most take an impressive range of journals, newspapers and periodicals, along with government reports on a range of topics. Of course, in addition, most have computer terminals that can give you access to the internet and specialist databases. Many libraries also have large stocks of recordings of educational material.

Sources

1 Tutors' recommendations
2 Bibliographies
3 Libraries:
    3.1 Journals
    3.2 Newspapers and periodicals
    3.3 Government reports
    3.4 Internet
    3.5 Specialist databases
    3.6 Recordings of educational material

One of the richest sources is found in your own mind

For most of us this list just about covers the range of sources available to us. But it ignores one of the richest sources of ideas and evidence, mainly because we're not accustomed to recognise it as such. Each day we talk to friends and acquaintances, we listen to the radio and watch TV, or we just sit thinking as we drive home, or on a bus or train. On all of these occasions our minds are taking in ideas and processing them into complex, self-organised structures. This is rich material that we ignore at our own cost. Just because it doesn't come from an authoritative book or article, or from a knowledgeable tutor, doesn't mean it's not full of insights that the mind will feed on to produce interesting and useful structures of ideas.

Our minds are constantly processing ideas into complex structures: a rich source of interesting insights.

Take those moments in the day when we're alone with our thoughts without any interruptions from friends, our smartphone, the TV, the radio or a book we ought to read. It's just us and our ideas as we travel home. On most of these occasions it's difficult in retrospect to recall exactly what we were thinking. This in itself is not always a bad thing. Such moments of reverie are the time when the mind can process the material it's taken in during the day and organise it into structures that we can use.

But on other occasions, rather than whiling away this valuable time with just empty static in your head, it's useful just to set yourself a topic to think about and sort out as you sit there – in fact more useful than most students ever imagine. It's the time when you can do some serious thinking for yourself, not in response to someone else, a book or a tutor, but responding to your own ideas and your own original insights. You will be surprised at the results, maybe not immediately, although that's quite likely, but certainly a few days later when all sorts of ideas, insights and structures will appear in your mind and you'll wonder where you picked them up from.

Tapping into your own ideas

PRACTICE EXERCISE 18

Sit down with a blank sheet of paper; take one of the following issues or one from a course you're studying; and write down the points for and against the argument presented.

Give yourself 30 minutes free of all distractions. As you produce each point or argument, ask yourself if it needs analysing into its component points. If it does, analyse it. Be as exhaustive as you can in an effort to empty your mind of all your ideas on the issue.

Issues:

1 There are not enough medical resources to meet all our needs, so we should put those whose illness is self-inflicted at the bottom of the waiting list.
2 Education in schools today is more about testing than teaching.
3 Bribes, gifts and commissions should be accepted as normal, justified methods in the modern business environment.

Some students plan whole essays in their head. Others give themselves a difficult problem to sort out or a complicated argument that they've never really understood before. And, without the usual distractions, like their books and other sources of reference they've come to rely on whenever they want to solve a problem, they sort it out on their own terms. Or, failing that, they at least discover for the first time what the problem is.

But it's not just these quiet moments that are a rich source of material and insights. When we discuss topics with friends we find ourselves using what we've read in books and articles, in the course of which we produce interesting ideas and arguments without any conscious prompting. Each day in newspapers we come across new evidence for something we've been studying, or interesting quotations that would support an argument we're planning to use in an essay. And, of course, there are those really special moments when we have a sudden dramatic insight, when we suddenly see something that's been troubling us for some time, clear and in sharp focus for the first time.

Spend just 30 minutes alone each day without any distractions to ...

1 Plan an essay.
2 Sort out problems.
3 Record ideas that may have come to you during the day as you discussed things with friends.
4 Note evidence and quotations you pick up from newspapers.
5 Catch insights as they come clearly into focus.

Carry a notebook

On all of these occasions we need to have our retrieval system well worked out. In particular, we need to have with us at all times a small notebook or access, through a smartphone or tablet, to an electronic equivalent, such as Online Notebook, in which we can note our sudden insights, or just work out our arguments and plans. This represents the internal monologue we have with ourselves on the subjects we're studying. It may be buried deep, but it's there. Although for some it's louder than for others, we all need to cultivate a system for tapping into it, so we can make the best use of its insights.

> We all need a system for tapping into our internal monologue to make the best use of its insights.

The point is that the most thoughtful and creative insights come to us not in the customary learning situations, such as lessons or as we work at our essays, but when we're off guard. And if we fail to live with this internal monologue and organise ourselves to use it, we'll lose a wealth of ideas and insights, which are essentially *ours*. You can always follow these up later with further research, but if you fail to record them the moment they occur, you will almost certainly forget them. Even if you're able to recover a small fragment of them sometime later, the most valuable part, the insight, the form that the idea took in the first place that forced it to the surface, will be lost to you forever. And it's this that made it vivid and clear for you and will, in turn, make it vivid and clear for others too. Once this has gone it rarely returns.

- Use a notebook to tap into your ideas as your mind sorts them out.
- Here you will find a wealth of original ideas that are genuinely yours.
- Record the ideas as they occur, otherwise you will lose the insight that made them vivid in the first place.

Keep a journal

Nevertheless, this is not the only way in which you can tap into more of your own thoughts. Probably the most useful method is to set up your own journal, either manually, in a computer file or online, in which you give yourself the opportunity of writing, say, two or three times each week for at least half an hour each time.

Unlike a conventional diary where you describe the events that have occurred in your life, a journal gives you the opportunity of writing exclusively about your ideas and their development. For most of us, opportunities to write in this free, unconstrained manner are rare: we're usually working with books, or with our notes, so the ideas that are genuinely ours, untainted by what we're reading or referring to, rarely reach the surface of our consciousness, although they're always there.

Index-card systems

To complete the system, back up the notebook and the journal with an index-card system divided into sections for each topic on the syllabus. You can set this up manually or online, using systems, such as Dropbox and Google Docs. Whenever we come across an interesting idea, an isolated statistic or a useful quotation, it's very difficult to know exactly what to do with it. Do you write it up on a sheet of paper? But if you do, where are you going to file it? And it's all too easy to lose just one sheet. To cope with this we need a simple, flexible system that we can use to catch all those isolated items that we would otherwise lose or not know what to do with. The index-card system, in whatever form, manual or electronic, fulfils this role perfectly.

Using just one card for each item (a quotation, an idea, an argument or a set of figures), you have a retrieval system that makes it very easy to find what you want whenever you want it, particularly when you come to revise for an examination, or set about the research for an essay. Once you've worked with a system like this for a few months, you'll wonder how you ever lived without one.

Recording isolated material	PRACTICE EXERCISE 19
Over the next week tick the relevant box below, each time you come across material that you would like to retain, but have nowhere to record it.	

An interesting idea	
A quotation	
Figures, statistics	
Examples	
The title of a book or article	
Miscellaneous items	

Equally important, most students find a card system frees them from the authors they read when they come to write the essay. First, because they are restricted by the limited space to noting only the ideas they need, they avoid getting trapped within the complex web of the author's arguments. And second, because each item is recorded in isolation, free of its context, they can take each idea in the order *they* want to, and not in the order their authors presented them.

A good card system also helps you avoid the temptation to plagiarise, which will not only unbalance your writing, but break up the flow of *your* words and ideas, making it increasingly difficult for you to keep control of your structure and, therefore, the relevance of your arguments. Even more important, it will make it difficult for you to develop your own ideas. Once you've accepted an author's statement as the undisputed authority, you're left with no good reason to discuss or challenge it.

Plagiarism ...

- Unbalances your essay.
- Breaks up the flow of *your* words and ideas.
- Makes it difficult to control the structure of your essay and, therefore, the relevance of your arguments.
- Makes it difficult to develop your own ideas.

A card system gives you the opportunity to record your sources accurately at the top of each card or electronic entry, and with the limited space it forces you to put the ideas into your own words. If the phrase or section in the text is so telling that no summary in your own words will capture the idea, then you're restricted to recording only short quotations of a sentence or two, which must be chosen with much greater care.

Index-card system

1 Catches all those isolated items we might otherwise lose.
2 Makes it easy to find what you want whenever you want it.
3 *You* decide on the order of your ideas, not the authors you read.
4 It helps you avoid plagiarism.

The project box

Finally, you might borrow an idea from professional writers. It's not unusual for writers to use a project box or file for the job they're working on. Into this they will put anything that comes to hand which might be useful in the future when they get around to organising the piece they've planned to write. You can do the same. Take a file, or even an actual box, and for all those items you come across online create an equivalent folder on your computer or online with a storage system, like Dropbox. Use these just for the essay you're going to have to write, or the topic you're about to study, and whenever you come across something that might be useful, drop it in. It may be an article taken from a newspaper or magazine; it may be notes taken from a TV programme; it may be anything that just stimulates an idea that you might otherwise forget.

This has all sorts of advantages. On a practical level, the very fact of having a box or file of this kind will in itself generate material that we would not otherwise have noticed. Knowing that we have something into which we can throw material of all different kinds is all the encouragement most of us need to set about noticing and collecting it wherever we can find it.

- Knowing that we have somewhere to put material, we notice and collect more.
- It prepares the mind to work on the project continuously even when we're not consciously thinking about it.

But equally important, it prepares the mind not just to recognise material when we see it, but to work on the ideas continuously – to see the essay as a developing project to be worked on even when we're not consciously thinking about it. We learn to regard our work as more like open-ended, ongoing projects, which we can't just switch off as soon as we leave the seminar or tutorial, or put down a book. It encourages us to develop our ideas over time and beyond the normal confines of study.

Summary

1 To generate more of our own ideas we must have an effective retrieval system.
2 With a flexible, effective system we are better able to catch our best ideas and produce work that is not predictable and imitative.
3 One of the richest sources of ideas is your own mind and experience.
4 Carry a notebook and keep a journal to catch your best ideas.
5 Keep an index-card system and a project box to catch isolated items you might otherwise lose.

The next stage

Reorganising your pattern of study in the ways I've suggested in this stage can noticeably improve your work within a short time. The most immediate impact will be on your ability to process ideas actively and to access your own ideas, rather than simply reproducing those you find in your sources. Moreover, with a more sophisticated retrieval system you will find you have at your fingertips a wealth of interesting material for your essays. This will give you more opportunity to develop those abilities that your syllabuses set out to assess.

As we've seen, a key element in this has been our organisation. And this is no less true of the next stage of essay writing: planning. Examiners regularly report that students lose marks not because they don't understand the subject, nor because they lack the ability, but because their poor organisation has resulted in essays that are irrelevant and confusing. And, like the organisation of our retrieval system, the results of well-organised planning can be almost immediate. Students accustomed to getting just average marks for their essays find themselves regularly getting marks that are two or three grades higher.

Planning

Introduction

As a result of what we did in the last stage, you should now have a wealth of material to work with. Moreover, you should feel more confident not just that you understand it well, but that you've successfully integrated it with your own ideas and made it your own. You've processed it thoroughly at all levels: for comprehension; for analysis and structure; and for criticism and evaluation. This should have left you with clearly structured notes taken from what you've read, which also record your own responses to the ideas in the form of criticism and evaluation.

What's more, you've now organised your retrieval system to ensure that you catch the best material, including your own ideas, wherever and whenever it presents itself. You are, then, in a much better position to meet the demands of an essay that asks you to use the higher cognitive abilities: to criticise, discuss and evaluate a claim or an argument. Given this, you can now move on to plan your essay – a stage that many regard as the most important, yet the most neglected. In this stage we will look not just at planning the essay, but at how this can improve your memory, your revision for the exam, and your exam technique.

Planning the essay

Without a plan you will always struggle to produce your best work. The plan gives your essay a clear structure for your tutors to follow as they navigate their way through ideas and arguments that are unfamiliar to them. Without this you're likely to lose them, and if they can't see why your arguments are relevant, or they can't see what you're doing and why, they cannot give you marks, no matter how good your work might be. Even your weakest arguments gain strength from planning. A carefully planned structure, which is clear, logical and relevant to the question, lends support to an argument that, on its own, might not be completely convincing.

Without a plan ...

1 You're likely to lose your tutors.
2 If they can't see why your work is relevant they won't give you marks for it.
3 Even weak arguments gain strength from a carefully planned structure.

In this stage we will look at the benefits of rehearsing your arguments in detail before you write, by planning an essay we interpreted and brainstormed in the first stage. In this way we are able to make sure that all of our arguments are relevant, that they are clearly and consistently argued, and that we have sufficient evidence to support them. It also reduces the risk of omitting some really important section or argument that is central to the issues raised by the essay.

What's more, by rehearsing your arguments in detail you will avoid the problem of trying to do the two most difficult things in writing at the same time: pinning down your ideas clearly, and then summoning up the words and phrases that will convey them accurately.

The benefits of rehearsing our arguments in a detailed plan:

1 We make sure all our arguments are relevant.
2 That they are clearly and consistently argued.
3 That we have sufficient evidence to support them.
4 That we haven't omitted some important section.
5 That we avoid doing the two most difficult things in writing at the same time: pinning down our ideas clearly and communicating them accurately.

To do this effectively we have to work through two stages: editing and ordering the ideas. We will see that if the essay is to succeed we have to learn to be ruthless in cutting out irrelevant material that we may have worked hard to collect. Otherwise we will pass on problems to later stages and, if they're not dealt with there, they will seriously weaken the clarity and logical structure of our essay. They will cloud the structure with unnecessary distractions that weaken our arguments and break up the logical sequence we've worked hard to create. The same applies to ordering our ideas, if we are to create logical coherence and give our essay more persuasive force.

Irrelevant material:

- Weakens the clarity of our essay.
- Clouds the structure with unnecessary distractions.
- Breaks up the logical sequence of our ideas.

Planning for the examination

However, the value of planning stretches beyond this. The plans we produce for our essays provide the core of our revision material, making it much easier for us to recall the arguments and evidence we need to use in the exam. We will look at ways in which we can improve our revision for exams and our exam technique by planning the typical questions that are set on the topics on the syllabus.

This will involve looking at how the memory works and what we can do to improve it by learning to structure our ideas as we do in our plans. On the companion website (www.howtowritebetteressays.com) you will find more on this with techniques and exercises you can use to improve your recall.

Planning: Getting the Highest Grades

In this chapter you will learn:

- how you can avoid losing the reader by planning carefully;
- how to strengthen your weakest arguments through planning;
- how to rehearse your arguments in detail before you write.

After completing the first two stages (interpretation and research), the plan of the essay should now be taking shape within your mind. In many cases it may not be very different from the original pattern notes you generated in the brainstorming session prior to the research.

The importance of planning

Nevertheless, careful thoughtful planning, in which you rehearse your arguments in as much detail as you can muster, is vital. It will not only improve the structure of your essay, making it more coherent and logical, but it will make the business of writing a lot easier. Indeed, it is always possible to tell the difference between an essay that has been planned and one that hasn't.

Avoid losing your reader

Reading somebody else's work is like entering an unfamiliar city: you can get lost easily, you're dependent upon others to give you directions and, even worse, you really don't know why you're there in the first place, unless somebody else tells you. The plan of the essay, therefore, represents the city map, and the introduction and the 'topic sentence' at the beginning of each paragraph (Stage 4) are the writer's attempt to let readers know where they are being taken, which turnings they will be taking along the way and why.

Without the plan and its clear development in the body of the essay you will most certainly lose the examiners reading your work, and if they are lost they cannot give you marks, no matter how well argued your point is, or how skilfully it is supported by evidence. If they cannot see why a passage is relevant, they must ignore it. They are not expected to make great efforts on your behalf to try to make sense of your work, to fill in the gaps that you've left. They must accept it on face value, otherwise they could find themselves spending more time on your essay – making more allowances for what they thought you meant to say – than on the work of other students.

> Without the plan and its clear development in the essay you will lose the examiners, and if they are lost they cannot give you marks.

Examiners regularly report that students fail examinations, or just do badly, not because they don't know the subject, not because they haven't got the abilities, nor even because they haven't done the work, but because they lose the reader, who is unable to discover why their work is relevant to the question. Almost always this comes down to a lack of planning.

The comments of one professor at Harvard are not untypical:

One common problem is the meandering paper, one that wanders from one thinker to another, from summaries of concepts to counterarguments to restatements of the paper topic, without a clear plan or logical progression.[1]

Planning strengthens weaker points

In fact the benefits of this go even further. By providing your readers with a sequence of obvious logical steps, so they can follow your train of thought, you give yourself an invaluable safety net. In many cases a weak or poorly defined point will gain strength and precision from being a step in a clear logical argument.

We all experience this when we come across an unfamiliar word: in most cases we can deduce its meaning from the context in which it's used. Examiners are no different. When they read your essay and come across a set of phrases or explanations that seem unclear, if they are part of a set of arguments and points thoughtfully planned in a logical sequence, your meaning will probably be all too obvious. Your arguments will gain strength and clarity from the clear, well-planned context in which they are developed.

Rehearsing the detail before you write

But it's not just a clear logical sequence that's created in planning: we're also able to sort out the main ideas and the important details we need in order to explain, illustrate and develop them. Doing so reduces the risk of omitting an important section or argument that is central to the issues raised by the essay.

Even so, it would be unwise to be so rigid that you cannot move away from your plan. Some new idea or relationship may occur to you and you might need to reorganise your material to include it. But be careful that this is really useful material for your argument, and not just irrelevant padding. Ultimately, the test of good planning comes when you rehearse your arguments in detailed note form before you write. At this point you make sure you've predicted what you need and you've rehearsed how you're going to use it, so there should be no last-minute changes.

> Rehearsing your arguments ensures that you predict what you need and know how you're going to use it.

Equally important, planning in this way is indispensable if you are to understand the subject. By rehearsing your arguments in detail you process your ideas: you internalise them and make them your own. Without this you are likely to struggle to express them clearly and convincingly.

Rehearsing the detail ensures:

- That we have all we need.
- That we haven't omitted an important section.
- That we internalise the ideas, so we can express them clearly and convincingly.

Avoid doing the two most difficult things in writing both at the same time

It is always surprising to find how many students still choose not to plan and, therefore, force themselves to do the two most difficult things in writing both at the same time – that is, summon up the ideas and plan the order in which they ought to be developed, and at the same time search for the right words to convey them with just the right strength and nuance, in order to develop the argument in the direction they've chosen. This is a task that is virtually impossible for all but the most familiar subjects that we've written about many times before.

The two most difficult things in writing …

1 Summoning up the ideas and planning the order in which they ought to be developed.
2 Searching for the right words to convey them with just the right strength and nuance, in order to develop the argument in the direction you've chosen.

Rehearsing your arguments in linear form

Rehearsing our ideas in the plan calls for different skills and techniques from those used in the brainstorming stage. As a result, some students feel more comfortable rehearsing their ideas in linear form, rather than in the pattern-note form they used in the interpretation stage. There are clear differences between the two stages. Rehearsing ideas is a deliberate step-by-step process, unlike the imaginative flow of ideas in brainstorming. But remember the importance of flexibility. Some assignments lend themselves more easily to pattern notes throughout, while others call for a combination of the two.

In the examination under timed conditions, when you want to capture the ideas quickly as they come tumbling out, pattern notes are clearly the most useful. But outside of that, when you're writing an essay on a subject for the first time, you'll find the step-by-step patient rehearsal of your arguments in linear form gives you more control.

PRACTICE
EXERCISE

Rehearsing your arguments in linear form

Question

'Advertisers seek only to ensure that consumers make informed choices.'
Discuss.

In the interpretation stage you brainstormed this question in pattern-note form. With those notes in front of you now, convert them into linear notes, rehearsing your arguments in the sort of detail you would need if you were to write the essay.

Then compare your notes with those below. Your notes may not be quite so detailed, but it will give you a clear idea of the level of detail you need to aim for in order to answer most of the problems you're likely to face when you come to write.

Answer: linear plan – rehearsing the arguments

'Advertisers seek only to ensure that consumers make informed choices.' *Discuss.*

A Advertisement

1 Just informative:
       e.g. railway timetable
   (a) no catchy jingles – 'Let the train take the strain'
   (b) no persuasive messages – 'Children travel free'
   (c) just information:
       (i)   routes
       (ii)   times – departures and arrivals
       (iii) platform numbers

But intention = crucial characteristic:

       (i)   to demonstrate it's more convenient, efficient, and less stressful to travel
              by train
       (ii)   e.g. fête notice – nothing but information – but intention = to
              encourage people to attend, in order to raise funds for local causes

   2 Therefore, information = surface appearance
      • what matters = intention – to suggest/persuade us to adopt certain course of
        action

B Informative

      • all but a few = informative
   1 Some only concerned with giving information:
       e.g. public information – changes in regultns & rates of taxation
            govt. warnings – smoking, use of domestic fire alarms
   2 Others give information while covertly promoting their products:
      • information about:
   (a) New products & technology:
       (i)   computer tech. & software
       (ii)   telecommunications, e.g. mobile phones

(iii) entertainment/hobbies:
- digital tech. – TVs, cameras
- music systems

But rarely just information:
suggestion = we can't afford not to keep up with progress

(b) New designs:
e.g. fashions/clothes-household equipment – washing machines,
dishwashers, microwaves
Suggestion = we can't afford to allow o/selves to fall behind our friends & neighbours –
comparisons/envy/conspicuous consumption – you are what you own

C But not the 'only' thing they do:
- overt manipulation

1 Selective use of information:
- says what's good about the product, but omits the bad
e.g. car accelerates 0–60 in 6 secs – but omits to tell you that it has a record
of rusting in 5 years
e.g. the latest printer that can do more than any other printer on the market
– but omits to tell you that the print cartridge costs 5 times as much as
any other printer

2 Uses information out of context:
- uses only those comments that appear to be in favour of the product in a
report that is critical of it
e.g. a critical report by a consumer association
e.g. unfavourable comments of an art, literary or theatre critic ignored by
promoters who comb through the article for isolated expressions of
approval

3 Association:
- associates information about the product with strong feelings and desires
(a) Sex – associates product with sexual desires
e.g. cars – clothes – perfume – alcohol
(b) Status – respect for authority
e.g. prestige of science – laboratory coats worn by those promoting washing
powders, vacuum cleaners, dishwashers, detergents
(c) Popular/respected public figures
e.g. sports-men & -women/TV personalities selling mobile phones, health
drinks, clothes, deodorants, shampoos
(d) Prejudices:
(i)   sexual stereotypes
(ii)   class – accents
(iii) weight/size
(iv)   race
(e) Subliminal manipulation through association:
(i)   to reduce shoplifting – messages like 'I will not steal', 'I will be honest'.
1970s experiment = 30% reduction in shoplifting

    (ii) Dangers:
        (a) political & social manipulation
            re. Aldous Huxley, *Brave New World Revisited*
        (b) promoting commercial interests
            subconscious manipulation to buy unwanted products

4 Distorts:

  (a) archetypal characters & scenarios created to evoke predictable responses:
      (i)   that we all want to be slim – that large people are associated with social failure & self-indulgence
      (ii) that we all consider it a crisis to find that the dishes aren't clean when they come out of the dishwasher
      (iii) that we all believe if our neighbour were to discover that our kitchen floor was not spotless it would amount to a social disgrace
      (iv) induces us to feel bad about ourselves – discontent fuels consumerism

  (b) appeals made to some imagined social consensus – to 'basic' or 'shared' values:
      (i)   that we all want the fastest car on the road
      (ii) that we all want to keep up with the neighbours
      (iii) that we all worry about being seen out in last year's fashions

  (c) myths created and sustained by the media to sell products
      e.g. that housewives are paranoid about the whiteness of their wash and the cleanliness of their floors

Summary

1 The plan represents the map of the essay to guide readers through it without losing them.

2 The essay's introduction and the topic sentences at the beginning of each paragraph are the directions guiding the reader at each change of course.

3 Lose the examiners and you lose marks.

4 A clear, logical structure will support your weakest arguments.

5 Rehearsing in detail what you plan to write helps you sort out the main ideas and important details, and improves your understanding.

6 It also means you are not forced to do the two most difficult things in writing both at the same time.

In the next chapter

Now that you've done this you will be aware not only of the importance of working on your ideas in this sort of detail, but of the problems it presents in first editing your ideas and then ordering them. In the next chapter we will tackle these two problems in more detail.

Note

1   Michael Sandel, *Writing in Moral Reasoning, 22: Justice* (Cambridge, MA: Harvard University, 2000).

Editing and Ordering Your Material

In this chapter you will learn:

- how to edit your material to create a structure in your essay that is clear and logical;
- how to order your ideas to develop arguments that are consistent and persuasive;
- how to make sure tutors are left with the right impression of your work.

Planning your essays in this way involves routinely working through two quite distinct stages: editing and ordering your material. Neither of them can be rushed: you must work through them carefully and deliberately.

Both call for what you might describe as the personality profile of a military planner: inexhaustible supplies of quiet patience matched by cool ruthlessness. There will be ideas, arguments and evidence with which you have developed a strong emotional bond, but you may have to cut them out and abandon them without a tear if the essay is to succeed. However painful it is to realise that some of the material you've worked hard to collect is irrelevant to this essay, you cannot shirk the responsibility. If you do, you will pass on problems to later stages and, if they're not dealt with there, they will seriously weaken the clarity and logical structure of your essay.

> Abandon material that is irrelevant to the essay, otherwise it will seriously weaken the clarity and logical structure of your essay.

By the same token, try to avoid the exhaustive answer in which you try to impress your tutor by putting in everything you know. You're being assessed on your abilities to interpret issues and make a judgement as to what's relevant to them. Don't sacrifice this ability for the chance to impress someone with how much you know. Your abilities to evaluate and discuss issues involve more complex skills, and therefore attract higher marks. Without spelling it out, you can always make your tutor aware that you know so much more, but you realise it is not relevant to the particular issues raised by this question.

- Cut out material that is not strictly relevant, even though you may have worked hard to gather it.

- Leaving it in will cloud the clarity and seriously harm the logical structure of your essay.
- You will earn more marks by showing tutors that you can interpret complex issues and write relevantly than you will by impressing them with how much you know.

Editing

Unless you've spent enough time interpreting the question, editing the material you've collected can be a tortuous nightmare. We are all quite naturally reluctant to give up material that we've struggled hard to uncover and record, especially if it includes particularly interesting points that we know will impress our reader. It's not surprising, then, that without a clear criterion by which you can decide what's relevant and what's not, you will find it difficult, if not impossible, to resist using material that's not relevant.

This will have the effect of clouding the structure of your essay with unnecessary distractions that weaken your arguments and break up the logical sequence you've worked hard to create. On the other hand, however, with a clear interpretation of the implications of the question, it is so much easier to be uncompromisingly ruthless with your material.

> Remove all irrelevant material which will otherwise obscure the structure with unnecessary distractions and break up the logical sequence of your arguments.

Ordering

Although you don't have the same distressing problems of ditching material you've become attached to, you still need an iron will in ordering your ideas if you're to avoid the same problem of being dictated to by your sources. It can simply be very difficult to abandon the order in which we recorded the notes in the first place.

> Impose your own order on your material, rather than follow the order in which you recorded your notes from your sources.

The simplest way of ordering our ideas, requiring little thought from us, is to describe some thing or event. Beware of this! Not only does it result in answers that are largely irrelevant, but we only use the simplest of our abilities, for which we will receive much lower marks.

> Unless you're asked for one, avoid descriptive answers ...
> - They are irrelevant.
> - They only demonstrate the simpler abilities and attract, therefore, much lower marks.

With the sort of question that asks us to discuss or critically evaluate a claim, be even-handed in presenting both sides of the issue. Even though you may have limited sympathy for one side, play devil's advocate and present it as strongly and as persuasively as you can. This way your tutors will know that you are aware of all the issues and you're not blinkered.

Equally important, they will realise that you have that exceptional ability and flexibility of mind to argue against yourself – to be self-reflective. As a result, you will show that you are not trapped by your own ideas; that you can think outside of them and accept new ones. In the process you'll demonstrate that you are an accomplished and mature thinker.

> Playing devil's advocate and arguing against that side of the argument for which you have most sympathy demonstrates that you are a mature and accomplished thinker.

But whatever the type of question, in general it makes sense to arrange your ideas in ascending order: from the simplest to the most complex; from the least persuasive to the most persuasive. In questions that ask you to discuss a claim or an argument there will be two parts dealing with each side of the argument, but within each part order the ideas in ascending order.

Logically this makes sense, particularly if the clarity of your most complex arguments depends upon how convincingly you've used your simpler, more obvious arguments to build a basis for them. But it also makes psychological sense in that in dealing with the most subtle and impressive arguments at the end of the essay you leave your readers with the impression that the whole of your essay was of that quality. Hopefully, you will have left them with a well-developed, interesting argument to think over as they consider what mark to award you.

Editing and ordering your material

PRACTICE EXERCISE 21

Question

Are there any circumstances where the individual is justified in refusing to obey a law?

Interpret the question above as you did in the first stage: write a statement outlining as fully as you can the meaning and implications of the question. For this exercise you don't need to brainstorm the question as you are given, below, a set of notes to edit and then order into a plan for the essay; but your interpretation should give you a clear idea of what you expect to see as relevant to the question.

Once you've done this, go through the notes below, deciding what you think is relevant and what needs to be cut. Then, order what's left into a plan in linear-note form, indicating how you would tackle this essay.

After you've completed it, compare your plan with the one given below (pp. 133–34).

The notes

1 Outline the main types of law – common law – judicial precedent – statute law – conventions

2 Refusal justified when:
 (a) Government has no popular legitimacy – lacks majority support – authoritarian governments
  e.g. South Africa/apartheid
 (b) Government is legitimate, but the majority tyrannises a minority
  e.g. Germany – Nazi Government – 1935 Nuremberg Laws
  e.g. USA – 1960s Civil Rights – segregation – M. L. King
 (c) Government extends its powers too far – restricting the liberties of the individual unnecessarily
 (d) There is a conflict between the legal and moral obligations of the individual. Question: Which takes precedence?
  e.g. moral obligation to help a friend by not turning him over to the police, who believe he has committed an offence

3 Give the reasons why Mahatma Gandhi deliberately broke the law in non-violent direct action to bring about the peaceful withdrawal of British power from India.

4 Problem = when government is legitimate and the law conflicts with individual conscience and principles, such as pacifism.
  e.g. Quakers refusing to pay that proportion of their taxes that is spent on nuclear weapons

5 Danger = social breakdown – it allows individuals to pick and choose the laws they will obey and those they won't.

6 Describe the campaign of civil disobedience launched by the suffragettes in 1906 to get the vote for women.

7 Note the arguments put forward by A. V. Dicey for the importance of the Rule of Law in ensuring regular, non-arbitrary government.

8 The government should only restrict the freedom of individuals when their actions are likely to cause harm to others (John Stuart Mill):
 (a) If you shout offensive racial remarks at people in public the government should intervene to restrict your doing this.
 (b) You have freedom of speech but the government should restrict this freedom if you publish pornographic material that can be shown to cause people harm, e.g. rape, child abuse, etc.
 (c) The government should intervene to prevent employers sacking staff for no reason at all without any hearing or compensation.
 (d) The government is justified in restricting your freedom when your actions cause physical harm to others, e.g. passive smoking.

9 But should the government be free to intervene and restrict your freedom when your actions cause harm to yourself only, e.g. smoking, wearing crash helmets?

10 Give an account of the ideas of those who have made important contributions to the debate:
>   Socrates
>   Henry Thoreau
>   Peter Kropotkin
>   Martin Luther King
>   John Rawls

The plan

Question

>   Are there any circumstances where the individual is justified in refusing to obey a law?

1 Problem: Government encroachment on our freedoms v. the danger of social breakdown if individuals are allowed to pick and choose the laws they will obey and those they won't

2 Government with no popular legitimacy – lacks majority support:
>   Refusing to obey the law = justified
>   - authoritarian governments, e.g. South Africa/apartheid

3 Government is legitimate:

(a) But the majority tyrannises a minority:
>   Refusing to obey the law = justified
>   e.g. Germany – Nazi Government – 1935 Nuremberg Laws
>   e.g. USA – 1960s Civil Rights – segregation – M. L. King.

(b) Problem = when government is legitimate and the law conflicts with individual conscience and principles.
>   e.g. Quakers refusing to pay that proportion of their taxes spent on nuclear weapons, because of pacifist principles

4 Conscience/principles: Problem = Government extends its powers too far – restricting the liberties of the individual unnecessarily.

(a) Extent of power 'harm' – Governments should only restrict the freedom of individuals when their actions are likely to cause harm to others (John Stuart Mill):
>   (i)   But should governments be free to intervene and restrict your freedom when your actions cause harm to yourself only, e.g. smoking, wearing crash helmets?
>   (ii) Governments are justified in restricting your freedom when actions cause physical harm to others, e.g. passive smoking.
>   (iii) Justified if you cause psychological harm? e.g. If you shout offensive racial remarks at people in public?

    (iv) Moral harm? You have freedom of speech but the government is justified in restricting this if you publish pornographic material that can be shown to cause people harm, e.g. rape, child abuse.

    (v) Economic harm? The government is justified in restricting the freedom of employers to sack staff for no reason without any hearing or compensation.

(b) Precedence – Question: Where there is a conflict between the legal and moral obligations of the individual, which takes precedence?

        e.g. moral obligation to help a friend by not turning him over to the police, who believe he has committed an offence.

1 Editing

Of course, as you haven't made these notes yourself, you can only take them on face value: you cannot go beyond what's given in the belief that if you search you may find something that's relevant. In fact, not being able to do this makes it easier for you to decide what's relevant and what's not.

1.1 Dumping material

We can all appreciate how difficult it might be for someone who has done the research to dump material like that contained in items 3, 6 and 10. If you have slowly worked your way through passages that are very closely argued, taking out a lot of material that you thought might be useful, it will be hard to ditch it. It's not that it's irrelevant, but it has to be used with more discrimination than is proposed here, which appears to be a straightforward description of the material. Far better would be to select from the material quotations and evidence that would support the arguments you want to make elsewhere in the essay.

1.2 Description for the sake of description

In fact the same can be said for items 1 and 7, both of which again appear to be descriptions for the sake of description. It might be useful to know the different types of law and Dicey's arguments for the importance of regular, as opposed to arbitrary law, but you will have to make this case out: you will have to justify why you think this is relevant. For example, there may be different implications for the question depending on the type of law involved, although on the face of it this appears unlikely.

2 Ordering

Having edited the material, you are now left to order your ideas from the simple to the complex and, as in this case, from the peripheral issues to those that are central. It seems that the best strategy is to work from those situations in which there appears least doubt and very limited discussion as to whether disobedience is justified, to those cases where there is real doubt. In this way you will ensure that your essay delivers you at the point that gives you the opportunity to discuss all the important issues.

2.1 The simpler cases

The obvious starting point, then, is with those governments who pass unjust laws or laws that lack the legitimacy of popular support. Few of us would not see some justification in the actions of those, like Steve Biko and Nelson Mandela, who refused to comply with laws passed as part of the apartheid policies of the South African government, which was supported by only a minority white population.

The more difficult case is that of a democratically legitimate government, such as that in Germany during the Third Reich, which passed policies aimed at the minority Jewish population, denying them rights as citizens to practise their profession and to marry non-Jewish persons. Yet, again, few of us would have much difficulty in commending those who bravely refused to comply with the law and rescued Jews who otherwise would have been sent to extermination camps.

2.2 The most complex

So, perhaps the most difficult case that raises the issues we all have to consider is one that avoids both of these problems: that raises the question of a legitimate government that is not tyrannising a minority, yet is passing laws that conflict with what we consider to be our moral obligations. In short, what should we do when our moral obligations conflict with our legal obligations?

This, in turn, appears to raise two distinct issues. The first can be described as the extent of government – the claim that a government can only rightfully restrict the freedoms of individuals when their actions do harm to others. Of course, this part of your discussion will turn on the various interpretations of the concept of 'harm': physical, psychological, moral, economic and so on. The second problem is that of precedence: when there is a conflict, which should take precedence, our moral or our legal obligations?

In your own work

Now that you've completed two practice exercises, on editing and ordering your material, and on rehearsing your ideas in detail, it's time to do the same with the question you originally chose from one of your courses. You've interpreted this question and completed the research on it. In the following exercise you are creating the plan from which you will write the essay.

Editing, ordering and rehearsing your arguments   IN YOUR OWN WORK

First, edit your material, cutting out any ideas you think are irrelevant to the question. Be ruthless. Even though you may like some of the arguments, because you know they will impress the reader, or because they have the sort of impact you want, cut them out if they are not strictly relevant to the issues raised by the question.

Then, order your ideas, paying particular attention to ascendancy and fluency. Start with the weakest or the simplest argument and move to the strongest. Try to envisage how you will move from one idea to the next.

Think about the types of transition you will use to create fluency between paragraphs (e.g. 'However', 'Therefore', 'In contrast').

Once you've got the overall structure clear, move to the content of the essay. Your aim is to see clearly how you will develop your arguments: how you will analyse points and concepts, make contrasts and comparisons, synthesise ideas from different sources, extend arguments consistently, and illustrate and support your points with evidence. So, as you go through the plan try to get an accurate measure of each argument, the links between them and the logical flow of the whole essay. You're trying to put yourself in the position of writing the essay without actually writing it. In this way you will confront all the problems now before you write – there will be no nasty surprises.

Finally, when you've finished, check that you've left nothing out: that you've answered the question relevantly and completely; that you haven't overlooked a major section or issue raised by the question; and that you haven't left important points vulnerable without sufficient evidence.

Summary

1 Be ruthless with your material, ditching anything that is not strictly relevant.
2 To do this well you will need to have interpreted the question well in Stage 1.
3 Be careful not to obscure your structure and weaken the logical sequence of your arguments with irrelevant distractions.
4 Impose your own order on your ideas rather than follow the order in which you recorded them from your sources.
5 As a general rule arrange your ideas so that you develop your arguments by moving from the simplest to the most complex.

In the next chapter

In this exercise we've gone as close as we can to writing the essay without actually doing so. There are very few essays that don't benefit from this. If we fail to do it, there will always be unforeseen problems that slow down our writing and break up the flow of our words. Even more important, as we will see in the next two chapters, having rehearsed our arguments we will be left, for each question, with plans that will be invaluable in the exam, when we have to reproduce the arguments under timed conditions.

Revision: Planning for the Exam

In this chapter you will learn:

- how to prepare for the examination;
- how to use plans as your core revision material;
- how to take much of the stress out of revision and exams;
- how to structure your ideas to improve your memory.

Prior to the fifteenth century everything had to be memorised: speeches, prayers, sermons, scholarly tracts and, of course, the Bible in its entirety. Then, in the fifteenth century, came the first printed book, the Gutenberg Bible. This was the first external memory. Since then millions of books have been published, including dictionaries and encyclopaedias, and now we have the internet and the various digital forms of external memory. Consequently, we no longer train our natural memories in the way that medieval scholars used to do.

Phone numbers and birthdays   EXAMPLE

According to recent surveys a third of British people under 30 can't remember their own land line number without consulting their smartphones and 30 per cent of adults can't remember the birthdays of more than three immediate family members.

All of our memories are bound together in webs of association, clear structures of interconnected ideas. We remember things in context as part of a structure: we are pattern thinkers. We struggle to remember isolated items, like those on a simple, unstructured list. Numerous psychological experiments have shown that, on average, the longest sequence of things a normal person can recall is about seven items. So, to recall information we need to create clear structures. The more tightly we can embed information in a familiar structure of ideas, the more likely we are to remember it.

Planning improves your memory for the exam

The clearest example of this in our own work is the plan we create to write our essay. Each time we create a plan, we embed the information we need to remember in a structure that we can then remember. In fact, this is no different from the way we would work normally in our everyday lives. Think how difficult it is to remember isolated items, like those things you've got to do throughout the day, or a quotation, or a few lines from a play. Presented with this sort of task, our minds attempt to create a structure, either out of the thing itself, like a telephone number we remember because we can see groups of repeated numbers within it, or by relating it to other structured information we already have.

> We only remember by creating structures.

This explains why it is that those with the most active minds, those people who are genuinely interested in a subject, can remember a surprising amount of detail, over a wide range of topics. Because they are interested in a subject, they ask more questions and to answer these they generate more structures that they can then recall.

We all know friends who might not seem particularly bright in class, but who can recall a staggering amount of detail if you get them on a subject they find really interesting, like basketball, cricket or football. With unerring accuracy they can tell you the batting averages of players, how many times a particular team has won a particular trophy, who scored most goals or made the most runs in a season, and so on.

- Memory works by creating structures out of what we have to remember or by relating it to structures we already have.
- Therefore planning, by creating structures, helps us recall what we need in exams.
- People who are interested in things create more structures, so they remember more things.

Having a need to remember is the secret to learning and remembering

The point is that we only learn when we have a need to. Those people who appear to know and remember a great deal are just good at creating needs. Our friend, who might not do well in his college work, can show all the intellectual skills when it comes to cricket or football, because he's interested in these subjects and, therefore, he's better at creating the need to know. Once we've created these we become active, not passive, processors of ideas and information, and we begin to create structures out of what we know. Our minds then take over and begin to self-organise, generating even more structures, which attach to those we first created. And before we know it we can recall a vast amount of material, which we never thought possible.

Create a genuine need to know something and before long you will surprise even yourself with what you can do. You will be able to create and reproduce the most complex structures of ideas. You will be surprised how well you can analyse the most difficult argument or concept, and remember a vast amount of material you never believed possible. You will begin to generate your own ideas and create thoughtful, well-constructed arguments. And it will happen, almost without you realising, as a result of knowing just two things: *how* to create structures, and the *need* to create them.

Needs and interests

> 1 We remember things when we have a need to, so those people who are good at creating needs remember more.
> 2 We create the need to know more about something once we are genuinely interested in it.

To illustrate the point, take the following simple task.

Remembering through structures

PRACTICE EXERCISE

22

Here is a list of ten items you've got to purchase at the local supermarket. Look at them for about 30 seconds, committing them to memory. Then cover them and try to recall them.

carrots	butter
yoghurt	milk
tomatoes	gin
beans	cheese
wine	potatoes

Most students are able to recall six or seven items, but only those used to the most active form of processing get all ten. What most of these do is to process the list into a structure, something like the following:

1 Vegetables:
  (a) carrots
  (b) tomatoes
  (c) beans
  (d) potatoes

2 Dairy products:
  (a) yoghurt
  (b) butter
  (c) milk
  (d) cheese

3 Drinks:
  (a) wine
  (b) gin

With this, the mind has a much simpler job: instead of having to remember ten items it only has to remember three, knowing that once these have been recalled the rest will come without a problem. In fact, this is no different from what you would have done normally if you were, indeed, shopping for these items. It would make obvious sense to group the items in this way so you could reduce the number of times you had to move between sections of the supermarket. You would know there were four things you needed to buy at the vegetable section, before you moved on to the next, and so on.

> **Memory**
>
> 1 We remember things by creating a structure out of them.
> 2 We remember wholes rather than isolated facts or lists.
> 3 The best structures are those that fit into what we already know.

Planning the typical exam questions

Given the importance of structures and planning it makes sense to prepare for the examination by planning all the typical questions that are set on each of the topics on the syllabus. Once you've done this, when revision comes around, all you need to do is commit them to memory and test yourself to see if you can recall them within ten minutes under timed conditions, as you will have to do in the exam.

The most well-organised tutors will give their students a course outline of all the topics on the course and then get them to list under each topic all the questions that have been set on each one. This will mean going back a number of years over past papers. In fact, it's more than likely that those tutors who teach a course year in, year out will have already done this for students. Each year all they will need to do is to bring the list up to date with the most recent questions.

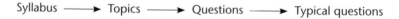

Syllabus   ⟶   Topics   ⟶   Questions   ⟶   Typical questions

When you analyse these lists into distinct types of question you will find that for each topic there are usually four or five typical questions that regularly appear. It's these that you need to plan. Your tutors will have their own plans for these and they will no doubt give you a copy when you've done yours, so that you can compare them and make adjustments if you need to.

The plans become your core revision material

Once this is done you will find these plans represent the core material for your revision. In my revision classes we timetable well in advance the topics we will be revising on any given day in the run-up to the exam, so that everybody comes prepared with their revision done and their plans stored in their memories. Then we produce our lists of typical questions for that topic, from which I select a question and give the students ten minutes to produce a plan, in the same way they will have to in the exam. We all then take a blank sheet of paper and try to produce our pattern- or linear-note structures, whichever we've chosen as the right format for that question. Having completed that, we compare our results. Then we go through all the remaining typical questions on our lists in the same way.

As a result, revision takes on a far less daunting, less menacing presence. In effect the students know that if there are, say, six topics that they know will come up on the paper, and there are four typical questions on each topic, then they have just 24 essay plans to commit to memory and recall under timed conditions. Most of them cope with this without any problem. Certainly it is much more manageable than the heaps of unstructured notes they might face otherwise.

Revision

1 Plan each typical question.
2 Commit them to memory.
3 Recall them in ten minutes.
4 Do timed plans for all the typical questions as a key part of your revision strategy.
5 Even if you don't get the exact question in the exam, the structured plans will help you recall what you need.

To make revision even easier, throughout the year we have regular sessions of this. As we complete each topic on our syllabus, time will be set aside so that students can do timed essays and timed plans. As a result, by the end of the course they will have written or planned every typical essay question under timed conditions. Most students will know them well, and have very little trouble recalling and writing them in the exam.

Even if you don't get in the exam exactly the question you've revised, your structured plans will help you to recall all the material you need to answer the question. It may be that you get a hybrid question that calls upon you to select from more than one structure and then combine the relevant parts into a new plan. It's probably true to say that at least 80 per cent of success in any exam is due to organisation, and the major component of this is the structured plans you create throughout the course and then commit to memory, so you can recall them in the exam.

A note of caution

Even so, one note of caution should be sounded: try to avoid pouncing on a question in the exam and then giving your prepared answer regardless of it. It's all too easy to look at the paper and say to yourself, 'Great, there's a question on X. I've revised that', and then set about producing your plan without carefully reading and interpreting the question. Nor are questions just an open invitation to write what you know about a subject regardless of the question. Although you're probably well aware of the dangers already, you'd be surprised just how many intelligent students do just this under the pressure of a timed exam.

Typical questions

PRACTICE EXERCISE
23

Take just one topic on your syllabus, preferably one that you've already covered, with which you're fairly familiar.

You've already collected some past papers. Usually around ten is sufficient to identify the major issues and approaches to the topics, which form the basis for questions.

List all the questions that have appeared on the topic you've chosen, recording the date on which they appeared. You should now be able to see recurring types. Some may appear every year, others once every two years. But it should be clear that there are only a limited number of types of questions, say four or five.

If you find that you have many more than this, it may be because you don't realise that a question, differently phrased, is in fact the same as another. This is often the case. Sometimes it's not until you try to plan it that you realise it's taking the same pattern as another. Therefore, if in doubt, try planning those you're not sure of.

Summary

1 Prepare for the exam by planning all the typical questions.
2 Planning improves our recall in exams by creating structures, rather than our trying to remember isolated facts or lists.
3 Test yourself to see if you can recall each plan in ten minutes, as you will have to in the exam.
4 Do this regularly throughout the year as you complete each topic.

In the next chapter

Planning in this way makes our revision and the exams themselves so much simpler. In the next chapter we will look at what you can do to make sure that you're able to reproduce the same quality of essay within the exam as you can outside.

Exam Technique: Planning in the Exam

In this chapter you will learn:

- about the importance of planning in the exam;
- how to plan in the exam;
- how to ensure that you have everything you need at your fingertips;
- how your plan itself may earn you valuable marks.

By the time we get to the examination it's not unreasonable to think that we have done everything we can do in terms of revision and preparation, and now it's just a matter of performing well on the day. But that's not exactly the case. Our approach to the exam and the way we organise ourselves to set about answering the questions will make a significant difference to our performance. At the heart of this, affecting everything we do, is the importance of planning each essay that we have to write. If planning is vital for the writing of an essay you complete in your own time, it is even more important for your performance under timed conditions.

The importance of planning in the exam

Some students claim they simply haven't got sufficient time in the exam to plan for five to ten minutes for each essay. Yet if you observe their behaviour during the exam it becomes clear they still have to plan, but in the least effective way. They will head straight into the essay without much deliberation, then they will stop at the end of the first paragraph to think about what they will do in the next paragraph. One to two minutes might pass before they head off again into their work, only to stop again for more thought to decide what they will do next. This happens, say, seven or eight times for each essay, amounting to 12 to 15 minutes of planning on the run.

As a result, they have, in fact, planned the essay, probably spending more time than they would have done if they had planned at the start. And, of course, they've planned in the worst possible way. Without doubt, ideas will have come to them out of sequence, making little logical sense to the examiner. In turn this will have dissipated any fluency they might have created. In contrast, if they had planned at the start, this would have left them free to write continuously and fluently, without interruption, until they had completed the question.

> If we fail to plan before we start writing, ideas will come to us out of sequence, breaking up the logic of our essay.

It's not difficult to see, therefore, that planning in the exam is vital to produce a well-written and fluently argued piece of work. Only by preparing a plan can you maintain control over your material and present your ideas in a logical, concise and coherent manner, with support from well-chosen, relevant evidence.

- Planning is even more important for essays in an exam.
- One way or another we all make plans.
- Planning before we write is essential to produce a logical, concise, coherent essay.
- Otherwise we have to interrupt the fluent, continuous flow of our ideas.

How to plan in the exam

When the exam begins, first read through the paper carefully, ticking all those questions that you could do. Then read it through again, selecting from these the strongest questions: those that you know you could answer best. Start with the strongest question and leave the weakest to last. Coping well with the first question will strengthen your confidence and settle your nerves.

With each question spend the first ten minutes writing down your plan. Don't get panicked into writing too soon, before you have exhausted all of your ideas and got them organised into a coherent, well-structured plan that answers the question with strict relevance.

> Don't get panicked into writing too soon. Make sure you have assembled all your ideas and organised them into a well-structured, coherent plan.

Indeed, there are compelling reasons for going even further than this. It makes very good sense to plan *all* the questions you have chosen to do, before you pick up your pen to write the first one. Each time you plan an essay you set your subconscious mind tasks to undertake and questions to answer. Except in the strongest of questions, which you know exactly how you're going to answer, there are always arguments, points, evidence and examples that you can't remember exactly.

This is understandable: you're trying to brainstorm, to get the ideas down as quickly as possible as they come tumbling out. Therefore, unless it's a central issue that will shape the whole essay, you don't want to stop the flow just to make sure you've got every detail on one particular issue exactly right; you can always come back to that after the flow of ideas has stopped. But at that point you may find you can't recall all the details you wanted to use. Nevertheless, by identifying the problem in the planning stage you will have alerted your subconscious and, while you're writing another question, it will be busy unearthing what you need. Then, when you come to write this essay, you will find the material that you couldn't remember there at your fingertips.

- Don't get panicked into writing too soon.
- Plan all the questions you've chosen to do before you write.
- This gives the mind sufficient time to sort through your data banks and come up with the ideas, arguments and evidence you need.
- Get all the points down in the plan as quickly as you can without interrupting the flow of ideas.
- If you fail to complete your essay you may get marks for your plan.

Planning in the exam   EXAMPLE

Let's say you're taking a three-hour exam in which you have to answer four essay questions, and you plan all four questions before you begin to write the first one. This will mean you will spend the first 40 minutes of the exam planning. Then, if you write your strongest question first and your weakest last, it will mean that your mind will have 2 hours 25 minutes to sort through your data banks and come up with those ideas, arguments and evidence that you weren't able to remember when you planned the weakest of your questions. Even with your strongest question your mind has 30 minutes, while you're planning the other questions, to find the few items that you couldn't recall.

A common-sense approach

The common sense of this approach is clear to most of us who have ever taken exams. We've probably all had the experience of coming out of the examination centre with a friend, comparing what each of us did. As we go over it, all sorts of things suddenly spring into our minds, things we should have included but didn't. In this situation what's happening is that either we haven't planned at all or we've planned each question just moments before we've written it. As a result, the mind has been set tasks to accomplish and questions to answer, but it has needed time for this, more than we have given it in the exam.

The sad irony is that over the next hour or so, as the mind comes up with what we asked it for, we'll recall a rich assortment of ideas, arguments and evidence, and we'll curse our luck for not being able to use it in the exam. But luck, in fact, had little to do with it; it was our organisation, or lack of it, that robbed us of the chance to get really high marks.

Each time we plan we ask our subconscious to dig up material that we can't immediately recall.

One final point to remember: in most systems, examiners will give you credit for a plan, if the essay is unfinished. In most examinations you cannot lose marks for a plan, however scrappy and indecipherable it may be. You can only gain marks. Therefore, if you run out of time halfway through a question, a clearly structured plan of what you would have done will earn good marks.

Revising and recalling plans

Now that you've planned your essay, the best test of whether it works, in so far as it's relevant, clearly structured and answers the question completely, is to try to recall it under timed conditions, as you will have to in the exam.

Spend 15 minutes committing your plan to memory. Concentrate on the main structure. If you can recall the key points that make up this structure, you will be able to recall the detail within it, if your arguments are organised in a clear, logical manner and they're relevant to the question.

After you've done this, put it aside for a day or so, but decide beforehand at what time you will come back to test yourself. Then, when you come back, take out a blank sheet of paper and give yourself ten minutes to reproduce the plan.

If the plan works, you will be able to recall, maybe not all of it, but at least the main structure. If you can't recall much at all, it may be due to technical reasons: the key words that trigger off your arguments aren't crisp and sufficiently memorable, or perhaps the structure is buried beneath too much detail. Make the necessary changes and try again.

You will know when you've got it right: you will be able to recall with complete accuracy all of the structure and most of the detail. Having done this once successfully, you will know what will work in future.

Summary

1 Planning in the exam is important to create essays that are fluently written and coherent.

2 Planning at the start leaves us free to write continuously without interruption.

3 It's important to avoid getting panicked into writing before you have assembled all your ideas and planned a well-organised, coherent essay.

4 In the exam, plan all the questions you've chosen to do before you write, to give your mind time to come up with everything you need.

The next stage

As we'll see in the next stage, by planning in this way you can begin to write introductions, conclusions and paragraphs with complete confidence. It is impossible to write a good introduction to an essay if you don't know what you're introducing. The same can be said for developing your arguments from one paragraph to another. Without a clear idea of the structure of your arguments and how you plan to move consistently from one idea to another, you will be forced to do this at the very same time that you're searching for just the right word or expression to convey your ideas with complete accuracy. As a result you're likely to do neither very well.

Writing

Introduction

As you've seen already, by breaking down essay writing into its stages we have been able to isolate problems as they arise in each stage and concentrate our efforts on tackling them. In this stage we will apply the same principle. First, you will learn how to find your own voice and then we will break down the actual writing of an essay into the framework and content of the essay.

Finding your own voice

Much of our academic writing seems to involve expressing ideas that are not ours in a language we do not command. We are encouraged to believe that there is a style of academic writing, a method of thinking and expressing ideas, which we must imitate. So we settle for just recycling the ideas of authorities, using their terms and forms of expression, which inevitably results in poor thinking and, consequently, poor writing.

However, if you can find your own voice, you can begin to free yourself from these beliefs, which make writing such a fearful exercise. You will begin to write in a style that is more natural, lighter and closer to the spoken word. Consequently, you will find you are more able to present your ideas and develop your arguments clearly, simply and economically, for which you are likely to be rewarded with higher marks.

The framework

There are few of us who could confidently claim that we have never had problems with the structural features of essays: introductions, paragraphs and conclusions. At least part of the problem is a lack of planning, which leaves us with no clear idea of the structure and content. It's impossible to write a good introduction if you don't know what you're introducing, and much the same can be said for paragraphs and conclusions.

Nevertheless, even with a good plan, most of us still have problems, because we're unsure what we're trying to achieve when we write introductions, paragraphs and conclusions. To cope with this, you will be shown a simple formula for each, which you can use as a model each time you write them.

To write good introductions, paragraphs and conclusions we need to know ...

1 The plan of the essay – its structure and content.
2 What we're trying to achieve when we write them.

With introductions you will be shown how to use your interpretation of the implications of the question and how to outline a map of the essay, to make sure you don't lose your readers as they try to follow your arguments and ideas. With paragraphs you'll be shown how to tie them into the introduction with clear topic sentences and transitions to create a taut, cohesive and tightly reasoned essay. You will also be shown how to develop your arguments in the body of the paragraph and support them with evidence. Similarly, with conclusions you'll be shown various ways of creating cohesion in your work by tying the conclusion to the introduction.

The content

In the second half of this stage we will examine the problems we all experience with our style. These can be difficult to pin down, particularly when they're bound up with the other problems we've examined in previous stages.

1 Simplicity

First we will look at the importance of simplicity, in particular the ways we can simplify our use of sentences and words, and what we can do to improve our writing skills to convey our ideas clearly and unambiguously.

You will be shown ways of avoiding heavy, unreadable prose and how to make your writing as light as your subject allows – more like talk in print. This is likely to result in not only a more enjoyable experience for the reader, but a memorable, effective piece of writing. By simplifying your writing in this way you will also be less likely to lose your reader.

1.1 Sentences

With sentences this calls for two things: keeping sentences relatively short and, wherever it needs it, using a logical indicator to make clear what you're doing. We will see that the problem here is not just that we fail to use these indicators, believing that the reader can follow our train of thought without difficulty, but that they get lost in our sentences. You will also be shown ways of experimenting, using the rhythm of your words and punctuation to convey meaning. This helps to create a rhythm that is nearer to the spoken word, and the nearer we approach this the easier it is to understand what we've written.

The closer we get to the rhythm of the spoken word, the easier it is for a reader to understand what we have written.

1.2 Words

Similar problems tend to arise with our use of words. We're inclined to overcomplicate, using complex, even abstruse, language. This can give rise to all sorts of problems, not least the use of jargon and other words that are empty of real meaning. Ultimately, clear and effective writing depends upon clear thinking. Language is the vehicle for ideas. If these are muddled and confused, then so too will be our language and style.

> Clear and effective writing depends upon clear thinking. Language is the vehicle for ideas. If these are muddled and confused, so too will be our language and style.

2 Economy

In addition to simplicity, we will also examine the other element of style, economy. We will look at the various ways we can improve our style, giving our writing greater clarity through a more economical use of language. We will also see how our use of evidence not only supports and illustrates our arguments, but makes our work more interesting and persuasive. All of this will be brought together in a practical way in the form of seven useful rules that we can use, day by day, to improve our style.

Referencing and bibliographies

You will also be shown how to avoid the danger of plagiarism by referencing the material you borrow. We will look at that most difficult of questions for most students: when do we need to cite sources and when don't we? You will be shown simple solutions that will help you avoid all the headaches this can entail. You will also be shown different methods of referencing and how to create a bibliography that is useful to both you and your reader.

Reflective writing

Finally, with more and more courses asking students to write reflectively on their learning and professional placements, we will examine the particular challenges this presents. In particular we will look at the best structure to adopt for each assignment, how to write each part and how to avoid the most common problems.

Finding Your Own Voice

In this chapter you will learn:

- how to find your own voice;
- how to organise your work to allow yourself to write as freely as possible;
- how to avoid just recycling jargon and complex abstractions;
- how to use your own voice to write more clearly, with a rhythm closer to normal speech.

Finding your own voice appears to be an act of deep introspection. In one sense, of course, it is. It involves reclaiming your mental space and the unique way in which you express your ideas from all those who pull you one way and another with their advice. It will bring a lightness of touch to your expression, a naturalness to your writing, nearer to the spoken word, that will help you to present your ideas and develop your arguments clearly, simply and economically. As all writers will tell you, once you have found it, never let it go.

Once you have found your own voice, never let it go.

The simplest way of reclaiming this territory is to get into the routine of regularly writing to yourself in your journal. As you know that you are the only person who will read it, you can develop your ideas with fewer restraints and explore the writer that has always been there in the shadows. Here you are likely to discover a mind that is perceptive, witty and intelligent. And then, after a few weeks of doing this, your own voice will begin to find its way into your essays. This works because we know our audience; we can envisage our reader, whom we can trust as a friendly critic.

Academic writing

By contrast, in academic writing our ideas are aimed at some unknown, anonymous reader, which encourages us to adopt a more universal, less personal form of communication. We are encouraged to believe that there is a style, a method of thinking and writing, which we must imitate. So we abandon our own voice and allow our own thoughts and ideas to recede into the background, while we settle for just recycling the ideas of authorities, using their terms and their forms of expression, even though they may mean very little to us.

Inevitably this results in poor thinking and, therefore, poor writing. As we depart from the spoken word, our writing becomes clumsy and difficult to follow. In effect, we express ideas that are not ours in a language we do not command. And not even the most accomplished writer can write well when she is expressing ideas that have no meaning for her. She will struggle to give shape to the ideas; her fluency of expression will break down; her sentences will no longer mean what she meant them to mean; she will become illiterate.

- We recycle the ideas of authorities and their forms of expression.
- This leads to poor thinking and writing.

What can you do?

The simplest solution, of course, is to have the confidence to use your own voice. But how do we develop this confidence? By concentrating on the following five things your confidence will grow and you will begin to hear your own voice coming through in everything you write.

What can you do?

1 Know your audience
2 Make contact with everyday reality
3 Write freely
4 Use the first person
5 Wherever possible avoid passive writing

1 Know your audience

The first thing to do is to have a clear idea of who you are talking to. As you do in your journal or in letters to friends, visualise your readers as a group of friendly critics – intelligent non-specialists, who might need just a little more translation of the technical aspects of your work. By translating them into more complete explanations you avoid the easy reliance on jargon and other literal shortcuts.

2 Make contact with everyday reality

Each time you find yourself just recycling complex abstractions and jargon, remind yourself to break it down into simpler, more concrete language that makes contact with our everyday experience. Whenever we fail to create this sort of bridge to our normal lives, it is difficult, often impossible, to understand what we're saying. It turns our writing into a foreign language that must be translated before sense can be made of it. It is as if we are writing for an exclusive set of code-breakers.

The key to this is to allow your own voice to surface as you did in your journal and in letters to friends. With the same audience in mind, use concrete everyday language to make what you say accessible to someone who knows nothing about it. When you cut language to the bone in this way, you discover what you really meant to say. Only at that point can you begin to build it back up with your own voice. And before you try to convince yourself that the ideas you are dealing with are too complex for this, tell yourself that there is not a single complex idea that is so complex that it cannot be expressed in simple, concrete language that we can all understand.

> There is not a single complex idea that is so complex that it cannot be expressed in simple concrete language.

It is revealing that in the acknowledgements to *A Brief History of Time*, Stephen Hawking concedes that the subject of his book is often made unreadable, not because of the difficulty of the subject, but because of poor writing. Referring to a book he, himself, had written on the same subject in 1973 he says,

> I would not advise readers of this book (*A Brief History of Time*) to consult that work for further information: it is highly technical, and quite unreadable. I hope that since then I have learned how to write in a manner that is easier to understand.[1]

Indeed, writing that is full of abstractions with few concrete referents holds very little actual meaning. Or more precisely, it could, in fact, mean anything. The information content of an argument is directly proportional to the range of possibilities it excludes: the more it excludes the more information content it has.

> If an argument does not forbid something from happening, it cannot be tested. Consequently, it could mean anything: it holds no meaning.

Like any scientific theory, an argument must forbid something from happening to allow it to be tested. If it cannot be tested, it could mean anything: it holds no meaning. Using concrete language excludes possibilities, it forbids certain things from happening, so that we can assess how probable it is that the argument is true. If it is composed just of abstractions, we cannot test it in this way, so we have to conclude that it is meaningless: it could mean anything.

Adorno   EXAMPLE

The following is taken from an essay on art theory.

Adorno's quote 'art perceived strictly aesthetically is art aesthetically misperceived', asks us through negation, to reject the past of the Kantian point of universality, and through the particular dialectical workings of Adorno, understand our present immanent with, the historical i.e. Kant's subjectivity and his pure aesthetic judgement, Adorno's reflexive objectivity and his 'fluid' conception of an autonomous artwork and the unknown of our social present.

You don't need to know anything about art theory and the philosophers to whom this refers to know that the meaning of the paragraph all depends on what is meant by abstractions like 'negation', 'our present immanent', 'autonomous artwork' and 'the unknown of our social present'. There are no concrete referents, so nothing is forbidden: they could mean anything.

Nevertheless, abstract concepts are important: they have the power to elevate an argument, lifting it beyond our particular concerns to levels of significance that help us advance our knowledge and solve fundamental problems. But they must be grounded in the concrete reality of our lives, otherwise the author is free to say what he likes.

> Whenever you use them, ask yourself, 'What difference do they make to our lives: how are we to come to understand the way they work in our experience?'

3 Write freely

In this book we have divided essay writing into five distinct stages. This spares us the nightmare we spoke of earlier – that of trying to do the two most difficult things in writing both at the same time:

1 summoning up our ideas and arranging them in a logical sequence and, at the same time,
2 searching for the right words that will convey the arguments accurately, at just the right strength, while developing them in the right direction.

In the same way, you will find there are advantages to be gained from splitting the actual writing into the two last stages: writing and revision. This helps you to bring your own voice to the surface and inject fluency into your writing that may not otherwise be there. To do this you must keep your inner editor at bay. We all have one; some are more persistent than others. They try to intervene whenever they can, but particularly when you start your work, or when you complete a significant section and sit back to bask in the glow of your achievement. At moments like these you will be tempted to read it all through to allow your editor to give his or her approval. Editors are persistent and, if you allow them to come in too early, they will overpower the artist.

To avoid this unwelcome intrusion, allow yourself to write freely without too much concern for style. You need to tell yourself that it doesn't matter if you don't get the wording exactly right on the first attempt. The emphasis should be on writing in your own voice and allowing your thoughts to flow freely, while you follow your plan and develop your ideas.

> Write freely without too much concern for mistakes to allow your own voice to surface.

Talk in print

The key to success here is to remind yourself that the best writing reads as though it is talk in print. The smoother the rhythm and the closer it is to our normal speech, the easier it is to read. You'll get your ideas across more effectively and you'll hold the attention of your readers. Of course, it will still be more formal than the way you normally speak: you must avoid slang and colloquialisms. But that's not to say you can't use a familiar phrase we all use in daily conversation. If it conveys your meaning more accurately and concisely than a more formal phrase, use it.

The problem with such phrases normally is that they reflect a 'habit' of thought, rather than real thought. So ask yourself, 'Does this phrase convey my idea accurately?'

and 'Is there a better phrase?' If it does and there isn't a better phrase, use it. As we have already said, keep in mind your audience: trusted friends who may not know your subject as well as you do. After writing freely in this way, when you move into the revision stage, you can clean up your work.

- Clearly separate writing from revision.
- Keep your editor at bay.
- Concentrate on writing fluently – don't stop to correct things.
- The best writing reads as though it is talk in print.

Talk in print

PRACTICE
EXERCISE

Read through the following passage and, where it departs from the rhythms of normal speech and becomes more difficult to understand, change it. Then check your changes with the answer below. You may not find that we have both made exactly the same changes, but you will most likely identify the same sections which you believe should be changed. Read through the passage again after you have changed it and see how it is more fluent and easier to understand.

24

Passage

Unlimited choice does not always maximise utility. We fear regret and disappointment after we've made our choice so much that we function more contentedly with limited choice which minimises the risk. Researchers have found that consumers continue to read advertisements for a new car after they've bought it, but will avoid information about other brands, fearing post-purchase misgivings. Indeed the fear of regret leads us into quite irrational behaviour. In another study it was found that shoppers who were offered free samples of six different jams were more likely to buy one than shoppers who were offered free samples of 24. It seems we are afflicted by decision paralysis if we are given too much choice.

Answer

Unlimited choice is not always the best thing. We fear regret and disappointment after we've made our choice so much that we are happier with limited choice which minimises the risk. Researchers have found that consumers continue to read advertisements for a new car after they've bought it, but will avoid information about other brands, out of fear that they will regret their decision. Indeed the fear of regret leads us into quite irrational behaviour. In another study it was found that shoppers who were offered free samples of six different jams were more likely to buy one than shoppers who were offered free samples of 24. It seems we cannot come to a decision if we are given too much choice.

4 Use the first person

Unfortunately students are often told that in academic writing they cannot place themselves at the centre of their writing; that they must avoid all forms of the first-person pronoun 'I'. Instead, you are told you must disguise your identity by talking about 'the author's opinion', 'in the opinion of the present writer', 'the author assumed that' or similar hedging devices, like 'It was thought that' and 'It was decided that'. As a result, your writing becomes anonymous. And with no identity, your own voice is silenced.

   Not only does this rob you of your own voice, it makes very little sense. Despite all your attempts to disguise your identity by referring to a third party, it is rare that anybody is actually deceived. We are all aware that when you refer to 'the author' you are referring to yourself. After all, your name is on the top of the essay. To suggest otherwise is to claim that someone else wrote the essay, as if you are shirking the responsibility for what you are saying.

> Your writing becomes anonymous. With no identity, your own voice is silenced.

Unfortunately, if the advice you receive from your department is to avoid the first-person pronoun, you may have no other choice. Instead, work on the other four things that I have explained in this chapter to make sure that your own voice comes through in your writing.

5 Wherever possible avoid passive writing

Similarly, many students are also advised that in academic writing they must adopt a passive writing style. Like avoiding the first person, this too can rob your writing of its clarity and introduce unnecessary ambiguity. It is also more impersonal and indirect, which makes it more difficult for you to use your own voice in your writing.

   As we will see in Chapter 32, the distinction between the passive and active forms is as follows:

Passive form	the receiver of the action or the action itself is the subject of the sentence;
Active form	the doer of the action is the subject of the sentence.

In the active form there is less ambiguity: your writing is more concise, clearer and more direct. By using a pronoun or noun at the beginning of the sentence to identify the person involved and an active verb to describe what she did, you can visualise the actual event in specific detail. In contrast, the passive form not only lacks precision, but is almost always less direct, positive and concise.

Active writing   EXAMPLE

1 Instead of saying, 'The test was carried out on the subjects of the experiment by the psychologist' you would say 'The psychologist tested the subjects of the experiment.'
2 And in both the active form and with the first person instead of saying, 'The survey was undertaken and the results published by the author of this report' you would say simply 'I conducted the survey and published the results.'

Your own voice and academic writing

To place yourself and your own voice at the heart of your writing resist the temptation to take the easy route by just recycling the language and style of specialists. All too easily this reduces academic writing to a turgid mass of poorly written prose that drowns us in the mire of ambiguous terms and convoluted sentences. Write with your own voice – let it prevail, even while you comply with the conventions that are imposed upon you. Only then will you begin to develop your ideas clearly and build the structure of your arguments confidently.

Summary

1　Find your own voice by regularly writing freely in your journal.

2　Instead of just recycling jargon, use concrete language to make contact with our everyday experience.

3　Separate writing from revision and write as freely as you can.

4　Try to write as close to the spoken word as you can without using meaningless slang and colloquialisms.

In the next chapter

This chapter has been all about how we can find our own voice so that we can begin to write in our own unique way with a lightness of touch that is closer to the spoken word, making it easier to read and understand. But that is just one part of the problem. We also need to liberate our thinking too while we write. As we will discover in the next chapter, for this we need to learn how to hang a question over what we write, so that we use the full range of our conceptual and creative abilities.

Note

1　Stephen W. Hawking, *A Brief History of Time* (London: Bantam Press, 1988), p. vii.

24

Suspending Your Judgement

In this chapter you will learn:

- how to ensure you use your higher cognitive abilities in your essays;
- the importance of suspending your judgement;
- why you should avoid telling your readers what to think;
- the difference between a debate and a discussion;
- how to cope with thesis statements.

In Chapter 9 we saw that essay questions at university set out to assess students not just on how much they know, but more importantly on how well they have developed and can use their higher cognitive abilities. These are the abilities to analyse concepts and arguments, to play devil's advocate and synthesise ideas and evidence from different sources to create new ways of looking at a problem, to construct consistent arguments, and to discuss and critically evaluate ideas and arguments.

But to use these abilities we must have the opportunity to think and for this we must suspend our judgement: things must be up for grabs. As Paul Tillich once said, 'The passion for truth is silenced by answers which have the weight of undisputed authority.'[1] Once we accept something as true, there is nothing more to think about, nothing more to discuss. Therefore, there is no opportunity to use our higher cognitive abilities to analyse, synthesise and evaluate.

> Unless we suspend our judgement as we write, we cannot use and develop our higher cognitive abilities.

Defending your own point of view

The same is true if you assume that essays are simply about making up your mind before you start writing and then defending that point of view. You no longer suspend your judgement and, consequently, you stop thinking: you close down your higher cognitive abilities. Having to think about a proposition is to accept that there is doubt about it – that the discussion has not ended with one point of view prevailing. Instead, it is up for grabs and we must explore all the alternatives, critically evaluate all the competing evidence and arguments, and analyse the important concepts that shape the problem.

Someone who has opinions has stopped thinking.

By contrast, someone who has opinions has stopped thinking: he has come to a decision; the process of thinking has come to an end. All that is left is to defend his conclusion, to win the argument by any means: by suppressing evidence that might weaken his case, ignoring arguments that conflict with his own and refusing to play devil's advocate.

Rather than discover the truth by using the full range of his conceptual and creative abilities to explore all available ideas and evidence, he closes down discussion. The bold, ambitious pursuit of truth, with the courage to propose new ideas and insights that many might find inconceivable, is swept aside for a negative, safely contained defence of opinion.

Avoid telling your readers what to think

So, even if you have a point of view, hang a question over what you write. This will also help you avoid telling your readers what to think. In this way you will allow your readers to think for themselves – to discover for themselves the points and arguments you're making. As a result they will feel more involved, finding themselves just as interested as you are in the different arguments you've made and the insights you've exposed. You will have written an essay that not only avoids passivity in the reader, but is interesting and thought provoking.

- Students who write essays just defending their opinions have stopped thinking.
- To think about a proposition is to accept that it is up for grabs: that there are issues to be discussed.
- To use and develop our higher cognitive abilities we must suspend our judgement.
- Avoid telling readers what to think. Allow them to find for themselves the value of the points and arguments you have made.

The thesis statement

However, advising students to hang a question over what they write can be confusing, particularly if their departments insist they write thesis statements. While most universities have a fairly broad and complex understanding of what they mean by a thesis statement, some insist on a more restricted interpretation, imposing a narrow range of expectations on students, who are told they *must* have a point of view, which *must* be stated in the introduction and then defended throughout the essay.

The thesis statement   EXAMPLE

As one university department puts it, 'form your own viewpoint and convince the reader that your viewpoint or perspective is credible'.[2]

This doesn't appear to be a strategy designed to produce imaginative thinkers with minds capable of suspending judgement as they think beyond their own biases and preconceptions, so why adopt such a restricted and defensive strategy for essay writing?

Why adopt such a defensive strategy?

As we've already seen, one answer, which makes this approach more understandable, is that many students come to university bringing with them a submissive attitude to authority, which encourages them to believe that to get good grades they must trade facts for marks and write the descriptive essay, even though they are asked to discuss and explore issues that have no right answers. At Harvard, students are warned,

> When you write an essay or research paper, you are never simply transferring information from one place to another, or showing that you have mastered a certain amount of material.[3]

Therefore, to overcome this submissive attitude students are told they must have an opinion of their own, which they must defend in their essays. However, as we have seen, this approach sidesteps the complex demands of an academic discussion, involving our higher cognitive abilities. Just defending a statement of our opinion is a much simpler task, involving less imagination and a more limited range of abilities.

Academic work

1 Doesn't just involve:
   1.1 Trading facts for marks in a descriptive essay.
   1.2 Stating a point of view and defending it.

2 Does involve:
   2.1 Analysing problems and concepts.
   2.2 Synthesising evidence and arguments from different sources.
   2.3 Discussing conflicting sides of an argument.
   2.4 Playing devil's advocate: empathising with those who hold different ideas for which you have least sympathy.
   2.5 Arguing the case consistently.
   2.6 Coming to your own evaluation.

A debate is not a discussion

In effect, by adopting this defensive strategy we abandon discussion in favour of the narrow intellectual demands of a debate. The objective of a discussion is to uncover the truth, to extend our understanding. It calls for an open, not a closed, mind.
We suspend judgement, hanging a question over everything as we analyse the concepts and problems involved, explore the full weight of the evidence, empathise with others, synthesise ideas and evidence from different sources, and discuss conflicting arguments. In short, we play devil's advocate. As the philosopher John Passmore said, 'Understanding, not victory, is the object of discussion.'

But as soon as we declare our opinion the search for truth is ended. It becomes a debate, in which we have one simple objective – to win the argument, usually by any means. As we saw earlier in Why Write Essays? (pp. xi–xiv), this may involve presenting evidence in the most favourable way to support our argument, suppressing evidence and arguments that might damage our case, exaggerating points, even making claims for which we have little evidence and failing to empathise with those who may represent interests that conflict with our point of view. Unlike a discussion, this is a convergent, not a divergent, activity: its objective is limited to winning the argument, not exploring all manner of ideas to uncover the truth.

One university department argues:

EXAMPLE

an essay has: an introduction which introduces your viewpoint (thesis or position), a body which develops and supports this viewpoint, and a conclusion which draws together the main lines of the argument to conclude that your viewpoint is correct.[4]

Everything is contained within the narrow confines of a simple objective: to convince the reader of a preconceived opinion. However, such an argument, in which you state your conclusion in the introduction and then make a series of points to back it up, is not an answer to most of the essay questions you will be set.

How to cope with thesis statements

Still, not all universities adopt this narrow interpretation of thesis statements, and in this may lie a solution. Those who advocate them often maintain they are necessary, because this is the only way to give your essay a structure in which to develop a coherent argument. If this is all we are after, there might be less of a problem.

As we've already seen in Stages 1 and 3, you can come to a clear interpretation of the implications of the question, from which you develop a clearly structured plan of the essay, without that entailing a viewpoint that you must defend. Indeed, two students can have an identical structure and plan, yet come to quite different conclusions. Structure does not depend on having a preconceived opinion; it just needs an interpretation of the implications of the question and a plan to go with it. In turn, as this means we have no need to set out to defend opinions which we have stated at the outset, we are free to suspend our judgement, on which all our higher cognitive abilities depend.

Harvard University Writing Center

EXAMPLE

Take the following example of a thesis statement from the Writing Center at Harvard:

Further analysis of Memorial Hall, and of the archival sources that describe the process of building it, suggests that the past may not be the central subject of the hall but only a medium. What message, then, does the building convey, and why are the fallen soldiers of such importance to the alumni who built it? Part of the answer, it seems, is that Memorial Hall is an educational tool, an attempt by the Harvard community of the 1870s to influence the future by shaping our memory of their times. The commemoration of those students and graduates who died for the Union during the Civil War is one aspect of this alumni message to the future, but it may not be the central idea.[5]

It gives structure, yet it suspends judgement and is not driven to prove one preconceived viewpoint. A question is hung over each sentence, with words like 'suggests', 'may not be' and 'it seems'.

As this suggests, essays are far more complex than just the defending of a preconceived opinion, like a defence lawyer attempting to persuade a jury. Genuine discussion, and the higher cognitive abilities that go with it, depend upon suspending judgement. As one tutor at the Writing Center argues, 'An effective thesis cannot be answered with a simple "yes" or "no." A thesis is not a topic; nor is it a fact; nor is it an opinion.'[6]

- We need to suspend our judgement if we are to use our higher cognitive abilities and get high marks as a result.
- This means hanging a question over the issues.
- For this a thesis statement is a means of giving the map of the essay – indicating its structure.

So, if your department does require you to write thesis statements, just clarify for yourself: does this mean I am expected to announce my opinion and defend it in the essay; or am I expected just to give a clear indication of the map of my essay, while I suspend judgement and hang a question over the issues involved?

Summary

1 To use your higher cognitive abilities you must suspend your judgement and hang a question over everything.
2 Someone who has opinions has stopped thinking.
3 To think about a proposition is to accept that it is up for grabs: that there are issues to be discussed.
4 It is not an answer to a question just to state your conclusion in the introduction and then set about defending it.
5 If you have to use thesis statements, use them to outline the map of the essay – its structure.

In the next chapter

Making clear the structure of your essay, then, does not depend upon you announcing your opinion in the introduction. In the next chapter you will see that the most effective introductions do two things: analyse the implications of the question and outline the map of the essay structure drawn from your plan.

Notes

1. Paul Tillich, *The Shaking of the Foundations*, 1949 (Harmondsworth: Penguin, 1964), pp. 118–21.
2. Jan Regan, *Essay and Report Writing: What is Expected of You?* (Lismore: Southern Cross University, 2000), p. 1.

3. Kathy Duffin, *Overview of the Academic Essay* (Cambridge, MA: Writing Center at Harvard University, 1998), p. 1.

4. Regan, *Essay and Report Writing*, p. 1.

5. Patricia Kain, *Beginning the Academic Essay* (Cambridge, MA: Writing Center at Harvard University, 1999), pp. 2–3.

6. Maxine Rodburg, *Developing a Thesis* (Cambridge, MA: Writing Center at Harvard University, 1999), p. 1.

Introductions

In this chapter you will learn:

- why so many of us struggle to write good introductions;
- how to write introductions that leave readers with no doubts about what you're doing and why;
- a simple formula for a good introduction.

There are very few students who wouldn't list introductions as one of the most difficult aspects of writing an essay. Much of this is due to the fact that most of us are unsure about what we should be doing in the introduction. If we don't know why we're doing something, what we're trying to achieve, we shouldn't be too surprised to find that we're not particularly good at it. But there's another reason why most of us are not good at writing introductions: we neglect Stages 1 and 3 (Interpretation and Planning). If we have very little idea what we're going to be writing, it's difficult to do a good job of introducing it.

However, even with a clear interpretation of the question and a well-structured plan it can be a problem, unless you set simple and clear objectives that you want your introduction to fulfil. These should include two things:

- the interpretation of the question (what is it getting at?);
- the structure of your answer; the map the reader is going to follow.

The interpretation of the question

The first question readers are going to ask themselves as soon as they begin to read your essay, before they even consider anything else, is 'Has the writer seen the point of the question?' In two or three sentences you need to outline the main issues raised by the question, which you will have uncovered in the interpretation stage. This may involve identifying the main problem or set of problems at the heart of the question, or it may involve pointing to the central importance of one or two concepts, which need to be analysed. But this does not involve discussing these problems or analysing the concepts in the introduction; it merely means you show your tutors that you have the ability to see the implications of the question, and point them in the direction you intend to take them.

- What is the question getting at? What is its point?
- Identify the main problems it raises.
- Point to one or two central concepts which will need to be analysed.

In the question we discussed in Chapter 2 you might begin with the following introduction:

Question

'Authority amounts to no more than the possession of power.' *Discuss.*

Most of us would no doubt agree that in the cases of police officers and government officials this claim is largely true: their authority does seem to derive exclusively from the power they have been given. Indeed, we acknowledge their authority because we are all too aware of the consequences of not doing so. But to accept that every case of authority amounts to no more than the claim that might is always right threatens the very existence of modern democracy along with its goal of balancing order with accountability and justice. Either way, whatever we're prepared to believe depends upon our understanding of the two central concepts, power and authority.

By identifying the major issues in the first few sentences you establish the relevance of these, and the relevance of your essay in tackling them. This is what writers describe as the 'hot spot': the first sentence or two in which you sell the subject, making it clear that you've seen the problem the question is getting at, and that you're aware of its importance.

The structure of your answer

Having done this you then need to outline in the broadest of details the structure of your answer, the plan you're working from. You don't need to do this in the authority/power question, because you've already done it by pointing to the central importance of the analysis of the two concepts. Again this need not be in any great detail, but it must provide a map so that your tutors are at no time unsure which way you're going and where you're taking them. At Harvard students are told:

A good introduction is successful because it allows readers to prepare themselves mentally for the journey they will undergo as they follow your argument through the paper. Like a travel guide, it enables them to recognize and understand the major points of interest in your argument as they go by.[1]

Remember, lose your tutors and you lose marks; it's as simple as that. Your introduction should point them in the right direction, giving them a clear idea of what is to follow.

- Give tutors a map of the structure of your essay.
- Let them know where you're taking them.
- If you lose them, you'll lose marks.

PRACTICE
EXERCISE

Write an introduction

Take the advertising question we considered earlier:

'Advertisers seek only to ensure that consumers make informed choices.'
Discuss.

Write an introduction that interprets the implications of the question and then outlines the map of your answer. When you've finished, compare your answer with the introduction below.

In this question our map might look something like the following:

Answer

Most advertising executives are willing to defend their profession by arguing that all they are doing is informing the public and in doing so protecting the democratic freedoms of individuals, in particular their freedom of choice. To a certain extent, of course, this is true: without advertising we would be less informed about new developments in technology, in fashion and in medical advances. Even government warnings about the dangers at work and in the home depend upon advertisements. But the key to this is the claim that this is the 'only' thing they do, when most of the public suspect their paramount concern is to manipulate consumers into buying products that they may not want or need.

This indicates what the reader should expect as the structure in the essay. One part will develop the view that advertisers are concerned with informing consumers. Then the structure will turn on the word 'only', leaving the writer, in the second half of the essay, to examine the way advertisers use information selectively and employ other devices to manipulate the consumer through appeals to sex, status and prejudices.

A simple formula for introductions

The real value of writing introductions in this way lies in the fact that most of us benefit from having a simple structure, a formula, like this to work from. As a result we're likely to feel more confident about what we're doing when we write introductions. They'll present fewer problems and they'll focus the reader's attention on the issues we believe are the most relevant.

Using quotations

Nevertheless, you may find as your confidence grows that you want to do more with introductions. You may decide to use a quotation to open up the issues raised by the question. This can have the twofold advantage of not just opening up the question, but setting it in the context of what the current authorities in your subject are saying about it. But it's worth sounding a note of caution. It can lead you to focus on the quotation, rather than the question you've been set. As a result your answer may not deal with the implications of the question fully and relevantly. So unless you're certain that it's relevant and goes to the heart of the question, opening up its implications, it may be best to avoid it.

Setting the problem in context

Alternatively you may want to set the problem in the context of recent history.

EXAMPLE

In the following question, which asks you to consider the inevitability of progress, you could begin with this:

Question

'You can't stop progress.' *Discuss critically with reference to one major technology.*

Looking back at the early years of the industrial revolution in Britain it's tempting to view opponents of progress, like the Luddites who smashed the machines they believed were threatening their way of life, as naïve and short-sighted. But in this we ought to be cautious; after all, theirs might not have been opposition to progress as such, but to just one account of it. It's worth wondering what makes *our* view of progress, with all its alienation at work, dissipated communities, rising crime, social disaffection and persistently high levels of poverty and homelessness, any better than that of the Luddites.

Today the problem is the same. Developing countries in the Third World can claim to have learnt from the mistakes of Western industrialised countries. As a result their account of progress is quite different. So, while we might agree that 'you can't stop progress', there is no reason why we should accept the implication of this, that we have lost our freedom to choose. We may not be able to stop progress, but we can still choose the type of progress we want.

Doing more with introductions in this way carries with it the danger of obscuring the original intentions: to reveal the implications of the question and outline the map of your answer. In this case it was wise to split the introduction into two paragraphs to give us a chance of making the structure clearer in the second paragraph. But there are no hard and fast rules to this. Just keep in mind the simple structure on which you are weaving these improvisations and avoid allowing the introduction to become so long and complex that it obscures the simple intent that lies behind it.

Summary

1 To write introductions well, adopt the simple formula.
2 Do two things:
   2.1 Interpret the implications of the question, so tutors know you've seen the point.
   2.2 Outline the map of the essay – its structure.
3 At all costs, don't lose tutors, otherwise you will lose marks.

In the next chapter

The same advice applies equally to paragraphs. As we will see in the next two chapters, they, too, have a simple formula.

Note

1   Julie Lynch and Jennifer Ritterhouse, *Writing at Harvard* (Cambridge, MA: Writing Center at Harvard University, 2000), ch. 2, pp. 2–3.

26

Paragraphs – Topic Sentences

In this chapter you will learn:

- how to write paragraphs to produce a taut, well-argued essay;
- a simple formula for writing paragraphs;
- how to use 'topic sentences' and 'transitions'.

The main body of the essay

Most students struggle with the problem of how to build the structure of their arguments in their essay. Now that you have outlined the plan of your essay in the introduction with the broad map of what is to follow, you can begin to build the structure of your arguments more confidently. Yet still, this depends upon knowing how to construct each paragraph so that you develop in your essay the tautness of a well-planned, cohesive piece of reasoning. Often essays fail because they read like a loose list of isolated paragraphs each dependent upon itself, and not supported by those that preceded it.

To avoid this, tie your paragraphs in with the major issues you identified in your introduction as being central to the question. You will be picking these issues up anyway as you follow the structure of your plan, but as you do so make it clear to the reader that you are following the map you outlined in your introduction. In this way you not only maintain relevance throughout, but by tying each paragraph in with the introduction you create a cohesive piece of work. Its structure will be taut, giving the essay the feel of being well organised and tightly reasoned.

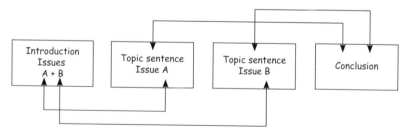

Tying in paragraphs with the introduction

Of course, this doesn't mean you should announce clumsily that this is what you're doing, repeatedly making the same sort of reference to your introduction at the beginning of each paragraph. This would be tedious and the reader would begin to suspect that your concern was for form rather than content. It can be done more subtly than this, as we will see later in this chapter and in Chapter 34. The important thing to remember is that in the first sentence of each paragraph, the 'topic sentence', the reader needs to be informed about what you're doing in that paragraph, and why it's relevant to the issues you identified in your introduction.

In the topic sentence the reader needs to be informed about:

1 What you're doing.
2 Why it's relevant.

Nevertheless, there is a qualification to this we need to mention. Not every paragraph needs to be tied in with the map in your introduction. Some of the major issues in the essay will take a number of paragraphs to develop. Therefore, in this case, you only need to tie in with the introduction the first paragraph of each major section. The paragraphs that follow will then have to be tied in with this paragraph to create fluency and cohesion.

> You need an effective 'transition' at the beginning of each paragraph to indicate to readers the course of your argument.

This raises an important issue, as we will see later in this chapter. In order to create a taut, cohesive piece of work, each paragraph has to have a clear connection with the one that preceded it. To make sure of this you will need to have effective 'transitions' at the beginning of each paragraph to indicate to readers the course of your argument. From this they should be able to see that this is an extension of the previous paragraph, or that you're making a comparison, or that you're illustrating the point you've already made, and so on. In some paragraphs it will be obvious what you're doing and there will be no need to announce it, but if in doubt use a transition. In Chapter 34 you will find many of the most common transitions we can use for this purpose.

- Try to avoid the essay that reads like a loose list of isolated paragraphs.
- Use the topic sentence to tie paragraphs in with the major issues outlined in the introduction.
- Use transitions at the beginning of the topic sentence to create fluency and cohesion between each paragraph.

If you read the sample essays that you can find in the revision stage, you will see how the topic sentences and transitions work in making your essay taut and cohesive. It's clear where every part fits in and readers are never lost as they move smoothly and consistently from one part of the argument to the next. Compare the revised versions of the essay with the unrevised original by going onto the companion website (www.howtowritebetteressays.com).

A simple formula for paragraphs

As we've already seen with introductions, we do most things much more effectively if we know what we're doing and why. But for many students paragraphs are a complete mystery.

This shows up in their concern over the length of paragraphs. Some suspect that theirs are either too short or too long, while others confess that they decide to end one paragraph and begin another on a mere whim. In fact, although this may not appear too helpful, the best advice is simply to vary their length. It will make the essay more interesting to read as you break up the otherwise predictable rhythm of your writing.

> Vary the length of paragraphs. It will make the essay more interesting to read.

Of course, ultimately the key to the length of paragraphs lies in the logic of the essay as a whole. In other words, keep to your structure and at all costs let readers see that, as they move from one paragraph to another, they're moving from one section within the structure to another. For the same reason, avoid long, rambling paragraphs that obscure the structure. In fact, this is not as difficult to avoid as it might seem. Long paragraphs, in which you lose the thread of what the writer's doing, are like the long, rambling essay: the product of writing without structure.

You can build this structure into each paragraph by keeping a simple formula for paragraphs in your mind. Although it would be arrogant to lay down the law on the structure of paragraphs, as it would be with introductions, it helps to have a simple formula, particularly when you're unsure of what you're doing. As for introductions, you can always use the formula as the basis for improvisation once you've grown in confidence using it.

- Don't be afraid of varying the length of paragraphs – it will make your essay more interesting to read.
- Let the logic of the plan dictate the length of each paragraph.
- Stick to a simple formula for writing paragraphs.

Three parts

For this purpose remind yourself that there are three parts to a paragraph: the topic sentence; the development; and the evidence. This structure may not always be appropriate, you may need to adapt it, but if you remind yourself of each part, you will always be aware of the weaknesses you're allowing to appear in your essay when you omit one part. You'll be reminding yourself that if you do decide to leave one part out, you will have to address the problem later in the essay.

Paragraphs

Topic sentence
↓
Development
↓
Evidence

The topic sentence

The topic sentence, as its name implies, introduces the topic of the paragraph. But even more importantly, it establishes the topic's relevance by tying it in with one of the major issues in your plan, which you mapped out in your introduction. This is a key element in the scaffolding of your arguments. Without it you will struggle to construct your arguments clearly and then indicate to your readers what you are doing and why it is relevant. As we've already pointed out, by tying all the components tightly together in this way you create both relevance and tight cohesion within the essay.

EXAMPLE

For example, the paragraph after the introduction in the advertising essay might begin:

> As this suggests, at least part of the advertiser's role is to provide consumers and the public with information.

And, later in the essay, after you have examined the way advertisers manipulate through the selective use of information, you may go on to examine the other forms of manipulation by introducing it with the topic sentence:

> However, advertisers have developed still more effective forms of manipulation, particularly in their exploitation of the sex, status and prejudices of the consumer.

As this illustrates, the topic sentence is important to establish the relevance of the paragraph you are about to write in the context of the paragraphs that have already been completed. It is the scaffolding of your arguments through which you make clear to readers what you're doing and how they should negotiate it. You can create this scaffolding in the following three ways and in Chapter 34 you will find the key words that you will need to do it.

1 Remind the reader of the question

Perhaps the most common and effective way, as we've seen already, is to remind the reader of the implications of the question and the key issues running through the essay, which you analysed in the introduction. This not only creates a bridge with what you've already done, but establishes the relevance of what you're about to do. So, in the advertising essay one paragraph might be introduced with the topic sentence:

> Nevertheless the statement in the question seems to be right at least in one respect …

And another might read:

> But where the question appears to go too far is in arguing that informing the consumer is the 'only' thing that advertisers do.

But it's best not to do this too often: it quickly becomes very tedious to be reminded of the question over and over again.

2 Recap

Alternatively, you can recap what you've done so far with the sort of topic sentence that begins:

So far, we have seen that …

But, like reminding the examiner of the implications of the question, this too can quickly become tedious and clumsy.

3 List what you're about to do

You can also, of course, do the reverse: rather than recap what you've done, list what you're about to do. If you're introducing a major section in your essay, which breaks down into two or three subsections each with its own paragraph, you can list these subsections and then signpost each one as you pick them up and discuss them. So, you might recap by saying:

In the last section we did …

and then finish the sentence by signposting what you're about to do by saying:

… which leaves us with three main issues to consider: A; B; C.

Then, as you pick each of these up, you number them in the topic sentence for each of their respective paragraphs: 'First'; 'Second'; 'Third'.

Topic sentences

1 Remind the reader of the implications of the question – the key issues running through the essay.
2 Recap what you've done so far.
3 List what you're about to do and signpost subsections as you pick them up.

Transitions

However, as you can see from this, topic sentences have another important function: to indicate to your readers which way you're now going to take them. To do this you need a 'transition' at the beginning of the sentence. This can be a short phrase, like 'As a result', or a single word, like 'Nevertheless'. In the examples above we used 'As this suggests' and 'However'.

In effect these work as 'logical indicators': they indicate what you will be doing in the paragraph. You might be striking a contrast with what you've just done in the previous paragraph ('In contrast', 'However'). You may simply be extending the argument you've already developed in a slightly different way ('Moreover', 'Therefore'). Or you may want to strengthen your argument by developing a point that reinforces it from a different angle ('Similarly', 'Likewise'). In Chapter 34 you will find many of the most useful transitions arranged in categories according to their logical function.

Transitions

Contrast:	'In contrast' – 'However'
Extension:	'Moreover' – 'Therefore'
Reinforcing:	'Similarly' – 'Likewise'

In view of their importance, make sure your transitions do what you want them to do. Occasionally we find ourselves using weak transitions, which create only weak links and a weak essay structure. The worst are those we use for a list of points, words and phrases, like 'Also', 'Another point is' and 'In addition'. These have their counterparts in subjects, like history, where we resort to time to order our ideas, which we introduce with transitions like 'After', 'Then' and 'The next'. When you find yourself using this sort of transition, just check to see what's happening in your essay. More often than not they will indicate that you're no longer discussing issues by developing a critical analysis. Instead, you've slipped into a description of the issues or into a narrative of the events.

> Make sure your transitions do what you want them to do. Weak transitions create weak links and a weak essay structure.

The same warning about transitions doing real work applies to all those times when we've found ourselves pressing a transition into service to create fluency that simply wasn't there in the first place. If we haven't planned carefully enough, establishing clear intellectual links between paragraphs, our readers will not be fooled if we try to paper over the disjointed paragraphs with carefully chosen transitions. It will always sound false and manufactured.

However, if your essay is clearly planned, not all of your paragraphs will need transitions. There are going to be some that are set in the context of a clearly signposted argument or analysis, and it's all too obvious what you're doing. Nevertheless, don't forget these are important directions for tutors, who need to know which way you will be taking them as they try to navigate the unfamiliar terrain of your thinking. To take the city analogy again, they need to know at each intersection and every turning, which way you intend to go, otherwise you will leave them mystified and confused as to what you're doing, and they will be unable to award you marks, even though your work may be good. So, if in doubt, use one.

- Transitions are important indicators of what you're about to do.
- They are like street signs in a strange city.
- If in doubt, use one, otherwise you might lose the reader.
- But make sure they do real work and are not an attempt to create fluency between paragraphs where there is none.

Write the topic sentence

PRACTICE EXERCISE 26

Question

'Authority amounts to no more than the possession of power.' *Discuss.*

Look at the introduction we wrote for this question in the last chapter and our interpretation of it in Chapter 2. It's clear from the introduction that we are going to start by arguing that the proposition is true, if we take the concept of authority to imply someone 'in' authority. This section of the essay could be represented by the notes below.

As you can see, we could probably write this in two paragraphs. The first paragraph would deal with 'official authority', the sort given to people like the police and government officials. Taking this as our first paragraph after the introduction, write a topic sentence for it.

Once you've done this, compare your topic sentence with the one below.

The notes

Question

'Authority amounts to no more than the possession of power.' *Discuss.*

1 Proposition = True if authority is taken to mean 'in' authority:
   = authority amounts to the power to make things worse – to oblige people to
   comply with orders

   (a) Official authority – institutional power
          e.g. the police
       We accept this sort of power as authority, maybe because of
       (i)   our respect for the institution

             or, when this fails, e.g. an inner-city ethnic community feels unfairly
             targeted by the police,

       (ii) because of our fear of the consequences

   (b) Unofficial authority – 'Might is Right'
          e.g. the local gang leader
       Their influence over the local community may be due to
       (i)   respect for individual leaders

             or

       (ii) more likely it's due to fear of the consequences of going against their will,
             e.g. protection rackets

Answer

As this suggests, one way in which we understand the concept of authority is
represented by the institutional power of officials like police officers, whose authority lies
largely in their power to make things worse for us if we don't comply with their orders.

Summary

1 Tie your paragraphs in with the major issues you identified in the introduction.
2 Use topic sentences to do this and transitions to create fluency between your
   paragraphs.
3 Stick to a simple formula for paragraphs: topic sentences + development + evidence.
4 Make sure your transitions do what you want them to do: create fluency and
   point the reader in the right direction.

In the next chapter

The remaining two parts of the simple formula for paragraphs are development
and evidence. In the next chapter we will see how we can earn the highest marks
by showing the examiner in the development that we can use our higher cognitive
abilities, and can deploy evidence skilfully to illustrate and support our arguments.

Paragraphs – Development and Evidence

In this chapter you will learn:

- how to develop your arguments to get the highest marks;
- how to avoid answers that fail to use the abilities tutors are assessing;
- how to use evidence that supports and illustrates your arguments.

Once you've established in the topic sentence the relevance of the topic you're going to be dealing with in the paragraph, tutors can get down to assessing the quality of your work.

The development

It is here, in the development, that you show your tutor that you are capable of the sort of intellectual processing that was called for in the question by the 'instructional verb' (see Chapter 8). At this point it's worth reminding ourselves of the issues we raised when we first examined this. You'll remember we pointed out that all syllabuses are written in the context of six 'cognitive domains' – six intellectual abilities, ranging from the simplest, 'recall', to the more complex abilities, such as analysis, synthesis and evaluation.

Again, as we pointed out then, most of our problems, both in writing and in our study skills, begin here. We wrongly assume that education is exclusively concerned with the possession of knowledge, so we aim to produce evidence in our writing that we know a great deal, that we have good recall, the simplest ability, whereas we should be exercising the more complex abilities to analyse, to criticise, to synthesise ideas and evidence, and to evaluate arguments.

Instead of using our higher cognitive abilities, we assume the question merely wants us to show that we know a great deal and can recall it.

All too often, even though the question might ask us to discuss, analyse or criticise, we assume tutors merely want evidence that we can understand the subject. With this in mind, as we set about researching the essay, we begin to take vast quantities of irrelevant, unstructured notes from texts, arguing that we cannot possibly leave any material out, because these are the facts and we are required to show evidence that we can recall them all. As a result, we lose sight of the implications of the question and our need to address them relevantly, preferring instead to put everything into our essays as long as they are facts. We assume the more facts we put in, relevant or not, the more marks we will earn.

Similarly, although we're told to put arguments in our own words, it's difficult to shake off the belief that, as the texts we use are the source of right answers, of indisputable facts, we can do nothing else but copy them with complete accuracy and without alteration, because to change anything would be to make them less than right. So we copy into our notes large chunks of texts that we have neither structured nor processed in any way. As a result our notes assume the structure the author gives us, which might be quite irrelevant for our purposes in preparing to write this particular essay.

The way we understand the purpose of setting essays determines how we go about tackling them		
	Wrong	**Right**
Purpose	To assess our understanding, our knowledge	To assess our higher cognitive abilities
Notes	Vast quantity Irrelevant Unstructured	Selective Relevant Structured
Essay content	Everything goes in Irrelevant Plagiarism	Relevant to the question In our own words
Essay structure	Author's structure Inappropriate to the question	*Our* structure based on our interpretation
Abilities	Copying Reproducing Imitating	Analysis Criticism Evaluation
Processing ideas	Surface level	Deep level

Passive surface-level processing

In other words, we become passive 'surface-level processors': we neither exercise judgement as to the relevance of the material, nor as to the credibility of what is being said. We've ignored the instructions to use the higher cognitive abilities, to evaluate the ideas critically, and instead we've settled for the simpler task of copying, reproducing and imitating what we've allowed ourselves to assume is the unquestioned authority, the source of right answers. Not surprisingly, then, in our writing we're inclined to plagiarise large sections, believing that to alter anything would be to make what is otherwise a right answer less than right.

However, in universities the essays we write and the examinations we prepare ourselves for are not concerned with demonstrating recall or with reproducing faithfully what our authorities say. They're aimed at assessing the higher cognitive abilities, where we synthesise and analyse ideas, and evaluate arguments critically. Rather than accept that there are authorities that are beyond question, this asks us to criticise and evaluate received ideas and opinions – to accept nothing on trust.

> The examinations we prepare ourselves for at university ask us to criticise and evaluate ideas and opinions – to accept nothing on trust.

In this stage of essay writing, therefore, as we develop our arguments in the paragraph, it's important to remind ourselves that those who assess our essays are not concerned so much with right answers as they are with the abilities we use to reach our answer. Two essays can both receive the same high mark, even though they come to completely different answers. And, conversely, even though two essays may come to exactly the same conclusion, this doesn't mean they will be awarded the same mark: one might receive the lowest mark awarded, the other the highest. And, of course, it's equally true that even though a tutor might agree with your conclusion, he or she may still award you low marks. It's not the conclusion you reach that matters so much as the way in which you reach it: the way you travel.

- Tutors are not so much concerned to see if you have the right answers as they are to see the abilities you use to reach your answers.
- Their concern is with the way you travel rather than the destination you reach.

Travelling well

Given this, it should now be clear that in the development of the paragraph, tutors want to see you use these higher cognitive abilities. They will want to see how well you travel from the simple description of the case, to an analysis of its implications, to the criticism of each of these implications, to the evidence to support your view, and finally to your evaluation. In such a sequence you will have travelled far, and for this you will earn high marks.

Description ⟶ Analysis ⟶ Criticism ⟶ Evidence ⟶ Evaluation

Of course, it may not be possible to do all of this in one paragraph. After the analysis you may want to take up each implication as the subject for each subsequent paragraph.

Analysis
⟶ Implication ⟶ Criticism ⟶ Evidence
⟶ Implication ⟶ Criticism ⟶ Evidence
⟶ Implication ⟶ Criticism ⟶ Evidence

In this case, in one paragraph you would describe the implication, criticise it and show evidence for your view, before moving to the next implication in the next paragraph, where you would do the same, and so on. Then your evaluation may come two or three paragraphs later at the end of this section of your essay, when you've dealt with all the implications. Alternatively, it may come at the end of the essay, if this works better. As we will see when we examine the role of the conclusion, this is often the stage in which we can most effectively bring the various strands together and reach a measured evaluation based on the strength of the arguments and evidence we've considered in the essay as a whole.

The evidence

Given what we have just said about the development, the evidence should present few problems. Obviously, if the development of our argument is clear, the relevance of our evidence should be equally clear. We will have a much better idea of the sort of evidence we need to support and illustrate our arguments in the paragraph.

The problems come when we revert to the assumptions that tell us the only things worth anything in education are knowledge and facts. Then we can become obsessed with impressing the reader with our knowledge by presenting a wealth of facts irrespective of whether they're relevant or not. The paragraph becomes overloaded, burying the structure of our essay; the facts are out of proportion with what they ought to be to support and illustrate our argument; and readers become confused about what we're trying to do. They will assume that either they have missed something, or the structure of our essay has broken down.

Evidence – two problems:

1 Giving too much – confusing the reader by overloading the paragraph and burying the structure of our essay.
2 Giving too little – relying instead on unsubstantiated opinion.

Nevertheless, even worse is the problem of giving too little evidence. There are some students who, realising that they should not be taking authorities on trust, that they should be analysing, criticising and evaluating them, jump from a statement of the problem in the topic sentence to evaluation, without any attempt to analyse and discuss the issues. As a result, because there has been no development, the evaluation is usually neither measured nor thoughtfully considered.

In effect they've convinced themselves that the only thing of any value is opinion – their opinion. As a result they fill up each paragraph with a series of unsupported claims, for which they provide neither analysis, nor argument, nor, in our present context, any evidence. In the minds of most tutors this extreme of unsubstantiated opinion is probably worse than the other: blind acceptance and description of so-called right answers.

- Try to avoid overloading the paragraph with evidence to impress tutors.
- They will assume either that they haven't understood something or that the structure of your essay has broken down.
- Equally, avoid unsubstantiated opinion.

PRACTICE
EXERCISE

Write the development and the evidence

Question

'Authority amounts to no more than the possession of power.' *Discuss.*

Having written the topic sentence for the first paragraph after the introduction in the last practice exercise, now, with your topic sentence and the notes for the plan in front of you, write the development and the evidence of the paragraph.

Once you've done this, compare it with the answer below.

Answer

Even so, stability in any society depends on there being a large proportion of the community willing to obey these orders because they have respect for official institutions, like the police. When this fails we may be left with a very volatile situation in which people feel obliged to obey, simply out of fear for the consequences. For example, if an ethnic community in an inner-city area feels that the police are unfairly targeting them, in time they are likely to lose respect for the institution and for the individual police officer, whose only recourse thereafter is to implement the law by threats of force, rather than by appeals to reason and justice.

Look again at the sample essays in the revision stage, where you'll see the sort of improvements that can be made to an essay by addressing these problems. But first, for comparison, read the same paragraphs in the unrevised original essay on the companion website (www.howtowritebetteressays.com).

Summary

1 In the development, show tutors you have the abilities to analyse, criticise, discuss and evaluate issues.
2 Avoid simply trying to impress tutors with how much you know.
3 It's not the conclusions you reach, but the abilities you use to get there, that matters.
4 Try to avoid giving too much evidence: it might confuse the reader by breaking up the structure of your essay.
5 Equally, avoid giving too little, relying instead on mere opinion.

In the next chapter

If a large part of paragraph writing is about travelling well, conclusions are about arriving in style. As we'll see in the next chapter, there are a number of simple ways to ensure that your conclusion ties in with your introduction, producing an essay that is cohesive, tightly argued and a joy to read.

Conclusions

In this chapter you will learn:

- the most effective ways of writing thought-provoking conclusions;
- how to use conclusions to tie up your arguments into a cohesive, relevant essay;
- how to leave your readers with a sense of discovery – that they have read something worthwhile.

Although many people list introductions as the most difficult part of writing an essay, conclusions must come a close second, whereas, in fact, it should be the easiest of the three parts out of introductions, paragraphs and conclusions. Having got your readers safely to this point without losing them or confusing them as to the relevance of your arguments, there is little you can do now to weaken your work. Nevertheless, there are still problems we should avoid.

What should I do in a conclusion?

As we've seen with other aspects of essay writing, the source of many of these problems is that we are simply unsure what we should do in a conclusion, and if we're not clear what we're doing we are unlikely to do it well.

Giving our opinions

Some students are convinced they must finish on an upbeat note, with a clear, firm declaration of their opinion. If the question asks for your opinion, they argue, you must give it. The problem with this is that such a declaration of opinion may just come completely out of the blue. The essay may be full of the most skilful analysis and discussion of the problems, leaving you with no clear grounds for absolute certainty one way or the other. Therefore, to make a clear statement of your opinion, showing no doubt or uncertainty, would be inappropriate.

   The opinions you express in the conclusion must reflect the strength and balance of the arguments that have preceded them in the body of the essay. They must be carefully measured to match the discussion you have developed, and if you've genuinely discussed the issues and not just given a one-sided defence of your opinion, there may be no basis for a firm declaration of certainty one way or the other.

> The opinions you express must reflect the strength and balance of the arguments that have preceded them.

It's well worth reminding yourself that firm, clear opinions have no particular value in themselves. Anyone can express their opinions, and almost everyone does. Down at your local bar you can find people with opinions on just about everything, from the reasons why your local football team is doing badly this season to the ethical implications of human cloning. But you're not going to earn marks for your opinions. Marks are earned by developing your analysis and discussion of the issues, and then supporting them with relevant, well-chosen evidence. Most of us down at the local bar are rarely so scrupulous in our attention to the quality of our arguments.

Of course, if you do want to make clear your own opinions and, on balance, they reflect the preceding discussion, then do so. Failing that, if you are genuinely undecided, give a tentative conclusion couched in carefully measured qualifications that reflect the strength of your arguments.

- In a genuine discussion there may be no basis for clear opinions one way or the other.
- In themselves opinions have no particular value.
- If you want to express them, make sure they reflect the preceding discussion.

Summarise the main points

Anyway, in many cases there are far more important things you can do. In particular, you can allow your readers to come to their own opinions, helping them to do so by summarising the main points in the essay. To do this you will have to come to a measured judgement of what you believe to be the most important issues the essay has raised.

EXAMPLE

'Advertisers seek only to ensure that consumers make informed choices'. Discuss.

Go to the companion website (www.howtowritebetteressays.com) and read the unrevised version of the conclusion of this essay. Now compare this with the revised conclusion in the first sample essay (pp. 264–67) in the revision stage. Judge for yourself how well you think the author identifies the most important issues and then comes to a measured judgement that reflects the balance of the essay.

Pick up the theme raised in the introduction

But perhaps the most useful thing you can do in a conclusion is to tighten your essay up into a cohesive piece of work by picking up the theme you raised in your introduction, reflecting on it in the light of what you've discussed since. Tying up the introduction with the conclusion in this way lends greater cohesion to your work – it is satisfying to the reader to know that you have come full circle and everything has found its appropriate place.

EXAMPLE

For example, the essay that examined the possibility of stopping progress began in the introduction by referring to the activities of the Luddites in the nineteenth century during the British industrial revolution. It suggested that in hindsight they might be viewed as naïve and short sighted. Given this, you could conclude the essay by picking up this theme again. You might suggest that in the light of the discussion in the essay, rather than the Luddites, we might have more justification in accusing our own generation of naïvety and short-sightedness in how we define and measure progress.

The wider implications or future trends

As this suggests, the best conclusion is one that is as thought provoking as possible. As we've already seen, there are a number of ways of doing this. You could just restate the theme of the essay, or you could summarise the main points of the arguments you've developed.

Alternatively, you may want to suggest the wider implications, or what you believe to be the future trends: you may want to tell the reader what you believe has to be done to solve the problems you've discussed, or predict what might happen if the problems are left unresolved. This might pick up on the broader issues that go beyond the limits of the essay, but which you have suggested in the introduction might become our ultimate concern.

EXAMPLE

Say, for example, you were writing an essay on the ethical implications involved in human cloning. In the introduction you might have pointed to the broader, long-term fears that we might be encouraging the development of a world in which children can be manufactured by parents according to their own ideal blueprints, rather like going along to a genetic supermarket to select the characteristics you most want in your children. In the conclusion, after your discussion, you may have decided that this really is a problem that needs to be faced now before it is too late, or you may want to conclude that the problem has been overstated. Either way, both would work well as long as they don't go beyond the strength of the arguments and evidence you have presented.

Similarly, if you were discussing a literary text, you might suggest that the implications of the issues you've raised go beyond the scope of your essay.

EXAMPLE

For example, if you were answering the question, 'How can the description of the need for distance at the beginning of chapter 19 of *Adam Bede* square with the novel's more general emphasis on novelistic sympathy?' (Harvard), you might suggest that a study of George Eliot's other novels, such as *Silas Marner* and *Middlemarch*, would be interesting to see if this apparent contradiction runs throughout her work.

In a nutshell

You can do any of the following:

- give your opinions as long as they match the strength of your arguments;
- summarise the main points;
- pick up the theme of the introduction;
- suggest wider implications;
- predict future trends.

If you do nothing more in a conclusion, always try to achieve at least one thing: to wrap up the essay leaving your readers satisfied that they have read something worthwhile – leave them with a sense of discovery. Whether you use an idea that pulls everything together or extends it, or whether you tie up the essay by picking up an anecdote you've already used, let your readers participate, so that they feel they've been able to come to their own conclusion and have discovered something thought provoking and interesting.

The framework – introductions, conclusions and paragraphs

IN YOUR OWN WORK

We've now reached the point where we're ready to write the essay. In the last stage, you completed the plan of the essay you have chosen to work on. Now, with this in front of you, write the introduction to the essay, the conclusion and the two paragraphs that follow the introduction. Once you've finished writing the whole essay, at the end of the book, you may find that you think a little differently about the issues and you want to change the conclusion, but for this exercise write it now (you can always change it later if you want to).

Summary

1 Be reassured: if you have got your readers safely this far without losing them, there's little you can do in your conclusion to weaken your work.
2 You can express your opinions as long as they reflect the balance of your discussion.
3 Alternatively, you can summarise the main points, pick up the main theme you raised in the introduction, or suggest wider implications or future trends.
4 But, most of all, let your readers participate so they feel they have read something that is thought provoking.

In the next chapter

In the exercise involving your own work in this chapter you will have seen how much simpler essay writing can be if you have a clearly structured plan from which to write, and if you understand how the structural features of the essay work – introductions, paragraphs and conclusions. We can now turn, in the next five chapters, to all those problems that arise when we begin to develop the content of the essay.

Style – Simplicity 1: Sentences

In this chapter you will learn:

- the three guiding principles for a better style;
- how to avoid heavy, unreadable prose;
- how to write sentences that avoid the danger of losing your reader;
- how to use the length of sentences and punctuation to create the rhythm in your prose that is nearer to talk in print.

When some students reach this stage, all too often they're ready just to shrug their shoulders and give up on their writing, dismissing it despairingly with the words, 'I just haven't got a very good style, that's all!', as if this was somehow God-given, encoded into our DNA. It probably comes from our early schooling when children were given prizes for their compositions, and from that moment on we came to believe the world is somehow divided between those who have writing talent and those who have not – and there's not a thing we can do about it.

But this is just not so. There is much we can do to improve our style. The simplest thing is just to read more: the more literature we read, the better our style. Like the process of photosynthesis it filters down through our consciousness, enriching our thought processes and sharpening our use of words without us being aware that anything significant is happening. Get into the habit of reading well-written novels, so that you're always in the middle of reading one. Just 15 to 20 minutes a night before you go to sleep will in time have a marked impact on your writing.

Writing lightly – the guiding principles

Beyond this, there are some simple practical steps we can take. But first, we need to establish certain guiding principles, definite markers that we can use when we choose our words and phrases. After applying them in two or three essays, you should be seeing quite noticeable improvements in your writing.

Each of these guiding principles is focused on one pre-eminent goal: to avoid all heavy, unreadable prose. Make your writing as light as your subject allows. The result is likely to be a more enjoyable experience for the reader and a memorable, effective piece of writing. Keep in mind the three main guiding principles, which can be summed up in just three words:

- logic
- interest
- brevity

The first of these you've already met if you've planned well and written an introduction that lays out the logical map that you will be following throughout the essay. As we've said, as you pick up each topic in this map in the first sentence of each paragraph, indicating with transitions what you will be doing in the paragraph, the reader can follow you, step by step, without fear of being lost.

As to the second, interest, we shall discuss this in Chapter 33 when we look at the type of evidence you might use. For now, our concern is with brevity – saying what you want to say in the fewest possible words. Here lies what most of us mean when we think of style. It means simplicity and economy in the use of language.

Simplicity

The key to writing lightly is not to overcomplicate things – to remind yourself constantly that writing is nothing more than talk in print. Some of the best writing we've ever read seems to glide across the page as if it's just someone talking to you in the same room, even though the writer may be grappling with the most complex ideas and the deepest of emotions. When you read it, it seems the simplest thing in the world to do. But like most things that are done well, its simplicity disguises the hard work that's been invested: in this case in trying to overcome the difference between written and spoken communication.

Written v. spoken

We're all aware of the problems this difference creates for a student writing an essay. As we're not sitting next to our readers, we're not able to tell them what we really meant to say each time they stop to struggle with one of our more difficult expressions. This is made even more difficult if our work is being marked by an external examiner, who won't have the same familiarity with and sympathy for our ideas as our tutor does.

But perhaps the most elusive aspect of normal speech, that's difficult to capture in our written work, is any emphasis we might express through tone or gesture. This has to be conveyed through our choice of words and phrases, and through sentence rhythm and punctuation. And, of course, unlike the oral explanations we might give in answer to a question, in our written work readers can go at their own pace; they can even go back and re-read one of our arguments. All of which makes writing a much more concentrated form of communication than speech.

Emphasis we might express through tone or gesture has to be conveyed in writing through:

- words
- phrases
- sentence rhythm
- punctuation

Given these problems you couldn't be blamed for putting your hands up in despair; it seems a frighteningly difficult task. But the truth is it's a lot simpler than we allow ourselves to think. If, when we come to write, we have convinced ourselves that it *is* a difficult task, this is exactly what we will find. We'll tend to complicate the task unnecessarily, making it virtually impossible to do a good job. This is what Matthew Arnold says about style and the business of writing:

> People think that I can teach them style. What stuff it all is! Have something to say, and say it as clearly as you can. That is the only secret of style.

Sentences

Most students find writing difficult because they're convinced that it's much more complicated than Matthew Arnold describes it. And it always appears that way, when anyone explains what you should do and what you should try to avoid. But this is all part of an effort to get back to what will eventually come easily, if not naturally, which is to produce writing that is talk in print. This may seem difficult to start with, but it will get easier as you apply these basic guiding principles.

Long and complex sentence structures

For most of us the problems seem to start when we graduate from one level of learning to another. We convince ourselves that, as this involves understanding more complex ideas and arguments, we must therefore use long and complicated sentence structures, and difficult and unusual words to convey them. In reading students' work I regularly come across mammoth sentences of more than 200 words, with a confusing array of multiple clauses and phrases that come tumbling out on top of each other. Reading this, tutors are likely to be confused and lost amidst this jungle of words.

But, equally serious, they will probably walk away from this kind of essay convinced of three things:

1 that we are not clear about what we want to say;
2 that we haven't planned our ideas with any care;
3 that we didn't think through our ideas in the planning stage before we wrote them and are only now working through them for the first time as we write.

It should be obvious, then, that the key to writing sentences, as it is to writing paragraphs, is not to lose your reader. A complex sentence full of multiple clauses is a difficult and perilous terrain for readers to negotiate. Not only are you likely to lose them as they gingerly pick their way through it, but by the time they have reached the end of the sentence they will have forgotten your original point. To prevent this, try to do two things:

1 keep sentences relatively short; and,
2 wherever it needs it, use a logical indicator ('but', 'if', 'however', 'therefore', 'moreover', 'similarly', and so on) to indicate what you're doing.

Length

Take the first of these points – length. Wherever possible make your sentences short and their structure clear.

For example, read the following sentence:

> It is possible to argue that almost all advertisements, with the exception of a few, are informative, indeed, as we have already seen, some appear to be wholly concerned with this, although government bodies releasing warnings about smoking or the use of domestic fire alarms are clearly intent on changing our behaviour they are still concerned to give the public what they believe is vital information.

It's not difficult to see that it would benefit, first, by being broken up into three shorter sentences, and then, by our punctuating the last of these to make its structure clearer:

> It is possible to argue that almost all advertisements are informative. Indeed, as we have already seen, some appear to be wholly concerned with this. Although government bodies, releasing warnings about smoking or the use of domestic fire alarms, are clearly intent on changing our behaviour, they are still concerned to give the public what they believe is vital information.

In the second of the sample essays in the revision stage you can find other examples (pp. 279–83). Compare them with the original, unrevised version on the companion website (www.howtowritebetteressays.com) and see the difference.

When complex sentences can't be avoided

Of course, sometimes this just isn't possible: occasionally, to develop a complex argument you can't avoid using a complex sentence structure. But if this is the case, beware of the dangers and do all you can to make sure the sentence can be negotiated easily, without any danger of confusion, by using logical indicators and the signposts of punctuation to indicate the structure.

Make their structure clear through ...

1 Punctuation
2 Logical indicators

Indeed, as you grow in confidence you will probably want to achieve more than this with your punctuation – it will certainly pay dividends. Experiment using the rhythm of your words and punctuation to convey the meaning. The 'white space' you create through your use of dashes, colons, semicolons, full stops (periods) and commas helps to create a rhythm that is nearer to the spoken word. And the nearer you approach this the easier it is to understand what you've written.

In much the same way you can experiment using different lengths for your sentences to achieve different effects. Although shorter sentences are easier to follow, it's not necessary to make every sentence the same length. If your ideas are well thought out and organised logically – which they will be if you've planned your essay – your sentences will have a rhythm of their own. But remember, longer sentences tend to be soothing, whereas shorter sentences tend to be abrupt. So, if you want to get your point across in a way that makes the reader really think about it carefully, use a shorter sentence, particularly after developing an argument with a series of longer sentences. But don't overdo it – it easily devalues.

- Use punctuation to create a rhythm that is close to the spoken word.
- The nearer you approach the spoken word the easier it is to understand what you've written.
- Use different lengths to create different effects.

Logical indicators

As to the second point – the importance of logical indicators – the problem is not just that we fail to use them, believing that the reader can follow our train of thought without difficulty, but that they get lost in our sentences. When you read your work through, check that the logic is clear. If it isn't, try moving your logical indicator to a more important position in the sentence, say to the beginning. In the revision stage, if you find it still doesn't read logically and smoothly, read it out aloud, record it and play it back to yourself, or get someone else to read it to you. You'll soon recognise the abrupt transitions, the lost or missing words, and all the other problems that keep your writing from being talk in print.

In a nutshell

- Aim to create writing that is talk in print.
- Don't lose the reader in long sentences.
- Wherever possible, use short sentences with clear structures.
- Experiment with your punctuation, words and sentence length to create the rhythm of talk in print.
- Make sure your logical indicators don't go missing.
- Read it aloud to make sure it reads logically and smoothly.

Sentences

PRACTICE
EXERCISE
28

Read the following passage. At times you will find it difficult to understand its meaning exactly. Sentences tend to be long and confused, the punctuation is not as helpful as it could be, and logical indicators tend to go missing.

Without actually rewriting the passage – by just sorting out the sentence length, punctuation and logical indicators – make the passage more readable, more like talk in print.

When you've completed this, compare your version with the answer given below.

Passage

Rationing medical resources

As populations increase and their demands become more varied all governments are faced with the difficult question of how to divide available resources among those who need them. Unfortunately no resource is scarce or plentiful in terms of an objective standard, but only in relation to certain human needs.

But here lies the problem we seem to talk about three different things when we describe something as a 'need'. First there is the strongest case: the need for certain things, like food and water, to maintain the minimum biological levels necessary for survival. There are those things we need in order to maintain a good quality of life, like adequate education, housing and a clean environment, to which we believe we are entitled and there are those things we might describe as 'social needs' created by living in a particular society or part of the world where these things are normal. Some are created by advertising, others by governments and organisations that influence our expectations. Advertisers lead us to believe that we all need annual holidays, fast cars, the latest fashions, even smartphones and tablet computers, while governments promote our need for national identity and a sense of community.

But where does medical care fit into all this? We talk about our 'right to care', which suggests it is a basic survival need, even though throughout most of its history the human species has survived, and still does in many parts of the world, with only a fraction of what we accept in the West as minimum medical care. We are all universally entitled to 'first class needs', like food, for our survival, whether we live in the wealthiest districts of New York or in a shanty town on the edge of a sprawling African city. If the total world food supply were distributed equally among the entire world population everyone would be hungry many would be less hungry than before.

So, it seems much of what we describe as our right to medical care is in fact a 'second class need' to maintain quality of life. These are 'ordinary' procedures, like annual check-ups and emergency care, which as a result of living in a particular society we believe we have a right to all we have to show is that if we no longer had these it would involve a lowering of our quality of life below the minimum accepted level. 'Third class needs', would include the 'extraordinary' procedures regarded as a privilege, a relative luxury, like cosmetic surgery.

The distinction between 'ordinary' and 'extraordinary' is not always so easy to apply. For example, we might regard living to 85 as consistent with the present notion of quality of life if future medical advances allowed us to live well beyond this would our right to life beyond our 85th birthday remain a luxury, a third class need? Such complexities make the practical task of deciding how to distribute medical resources extremely difficult.

Answer

Rationing medical resources

As populations increase and their demands become more varied, all governments are faced with the difficult question of how to divide available resources among those who need them. Unfortunately no resource is scarce or plentiful in terms of an objective standard, but only in relation to certain human needs.

But here lies the problem: we seem to talk about three different things when we describe something as a 'need'. First, there is the strongest case: the need for certain things, like food and water, to maintain the minimum biological levels necessary for survival. Second, there are those things we need in order to maintain a good quality of life, like adequate education, housing and a clean environment, to which we believe we are entitled. And, third, there are those things we might describe as 'social needs' created by living in a particular society or part of the world where these things are normal. Some are created by advertising, others by governments and organisations that influence our expectations. Advertisers lead us to believe that we all need annual holidays, fast cars, the latest fashions, even smartphones and tablet computers, while governments promote our need for national identity and a sense of community.

But where does medical care fit into all this? We talk about our 'right to care', which suggests it is a basic survival need, even though throughout most of its history the human species has survived, and still does in many parts of the world, with only a fraction of what we accept in the West as minimum medical care. We are all universally entitled to 'first-class needs', like food, for our survival, whether we live in the wealthiest districts of New York or in a shanty town on the edge of a sprawling African city. Yet if the total world food supply were distributed equally among the entire world population everyone would be hungry, although many would be less hungry than before.

So, it seems much of what we describe as our right to medical care is in fact a 'second-class need' to maintain quality of life. These are 'ordinary' procedures, like annual check-ups and emergency care, which, as a result of living in a particular society, we believe we have a right to. All we have to show is that if we no longer had these it would involve a lowering of our quality of life below the minimum accepted level. In contrast, 'third-class needs' would include the 'extraordinary' procedures regarded as a privilege, a relative luxury, like cosmetic surgery.

But the distinction between 'ordinary' and 'extraordinary' is not always so easy to apply. For example, we might regard living to 85 as consistent with the present notion of quality of life. But if future medical advances allowed us to live well beyond this, would our right to life beyond our 85th birthday remain a luxury, a third-class need? Such complexities make the practical task of deciding how to distribute medical resources extremely difficult.

Summary

1 Try to make your prose as light as possible – as close as you can to the rhythms of speech. This way it will be easier to follow.
2 To avoid losing the reader, keep sentences simple and short, and use logical indicators to indicate where you're going.
3 Use punctuation to make the structure of sentences clear and to get nearer to the rhythms of speech.
4 Keep in mind, as you write, the three guiding principles: logic, interest and brevity.
5 Try to remind yourself that even the most complex idea and argument can be expressed using short and simple sentence structures.

In the next chapter

Now that you have completed the practice exercise in this chapter it should be clear to you just what a difference it can make to your writing to use shorter sentences, punctuation that indicates clearly the structure of the sentence, and logical indicators that point readers in the direction you want to take them. Similarly, in the next chapter you will see that by choosing your words and phrases carefully and deliberately you can convey the most complex idea using language that is simple and direct.

Style – Simplicity 2: Words

In this chapter you will learn:

- how to avoid jargon and other words that are empty of real meaning;
- the benefits of striving for greater clarity and precision in your use of language;
- about the dangers and benefits of using clichés in your writing;
- how to use words to convey your meaning accurately.

The same problems that make sentences difficult reappear in our use of words. We believe that as we advance to higher levels of learning we will need to use more complex, even abstruse, language. And it's true that as we graduate from one level to another we will be expected to use and explore more complex ideas and concepts, and these will demand a more subtle use of language and a more careful and deliberate choice of words and phrases. Clearly, words like 'nice', 'good' and 'bad' are inadequate vehicles for conveying subtle distinctions and for all but the crudest of meanings. But this doesn't mean that we're driven to using a plethora of multi-syllabled words or the most convoluted sentences that conceal more than they reveal.

Jargon

This can give rise to all sorts of problems, not least the use of jargon and other words that are empty of real meaning. The following sentences illustrate this. The first is taken from a student's essay, and the second, ironically, is drawn from material for a course on talking and writing.

> Negative feedback brings about an opposite action as a consequence of having sampled the output through the feedback loop.

> Concepts and the language that infuses and implements them give power and strategy to cognitive activity.

You can probably glean some sense from these sentences, but there will be few of us who don't have some problem unwrapping their meaning. They both suffer from the use of jargon, which has been substituted for genuine, explicable thought. In fact, as we saw in Chapter 23, in most cases when we're confronted by jargon, it's not surprising we fail to see the meaning clearly, because the truth is that it's not there to start with.

Jargon is more often a substitute for genuine thought.

And, even when there is meaning, the jargon only serves to obscure it. In these sentences, phrases such as 'negative feedback' and 'feedback loop', and words that are used vaguely, such as 'infuses', 'power' and 'strategy', are all substitutes for genuine thought. The authors have evaded the responsibility to think clearly about the subject, choosing instead to rely upon jargon to convey what meaning there is.

This underlines what we've emphasised in previous sections, that clear and effective writing depends upon clear and effective thinking. Language is the vehicle for your ideas: if your ideas themselves are muddled and confused, then so too will be your language and style. This brings us back to the interpretation and planning of the essay. Now that you've done these successfully, you're better placed to make clearer demands upon your style, and this is more likely to result in clarity and precision in your use of language.

- Just because we have to think about more complex ideas and concepts doesn't mean we must use language that is confusing and difficult to understand.
- We must take more care to choose our words and phrases to convey our ideas as simply and as accurately as we can.
- Clear and effective writing depends upon clear and effective thinking.

Choosing the right words

Nevertheless, that's still only half of the problem. Now that you've got the inside clear, your ideas, you need to be clear about the outside, your words. As you search for the right word, don't settle for something that doesn't capture your specific idea accurately. Of course, you don't want to interrupt your flow of ideas and words, and you can leave much of this tidying up to the revision stage, but you will need to get close enough to your idea to recall exactly what you were trying to say, when you come to revise.

So, when you find yourself using the familiar generality that approximates roughly to what you want to say, stop and search for a word that is more accurate and specific. Otherwise your readers will conclude that you simply haven't got the intellectual determination to pin your ideas down precisely or, worse still, that you have few interesting ideas of your own. Either way, they're likely to assume that the vague sweeping generalities you've used mean one thing, when you really mean another.

> Don't allow your readers to assume you haven't got the determination to pin down your ideas precisely, or that you have few interesting ideas of your own.

Choosing the right words

PRACTICE EXERCISE 29

As you read the following sentence, even though you may broadly agree with what it is saying, you can't place much significance in it, because it could mean a number of things to different people. The language needs to be more specific before we can be certain what the writer is trying to say exactly. Decide what questions you think should be answered to pin down exactly what the writer is saying, and then compare them with the list below.

'Modern business methods are destroying communities and exploiting the poor.'

Answer

1 What methods in particular?
2 In what way are they destroying communities?
3 What specific groups are being exploited?

Clichés

However, the benefits of striving for greater clarity and precision in your use of language don't end there. The more you force yourself to search for a word that is the perfect vehicle for your idea, the more you will have to draw on in the future. As a result, you'll be less likely to fall back on the familiar, reassuring, although empty, cliché. Like jargon, clichés are often a sign that you haven't pinned your idea down accurately, or that you haven't searched thoroughly for the exact word that will carry your idea perfectly.

And yet, as most of us know, it's not always easy to avoid clichés. Indeed, it may not always be wise to. Cutting out all the clichés in your writing can often make your prose sound stiff and cumbersome. A familiar cliché conveying just the right emphasis and meaning will help you produce prose that is nearer to talk in print, with a natural rhythm that's not strained and difficult to read.

> Avoid any word or phrase that fails to do justice to your ideas.

Unfortunately, however, all too often the impact is quite the reverse. An empty cliché, that does no real work beyond sounding cosy and familiar, can sap our writing of its life and vigour. If you want your ideas to have impact and your readers to appreciate that you really do have interesting and original ideas, then avoid any word or phrase that doesn't do justice to your ideas, and this includes clichés.

So ask yourself, when a cliché comes to you in the middle of a passage, does this convey what I want it to, or is this familiar phrase encouraging me to adopt a thought structure that I didn't want? And, of equal importance, will it lead my readers gently down a familiar path which I didn't really want them to go down? Like everything else in your writing, if you use a cliché, mean to do it: have a clear reason, a purpose, for doing so.

Clichés

1 They can be familiar and reassuring, but empty.
2 Without them our prose can sound stiff and cumbersome.
3 Make sure they do real work: that they do justice to your ideas.
4 Ask yourself: Does this convey what I want to say? Does it take my argument in the direction I want to take?

Style 1

In the last exercise you wrote the introduction, the conclusion and the first two paragraphs that followed the introduction to the essay you've chosen to work on. In this exercise write the next three paragraphs that follow on from the two you wrote for the last assignment.

Make sure that the structures of your sentences are clear and your words convey your meaning accurately.

After it's written, read it over to yourself aloud or get someone else to read it to you. As you listen to it, search for two things: first, any passage where the rhythm is clumsy and it's not possible to read it fluently; and second, places where logical indicators go missing, making it difficult to decipher your meaning.

Summary

1 Make sure your words are accurate and specific – that they do real work, conveying real meaning.

2 Although not all jargon is empty of real thought, ask yourself if there is an alternative that will convey your idea simply and accurately. Often jargon is a substitute for genuine thought, designed to impress the reader.

3 A familiar cliché can convey just the right emphasis and meaning, creating a natural rhythm in your prose that is nearer to talk in print.

4 But make sure that this is not just an empty habit of expression. If you use one, it must be the best, most accurate way of conveying your idea.

In the next chapter

Once you've completed the exercise in this chapter you will be more aware of just how effective these techniques can be in making your writing lighter, more like talk in print. Writing lightly often means catching the rhythms of speech and, at times, this can be done just by shortening a sentence, or moving a logical indicator, or using your punctuation to make more white space.

In the next chapter we will consider the other element of style, economy. We will examine the various ways we can improve our style, giving our writing greater clarity through a more economical use of language.

Style – Economy

In this chapter you will learn:

- how to make sure your arguments are not obscured by superfluous words and phrases;
- what we need to do to write clearly and concisely;
- how we can give our writing more impact;
- how we can learn the art of knowing what to leave out.

Improving the readability and impact of your writing

In the previous two chapters we examined the importance of simplicity in our writing, the first of the two elements of style. This brings us to the need for economy. Once you've thought your ideas through and planned them carefully, your major concern thereafter should be to express them clearly, concisely, with an economical use of words. In this lies the essence of what most of us understand by 'style' – what the Reverend Samuel Wesley once described as 'the dress of thought; a modest dress, neat, but not gaudy'.

Even so, many students still find it difficult to abandon the belief that somehow a good style is full of superfluous flourishes and 'tasteful' affectation. Nothing could be further from the truth. As the Reverend Wesley rightly points out, a good writing style is elegant, but not ostentatious. Each component of a sentence should have a reason for being there: it should have a clearly defined function. There should be no wasted effort: no unnecessary words or phrases that obscure the meaning of the sentence. Otherwise the clarity of your thought will be lost, leaving the reader wondering what it all means.

> There should be no wasted effort, no unnecessary words to obscure the meaning of your sentences and the clarity of your thought.

Understandably, in the discussions we have with people in our normal lives we all use superfluous words and phrases that cloud and obscure the issues. This is often necessary to give us the thinking time we need to summon up our thoughts while we speak. Modern politicians, confronted by a throng of probing TV microphones and a posse of journalists, have long learnt how to buy themselves extra thinking time with wordy phrases, like 'this moment in time'. But at least they have some excuse in that they need to buy time to gather their thoughts. For the rest of us, who can enjoy the luxury of careful, time-consuming thought as we write our essays, there is no excuse for phrases like 'most importantly of all', 'in modern America of today' and 'in future going forward'.

- Try to express your ideas clearly, concisely, with an economical use of words.
- Ask yourself, 'Is this phrase necessary?'
- If it is, ask yourself, 'Is there a better one?'
- Avoid those 'time-buying' phrases, like 'this moment in time'.

Knowing what to leave out

Along with simplicity, then, economy should be our paramount concern as we write. A. N. Whitehead described style as the ultimate morality of the mind. By this he implied that the mind should adjudicate rigorously on our use of words and our choice of phrases to ensure that each phrase has a well-defined function, that sentence structures are direct, and that words are chosen for their absolute economy of expression.

Indeed, knowing what to leave out is as important as knowing what to include. In effect, Whitehead's ultimate morality of the mind is the art of knowing what not to do. Therefore, if clauses and phrases can be summed up in a word, replace them. You'll be surprised by the effect. It's worth having a notice pinned over your desk reminding you constantly of the following key principle:

> The readability of your work increases in proportion to the unnecessary words you eliminate.

The significant words and ideas will stand out

But this is not the only bonus that comes from economising. Equally important, the really significant words will no longer be smothered, and your points and arguments will no longer be obscured by unnecessary words and phrases. They'll stand out more, and they'll have impact to make the reader think and wonder. Take the following sentences, remove the unnecessary phrases and see the impact. The resulting sentences are sharper and more direct.

Advertisers will tell you, if you're thinking of making a purchase, what's good about their product, but omit the weaknesses.

Advertisers will tell you what's good about their product, but omit the weaknesses.

A report from a consumer association might heavily criticise a product for one reason or another, but if it contains just a single sentence of praise, this is likely to find its way into promotional literature.

A report from a consumer association might heavily criticise a product, but if it contains just a single sentence of praise, this is likely to find its way into promotional literature.

Look at the unrevised essay on the companion website (www.howtowritebetteressays.com), where you will find other examples of phrases that add nothing to sentences and serve only to obscure their meaning. If you compare this with the second sample essay in the revision stage, you can see the difference it makes to take these phrases out.

All this means that as you write you should constantly censor yourself and monitor your choice of words, asking yourself, 'Is this word or phrase necessary and does it convey my meaning exactly?' Although this is difficult at first, it will get easier. And you've always got the revision stage to come when you can clean up your work.

Superfluous words and phrases

PRACTICE EXERCISE 30

We all fall into habits of expression, unaware that what we say could be said much more economically and, therefore, more clearly. Like many of our most inveterate habits it's difficult to correct them, because we're completely unaware of them. So, we have to take special steps to make ourselves more aware of them each time we write. We need to remind ourselves that we have a tendency to use a particular phrase or word, so that we can avoid it.

So, in this exercise read through the last three essays you have written and list all those words and phrases that are superfluous: all those that could be removed without affecting the meaning of the sentence. As you do this, also record how many times you use them in your writing. This will give you a clear idea of how inveterate these habits are. It will give a clear idea of what you must look out for as you write, so you can avoid them.

Eventually, you will automatically stop using these words and phrases, so that you won't have to constantly remind yourself. Nevertheless, it is a useful exercise to repeat after a certain time just to make sure you haven't developed alternative habits of expression that also need to be addressed.

Summary

1 Try to express your ideas clearly, concisely, with an economical use of words.
2 Remove all unnecessary words that obscure the meaning of the sentence.
3 Knowing what to leave out is as important as knowing what to include.
4 As a result, the significant words will stand out and your arguments will not be obscured by unnecessary words.
5 In turn this will make your ideas and meaning clearer, giving them an impact that will make the reader think and wonder.

In the next chapter

With many of the changes we make to the way we write essays, the improvements come gradually. As we practise our new techniques and skills we begin to see more structure in our essays and we lose fewer marks as a result of our arguments being irrelevant. We begin to see more of our own ideas coming through and we feel more confident about criticising and evaluating the arguments we find in authoritative texts.

But with most of the changes we make to our style, we feel the effects immediately. This is, perhaps, true most of all for those changes that ensure we use words more economically. You will see immediately that your ideas are clearer and more concise. As a result your essays will have an impact they may never have had before.

But we also need to do other, quite simple things that will also have an immediate impact. The problem is that we are given so much advice about how to improve our style that it's difficult to know where to begin. So, to avoid this and give you a clear idea of what you ought to work on, in the next chapter we will look at a simple set of practical dos and don'ts that you can follow routinely as you work.

Style – The Dos and Don'ts

In this chapter you will learn:

- a simple practical guide to improve your style;
- how to use the active voice wherever possible;
- how to avoid watering down your prose with too many adverbs, adjectives and prepositions;
- how to rely on nouns and verbs to carry your meaning;
- how to create fluency by using transitions.

All of what we said in the last chapter makes sense in general terms – it gives us a clear idea of what we need to do throughout our work to avoid heavy, unreadable prose. But it still helps to have some simple practical rules by our side to help us produce work that is light, concise and interesting; work that grabs the reader's attention and keeps it to the end of the essay.

To help you do this, try using the list below as a simple practical guide. It may not be possible to apply each rule all at once; you might need to concentrate on two or three of them, until they become established. Then you can move on to the others, until you're applying all of them in every piece of work. But you must try to keep your inner editor at bay as you write, so you can release your creativity. If you find the fluency of your writing begins to break up as you check on these things, remind yourself that you've still got the safety net of the revision stage.

Style – A practical guide

1 Choose the short simple word over the long obscure one.
2 Use the active voice.
3 Rely on nouns and verbs to carry your meaning.
4 Replace prepositional phrases with prepositions.
5 Create fluency through transitions.
6 Match your words to the strength of the evidence.
7 Know how much evidence to give.

1 Choose the short simple word over the long obscure one

If the short simple word carries the same meaning as the long obscure one, use it, otherwise you're in danger of producing prose that sounds unnecessarily pompous. But whatever word you choose, your primary concern should be to ensure the meaning is clear – avoid words that are vague, whether short, simple, long or obscure.

2 Use the active voice

In Chapter 23 we learnt the importance of using the active rather than the passive voice, wherever possible. All too often the passive voice produces passive readers, who sleepwalk their way through your prose. The active voice is almost always clearer and more direct, so there's no need, as many students writing academic essays tend to believe, to convert every sentence into the passive form.

In the active form it's the doer of the action who is the subject of the sentence, rather than the receiver of the action, or the action itself, as in the passive form.

Active:	the doer of the action
Passive:	the receiver of the action; the action itself

EXAMPLE

Passive:	The party was made more enjoyable by Rita's outrageous stories.
Active:	Rita's outrageous stories made the party more enjoyable.
Passive:	The blue getaway car was described by the bank clerk.
Active:	The bank clerk described the blue getaway car.
Passive:	An atmosphere of deep gloom is created by the novelist in the last paragraph of the chapter.
Active:	The novelist creates an atmosphere of deep gloom in the last paragraph of the chapter.

Notice how the passive form is almost always less direct, positive and concise. For example, you might say,

My first car will never be forgotten by me.

But when you convert this into the active voice, with the doer of the action the subject of the sentence, by being more direct it is more concise, and also more positive:

I will never forget my first car.

But that's not to say that the passive voice should never be used. There are times when what is done is more important than who did it. For example, the statement,

Professor Jenkins and Dr Taylor of University College, London, last month achieved the most significant breakthrough yet in the treatment of colon cancer.

would be better in the passive voice:

The most significant breakthrough yet in the treatment of colon cancer was achieved last month by Professor Jenkins and Dr Taylor of University College, London.

because the most important fact in the statement, what has been achieved, has been placed at the front of the sentence, and the doers at the back.

Passive or active?

Listed below you will find three pairs of statements. Rewrite each pair into a single sentence in either the active or the passive form. Choose which you think is the most effective in each case and then briefly give reasons for your choices.

Once you've finished, compare your choices and the reasons you've given with those in the answer below.

Statements

1 Nigel Brown scored the goal.
   The decisive goal was scored in the last minute of the game.
2 Chief Justice Taylor was driving home.
   He was stopped by the police and found to be driving under the influence of alcohol.
3 John Douglas was stopped on his way home and robbed at knife point.
   He was robbed by a gang of eleven-year-olds.

Answers

1 Passive sentence: The decisive goal was scored in the last minute of the game by Nigel Brown.

   Reason: The most interesting fact in these two statements is that the goal was scored in the last minute of the game.

2 Active sentence: While he was driving home Chief Justice Taylor was stopped by the police and found to be driving under the influence of alcohol.

   Reason: The most interesting fact is not that someone was caught driving under the influence of alcohol, but that it was a prominent member of the judiciary.

3 Active sentence: A gang of eleven-year-olds stopped John Douglas on his way home and robbed him at knife point.

   Reason: That he was robbed by a gang of eleven-year-olds is more interesting than the fact that he was robbed at knife point.

3 Rely on nouns and verbs to carry your meaning

In Chapter 34 you will find an explanation of why nouns and verbs are the most important words in a sentence and lists of strong ones from which you can choose to replace weak ones.

Verbs

Wherever you can, try to build sentences around verbs that are specific and active. Weak verbs have to be shored up by adverbs and adverbial phrases that can water down the image. However, beware of your choice of verb: don't overstate the case by choosing one that is too strong.

In the following sentences, by replacing the weak verb and its adverb with a stronger verb, the sentence is made sharper and its meaning clearer.

> Yet we still might be right in thinking suspiciously that behind all this information lies a covert message.

> Yet we still might be right in suspecting that behind all this information lies a covert message.

> Our desire for status and our respect for authority has given advertisers an effective way of deceptively taking advantage of our feelings to promote all manner of products.

> Our desire for status and our respect for authority has given advertisers an effective way of exploiting our feelings to promote all manner of products.

Nouns

In the same way, make sure the nouns you use are specific and definite, not general. They must produce a clear image. Like the use of adverbs, if you have to use adjectives to shore up your noun, modifying or qualifying it, you've probably chosen the wrong one in the first place. The danger is that your meaning will lose impact, or will be difficult to see, beneath the camouflage of adjectives and adjectival phrases.

In the following sentences, by replacing the noun and its adjective with a single noun that is more specific, a clearer image is produced, one which carries much more meaning.

> By appealing to their strong tastes advertisers successfully bypass the consumer's capacity to make rational choices.

> By appealing to their passions advertisers successfully bypass the consumer's capacity to make rational choices.

It's not just tastes that you're discussing, but passions – a particular type of taste which is much stronger than all the rest, at times even irresistible.

> They may give us information on the latest technology, but they are also covertly suggesting that we can't afford not to keep up with the latest developments.

> They may give us information on the latest technology, but they are also covertly suggesting that we can't afford not to keep up with progress.

It's not just the latest developments, but the whole idea of progress and whether this is necessarily a good thing.

4 Replace prepositional phrases with prepositions

In Chapter 34 you will also find lists of empty phrases and unnecessary words that frequently water down our writing, obscuring its meaning, along with prepositional phrases that can be replaced by simpler and more direct prepositions. Get into the habit of using these lists routinely to clean up your work and make your meaning clearer.

Like adverbs and adjectives, too many prepositional phrases water down your prose and obscure your meaning. Many of these we use in our normal speech simply because they give us more thinking time. But if you use them in your writing they will clutter up your prose and give the reader a bumpy, uncomfortable ride through your arguments and explanations. This will make it difficult for your reader to understand your meaning.

Therefore, wherever possible replace the prepositional phrase with a simple preposition.

EXAMPLE

Replace   'with regard to' with 'about'
           'for the simple reason' with 'because'
           'on the part of' with 'by'

This is not to say that such phrases always obscure your meaning, but you should pose yourself the question, 'Can I replace these with a simpler preposition without any loss of meaning?' If you can, do it!

You will also find, particularly in the revision stage, that it helps to collect prepositional phrases in your notebook. When we're asked to produce them, most of us are hard pressed to think of one. It helps, then, to list them in your notebook as you come across them in your reading, so you know what you're looking for when you come to revise.

Nouns, verbs and prepositional phrases

PRACTICE EXERCISE

Read the unrevised essay on the companion website (www.howtowritebetteressays. com) and note all those phrases that are cluttering up the text and ought to be removed, and the weak nouns and verbs that should be replaced with strong ones. Then read through the second revised sample essay (pp. 279–83) in the revision stage and compare those that you have identified with those that I have. Notice the difference this makes to the essay as sentences become clearer, sharper and more direct.

5 Create fluency through transitions

In Stage 3 (Planning) we discussed the importance of transitions in creating fluency between paragraphs, thereby giving your essay the coherence and continuity it must have to achieve a high grade. In Chapter 26 we also learnt of their importance as a means of giving your readers the literal signposts they need to negotiate your essay successfully without getting lost.

As you come across them in your reading, note how other writers link their paragraphs, perhaps even keeping a record in your notebook so you can use them yourself. Some of the most effective transitions are the most simple, indeed so simple that we hardly realise they are there at all. Demonstrative pronouns, like 'this', 'these' and 'those', slipped into a topic sentence create a bridge between two paragraphs, while hardly disturbing the flow of ideas. Others you'll find useful include 'Likewise', 'Correspondingly', 'Hence', 'Accordingly', 'Nevertheless', 'Incidentally', 'Otherwise', 'Nonetheless', 'Obviously'.

> Get into the habit of noting in your notebook the transitions that other writers use so you can use them too.

In Chapter 34 you will find a list of the most useful transitions arranged in categories according to their logical function. As you write your essay it is helpful just to get into the habit of referring to this each time you need to establish fluency between paragraphs or between two points as you build your arguments, so that you can indicate clearly the logic of what you are doing. You will also find there a list of very useful compound transitions.

Compound transitions

The more you look for transitions to record in your notebook, the more compound transitions you will come across. As the name implies, they are made up from one or more words or transitions. There is, therefore, an almost inexhaustible variety of them; indeed, you can make up your own as easily as you can collect them. Their value lies in giving you a much wider range of transitions to choose from, allowing you to navigate exactly the right passage through your arguments with just the right changes in emphasis and direction to reflect all the subtleties of your arguments.

And moreover   EXAMPLE

By combining two conjunctions, like 'and' and 'moreover', you create a transition that allows you to connect two points in a subtler and more effective way than either of the two conjunctions could have done individually. You are not just conjoining two points, but emphasising the point you are about to make.

Summary

1 Use the simple, practical guide to revise your essays, working on two or three rules first and then moving on to others.
2 As you write keep these in your mind, but try to keep your inner editor at bay so you allow yourself to write freely and fluently.
3 To make your writing clearer and more direct use a short, simple word rather than a long, obscure one and wherever possible use the active, rather than the passive, voice.
4 Try to avoid watering down your writing and obscuring your meaning by using too many adverbs, adjectives and prepositional phrases.
5 Try to get into the habit of collecting and using transitions to create fluency between your paragraphs and between points as you build your arguments.

In the next chapter

The final two rules in our practical guide concern our use of evidence. In the next chapter you will learn how to use evidence to change the pace of your writing and engage your readers in your arguments. You will see how your use of evidence not only supports and illustrates your arguments, but makes your work more interesting and persuasive.

Working with Evidence

In this chapter you will learn:

- how to use the different types of evidence to support your arguments effectively;
- how to make your work more readable by varying the type of evidence you use;
- how to make the seven practical rules part of your writing strategy.

The last two of our seven practical rules for improving our style are concerned with the way we use evidence. Without doubt this is one of the most neglected aspects of our writing. We tend to assume that all we have to do is select our evidence and then insert it into our essay when our arguments need support.

Yet the evidence we use serves to do much more than just support and illustrate our arguments. Used thoughtfully, it can help us change the pace of our writing, making our essay more readable. And there is no other component of our essays that can so effectively engage our readers' empathetic responses. You will find, then, that by looking carefully at the way you use evidence, not only can you make your work more interesting, but you can give it real impact.

Evidence

1 Supports and illustrates our arguments.
2 Changes the pace, making our essays more readable.
3 Engages the reader's empathetic responses.
4 Can make our work more interesting, giving it real impact.

6 Don't overstate or understate: match your words to the strength of the evidence

Choose your words consciously and deliberately to convey accurately the strength of your ideas and the evidence that supports them. As we discovered in Chapter 16, the words that we use to do this are known as 'Qualifiers'. In the next chapter you will find lists of these that you can use to convey just the right strength when you present your evidence. Often, when we fail to think through our ideas with sufficient care, we're inclined to see issues in the form of simple absolutes: all/nothing, right/wrong, yes/no. But rarely is there sufficient evidence to support such claims.

There are, of course, categories of sentences in which you can use qualifiers like 'all', but they're more restricted than we generally acknowledge. Either they're sentences describing a particular known group of things, such as 'all of my friends', or 'all of the coins in my pocket', or they're trivially true, that is they're true *a priori*, by virtue of the meaning of their constituent parts.

Analytic propositions

These are known as 'analytic propositions' because their truth can be verified by analysing the meaning of their parts. For example, it would be quite correct to say that 'All bachelors are unmarried men', or that 'All cats are animals', or that 'All bicycles have two wheels', because this is what we mean by these terms. These sentences are true by virtue of what we agree to put into them in the first place. The fact that we agree the word 'bachelor' shall mean 'male' and 'unmarried' makes the sentence true. In the same way, when we unwrap the meaning of other words like 'cat' or 'bicycle', we find that their meaning too links two or more characteristics in 'all' cases.

Empirical propositions

Beyond these analytic propositions, we're faced with the problem of using simple absolutes, like 'all', in empirical propositions – that is, propositions that go beyond the meaning of the terms they use to make statements about the real world. As we've already seen, it's safe to use words like 'all' in sentences that make a claim about a particular known group of things, like your friends or the coins in your pocket. So you could safely say that 'All the people in this room are male', or 'All the members of the party voted for Mr X as their candidate', because the evidence for these claims is easy to verify.

Using 'all' statements

Safe for:

  1 Analytic propositions.
  2 Empirical propositions about particular known groups of things.
Less safe for:

  3 Empirical propositions involving an element of judgement.

But most of the claims we make are not like this: they involve an element of judgement on our part; they cannot be verified either by demonstrable fact or by analysis of the meaning of their constituent parts. They are claims like 'Nobody believes it's right to kill dolphins', 'Everybody agrees that terrorists should receive capital punishment', or 'At no time over the last seventy years has anybody seriously doubted the value of the automobile'. Each of these claims is too strong for the evidence we have, or even could have. You need find only one person who believes dolphins should be killed, or that terrorists should be sentenced to life imprisonment, or that the automobile has damaged the quality of our lives, to have disproved them.

Analytic or empirical?

PRACTICE EXERCISE

In the list below you'll find analytic and empirical propositions, including those that are demonstrable statements of fact and those that involve an element of judgement. Read them through carefully and decide which are analytic and which are empirical. Then compare your answers with those given below.

1 All triangles are three-sided figures.
2 All skyscrapers are tall buildings.
3 Every person in this room is a student.
4 A significant proportion of the adult population is illiterate.
5 My father's brother's son is my cousin.
6 Your father's brother's son is my cousin.
7 For most of the year it is very cold in Chicago.
8 $2 + 2 = 4$.
9 Two trees plus two trees is equal to four trees.
10 All men die.

Answers

1 Analytic
2 Analytic
3 Empirical
4 Empirical
5 Analytic
6 Empirical
7 Empirical
8 Analytic
9 Analytic
10 Analytic

Another sign worth sticking to your computer screen or pinning above your desk might read:

The more difficult I make it for tutors to dismiss my arguments, the higher my marks.

Clearly, then, you must make every effort to match the strength of your statements to the strength of your evidence, using qualifiers like 'much', 'many', 'some', 'frequently'. In this way you avoid the risk of overstatement, which will weaken your arguments and lead tutors to dismiss them for lack of sufficient evidence.

You can do this in three ways in descending order of evidential strength.

6.1 Hard evidence

This is the strongest form of evidence, which includes statistics, examples, quotations, even anecdotes. Obviously, wherever possible use this form of evidence to support your arguments. Although readers can challenge your judgements and the interpretation you place on this evidence, they cannot criticise you for dispensing mere opinion. The hard evidence you use shows that there are serious grounds for someone to consider the arguments and points you've developed.

Numerical data, diagrams and quotations

Even so, try to avoid using evidence like numerical data, diagrams and quotations as a substitute for your own arguments. They should support and illustrate your arguments, not replace them. Don't let them do the work for you. Introduce them carefully and integrate them within your arguments, rather than just state them and expect them to speak for themselves.

The best way to do this convincingly is to critically evaluate them, revealing what you believe to be their implications and their limitations. If you use graphs or bar charts, do they accurately represent the magnitudes or do they exaggerate? If you use empirical data, how is it collected? Are there problems with this which mean that it is not wholly reliable? This may mean that while we can draw some conclusions from it, we cannot draw others. Look at Chapter 16 to see the sort of mistakes that are made when we draw inferences from evidence.

> Critically evaluate your own evidence, revealing what you believe to be its implications and limitations.

By now you will have realised that there is a rich reward for this sort of critical evaluation, particularly when you show that you can be even-handed with the very sources you are using to support your own argument.

- Don't let them do the work for you: introduce and integrate them.
- Critically evaluate them – it will make your arguments more credible.

Examples

The same can be said for your use of examples: select and use them carefully. Wherever possible support your arguments with more than one, arranging them so that you start with one that has the most significant and far-reaching implications and then use those that are more specific, that have more limited application. It also helps their credibility if you can select them from a range of different sources. If they all come from reports of people in the same profession or political party, this will make them less persuasive.

- Use more than one.
- Select them from different sources.

6.2 Explication

However, often it's simply not possible to support an argument with the sort of hard evidence it needs. Nevertheless, you may still believe it's a valuable argument to develop, one that most people will accept for good reasons. It may not even be possible to gather any evidence of any kind to support it; it's just that most of us accept that it's reasonable to believe that this is the case. Of course, common opinion is not always common sense, but in these cases it is more a question of what makes *reasonable* sense.

For example, you might claim that most people believe that tobacco companies should not target their products at children. Now there may be no hard evidence for this claim: there may have been no surveys ever done, or government statistics issued about what people believe. Yet it's obvious you're probably right. All you can do, therefore, is to reveal the reasonableness of this claim through careful explication of your argument. In this way you show that your assumptions are reasonable, that they're based on common sense, and there are no flaws in your arguments.

In our claim about tobacco companies, for example, we might argue that most people are aware of the long-term health problems that smoking creates; that children are not in a position to evaluate all the information and make a free and informed choice; and that once hooked at an early age most smokers find it difficult to quit and, therefore, end up suffering from these health problems, some of which may be terminal. Given all this, it now seems a reasonable claim to make. It's founded on a common-sense understanding that you share with others, including the reader, and you've demonstrated that the case is argued consistently.

6.3 Report

However, if you lack hard evidence, or you're in a timed exam and you can't remember any, and you don't feel confident enough to argue for the reasonableness of your case, then you're left with only one alternative: shift the weight of responsibility from your shoulders onto someone else's. You do this by attributing the view to some named authority or, if you can't remember who advocated the view, to some impersonal authority, like 'many believe …', 'some people claim …', 'it is argued …' and so on.

Of course, if you're not writing a timed essay you will have the opportunity to name an authority whose argument it is. Still this may be a point that is useful to explain, but a digression to pursue in the context of this particular essay. If this is the case, you could report it, rather than develop and discuss it, but in your references cite the research that readers can follow for themselves.

In the advertising question you might argue:

By appealing to their passions and feelings advertisers successfully bypass consumers' reason and their capacity to make rational choices. The most successful form of this has been subliminal manipulation, where messages have been recorded onto sound tracks at low speeds. These can only be picked up by the subconscious, when the tape is played at normal speed, without individuals knowing that they've been manipulated. The same can be achieved visually by inserting isolated frames into a reel of film to suggest and stimulate certain behaviour.

You could then cite references for the reader to pursue:

For a more complete discussion of this see Karl Brinkmeyer, 'The Threats to Our Freedom', in *The American Journal of Psychology*, Jan. 2003, pp. 117–33; P. J. Foster, 'Advertising and Subliminal Manipulation', in *British Business Review*, 2001, vol. 1, pp. 103–13; B. R. Brainstowe, 'The Politics of Promotion', in *Political Review*, 2001, vol. viii, pp. 284–97.

Clearly this is the weakest form of support for your argument and, although it can be useful under timed conditions, you must be aware of the degree to which it weakens your argument. Hard evidence and explication will earn higher marks, because, as you take on the responsibility of defending the argument as your own, you are obliged to use your higher cognitive abilities to argue and justify it with evidence of the appropriate quality and strength.

In contrast, by shifting the responsibility to others you merely exercise your lower cognitive abilities: you're merely recalling and describing a case developed by somebody else. Nevertheless, without this, without any attempt to support your argument, it will be dismissed as merely a statement of opinions, of no particular value, beyond the fact that you can remember it. And, as we said before, anyone can express opinions.

Explication

PRACTICE EXERCISE

34

Listed below you will see three statements. Give three or four reasons why you think these might be reasonable statements to make. Most of us believe these statements are reasonable, but if you don't, set aside your doubts and give the sort of justification that you think someone could give who does in fact believe them. Compare your reasons with those listed in the answer that follows.

Statements

1   Most people believe we're right to try to protect the environment.
2   Most of us are opposed to the systematic use of very young children in the labour force.
3   Most of us accept that we should not be cruel to animals.

Reasons

1   The environment.
    Because of:
    1.1   the increasing levels of pollution;
    1.2   the rise in the incidence of health problems related to environmental pollution, e.g. asthma;
    1.3   the depletion of resources, like rainforests;
    1.4   the damage to the ozone layer and the related increase in skin cancer;
    1.5   the effect of changes in the ecological system, e.g. the changes in weather patterns which are widely held to be the result of greenhouse gases;
    1.6   endangered species whose habitats are disappearing.

2   Child labour.
    Because:
    2.1   children should be in education;
    2.2   children are easily exploited;
    2.3   they should have a childhood, rather than be forced into the adult world too early;

2.4   they are likely to work in dangerous and unhealthy conditions;

2.5   in some circumstances they will take work away from adult workers who need it to support their families.

3 Animals.
Because:

3.1   we believe we have a moral responsibility to try to maximise the well-being of all, not just promote our own self-interests;

3.2   this involves the moral obligation to minimise all unnecessary suffering;

3.3   all sentient beings – including animals – have a capacity to suffer as a result of physical pain, and emotional and psychological distress.

7 Know how much evidence to give

In view of what we've just said, the standard advice to novelists applies equally to those of us who write essays – wherever possible *show*, rather than *tell*. Don't just state that something is the case, demonstrate it with evidence. It's worth reminding yourself that you're not just describing an event, just explaining *what* happened; you're explaining *why* it happened – you're giving reasons that will, hopefully, convince the reader that you're right.

> Wherever possible, show rather than tell; demonstrate rather than state it.

Interest – evidence makes your work more readable

Equally important, this has a significant bearing on the second of our guiding principles (see p. 186) – interest. Quotations, statistics and anecdotes all make your work more readable. Not only do they break it up with changes of pace and content, but they allow the subjects to speak for themselves. Your readers can then respond empathetically and, with their emotions and feelings engaged in your work, this can lend untold support to your arguments.

But make sure the evidence you use has a point: that it is related to and reinforces your arguments. Any quotations, statistics or anecdotes you use must do real work. You may like a quotation for the impact you know it will have on the reader, or an anecdote for its pathos or poignancy, but if it doesn't reinforce a point or advance your argument, drop it. You'll always find a use for it later.

Don't overdo it

Similarly, don't overdo it with evidence. There's always the danger that you just might bury your readers under information, making it impossible for them to take on board everything you want them to, thereby wasting a lot of the good evidence you've dug up. If you pile one unrelated piece of information on another, your readers will have no means of dealing with it successfully. They will lose themselves and, in turn, you will lose marks; whereas, if you strip out all the unnecessary information, what remains will stand out and will have more impact.

As we've seen a number of times already, the key to this is structure. If your readers are clear what part the information plays in the overall scheme of things, they can process it successfully and put it in its appropriate place. But if the structure's weak, they'll have to re-read it to make sure they've understood it, or, if they're not so scrupulous, they'll just miss much of what you're saying. The key to this, then, is to create a clear structure within which you use only those facts, quotations and statistics that do real work, and write them out as succinctly as possible.

In a nutshell

- Show rather than tell.
- Make your work more readable by varying the type of evidence you use.
- Make sure your evidence does real work.
- Try not to bury your reader under an avalanche of information.
- Create a clear structure for your evidence so your reader knows how to process it.

Using the seven practical rules

All of this is a great deal to remember, particularly while you're writing. So don't, if it interrupts your creative flow. Just start by reminding yourself of two or three of the rules as you write. Eventually, with these well under your control, you can move on to the rest. And you've always got the revision stage after this to clean up your work. Indeed, you'll find as you revise one essay after another, all seven rules will gradually filter through into your writing. This is not to say you shouldn't bother to remind yourself that the active voice is better than the passive, or that nouns should be specific and definite, not general. If you can do this without interrupting your flow, then do it.

Style 2   **IN YOUR OWN WORK**

In this assignment finish writing the remaining paragraphs of the essay you've chosen to work on. Before you start, remind yourself of the seven practical rules we've outlined in this section. However, write as freely as possible: don't let your editor in to disrupt the flow of your ideas.

Once you've finished, put them aside for a day or so, then read them through to check how well you've done with the seven practical rules. For this exercise you're not actually revising them, but you should go through each rule to see if you could have done better.

Summary

1 Evidence is important to support and illustrate our arguments.
2 It makes our work more readable by helping us change the pace of our writing.
3 It engages the readers' empathetic responses.
4 But make sure you match the strength of your statements to the strength of your evidence.
5 And try not to overload your work with evidence, which obscures the underlying structure of your argument.

In the next chapter

We have now worked through the seven practical rules. To help you use them routinely every time you write, in the next chapter you will find useful tables that list transitions, qualifiers, strong nouns and verbs, and all those verbose phrases that can so easily clutter up our writing obscuring the structure of our arguments. All of this is designed to make it easier for you to deal with the problems we have identified and integrate the seven practical into your essay writing.

Choosing the Best Word

In this chapter you will learn:

- how to recognise the verbose phrases that clutter up our sentences and obscure the structure of our arguments and the clarity of our thinking;
- how to identify the strong nouns and verbs that we can use to make clearer our meaning and the direction we are taking the reader;
- how to choose just the right qualifier to convey the strength of our evidence accurately;
- how to find the best transition to make clear the connections between our ideas and signpost precisely the direction we are developing our arguments.

In the previous few chapters we have seen how important it is to choose our words carefully. We have stressed the importance of economising our use of words and simplifying our writing to ensure that our arguments are clear and effective. We have also seen how the clarity of our writing improves, if we can avoid the overuse of adjectives and adverbs, relying instead on strong nouns and verbs, and how we can use transitions and qualifiers to create consistent arguments that readers can follow easily.

But where can we find these words? Of course, you could always consult a good dictionary or thesaurus, but you need to have some idea what you're looking for. You could simply copy the style and use of words you find in academic journals, but then you might find yourself reproducing the same problems we have already talked about with the overuse of jargon and the cluttered obscure sentences that are difficult to understand.

To help you solve this problem, in this chapter you will learn how to de-clutter your sentences and you will find lists from which you can choose better words to develop your arguments clearly and effectively.

Verbose phrases

Each time we use more words than we need to convey our ideas we clutter up our arguments, obscure their structure and make it difficult for readers to understand our points. By cutting language to the bone, you reveal what you really want to say. As we said in Chapter 23, at that point you can begin to build it up using your own voice. The result can be quite transformative. As your readers are reading closer to the spoken word, they read faster, your meaning is clearer and your arguments have greater impact.

There are three things we can routinely do to de-clutter our work:

1 Cut out empty phrases
2 Replace prepositional phrases with prepositions
3 Identify our favourite unnecessary words

1 Cut out empty phrases

These are phrases that add little or nothing to the meaning of our sentences. We all use them in our everyday lives, but to make our arguments clearer we need to de-clutter our sentences by taking them out of our writing. Some phrases may, indeed, add something to the meaning of a sentence, but we need to ask whether they add anything significant. You are likely to find that your writing becomes clearer and has more impact as soon as you take them out. In the following list you will find your own personal favourites. Once you start looking for them, you will begin to see more in your writing that you can add to the list.

All things being equal
All things considered
As a matter of fact
As far as I am concerned
At the end of the day
For all intents and purposes
For the purpose of
In a manner of speaking
In my opinion
In the event of
In the final analysis
Kind of
The point that I am trying to make
Type of
What I am trying to say
What I want to make clear

Empty phrases

PRACTICE EXERCISE

Rewrite the following sentence taking out all the meaningless phrases so that its core meaning can be written more clearly and economically.

As a matter of fact, what I am trying to say is that the average person believes, as far as I am concerned, that there is kind of not enough consumer protection for all intents and purposes.

Answer

The average person believes there is not enough consumer protection.

2 Replace prepositional phrases with prepositions

In contrast, the following phrases do add something to the meaning of a sentence, but they could be said in far fewer words, making the sentence clearer and more direct. As you come across others in your own writing add them to the list.

Ahead of schedule – early
Arrived at an agreement – agreed
As a consequence of – because of
At the present time – now
At this point in time – now or at this time
Bright in colour – bright
Came in contact with – met
Costs a total of – costs
Due to the fact that – because
During the time that – while
For the simple reason – because
Give an indication of – show/indicate
In close proximity to – near
In spite of the fact – although
In the direction of – to or toward
In the vicinity – near
Large in size – large
Located at – at
On the part of – by
Smooth to the touch – smooth
With regard to – about
With the possible exception of – except

3 Identify our favourite unnecessary words

We all have favourite words that we use that add nothing to the meaning of our sentences. So, it's worth checking to see if we have become over reliant on them by putting them into the search function of our word processor to see how often we use them. Then we need to ask whether there might not be better words that more accurately convey what we want to say. The obvious candidates can be found in the jargon that plays such a large part in the subjects we are studying, but there are other words that we hear all the time, which seep into our writing, clouding our meaning and robbing our arguments of the impact they should have, words like,

Appropriate/inappropriate
Going forward
Iconic
Kind of/sort of
A lot

Then there are familiar, unnecessary words we use, without thinking, in combination with others:

absolutely essential/necessary	*joint* collaboration
advance warning	later *time*
added bonus	look *ahead* to the future
alternative *choice*	meet *together*
assemble *together*	might *possibly*
basic fundamentals/ necessities	*mutual* cooperation

brief moment
brief summary
careful scrutiny
close proximity
collaborate together
compete with each other
completely destroyed
confer together
consensus of opinion
contributory factor
cooperate together
crisis situation
depreciate in value
during the course of
each and every
eliminate altogether
emergency situation
end result
entirely eliminate
eradicate completely
estimated at about
evolve over time
exactly identical
favourable approval
fellow colleague
few in number
filled to capacity
final conclusion/outcome
final ultimatum
first of all
foreign imports
free gift
future plans
general consensus
general public
grow in size
had done previously
integrate together
join together

mutually interdependent
mutual respect for each other
natural instinct
necessary prerequisite
never before
new beginning/innovation
none at all
originally created/built
over exaggerate
past experience/history/records
period of time
personal opinion
pick and choose
plan in advance
polar opposites
postpone until later
present time
protest against
reason is because
reason why
refer back
regular routine
repeat again
revert back
small size
spell out in detail
still remains
sudden impulse
sum total
time period
true facts
two equal halves
unexpected surprise
usual custom
very unique
warn in advance
whether or not
write down

Strong nouns and verbs

As we saw in Chapter 32, the other way we clutter up our sentences is to use adjectives and adverbs to strengthen weak nouns and verbs that struggle to do what we want them to do. The best writing comes from strong nouns and verbs that catch the image of what we want to say precisely. Adjectives and adverbs only *tell* us things; nouns and verbs *show* us.

Adjectives and adverbs tell; *nouns and verbs* show.

Nouns and verbs are the most important words in a sentence. Nouns give your sentence a clear image, the sound foundations on which you develop your ideas, while verbs give your sentence its movement, its momentum. When your nouns and verbs are weak, your ideas are unclear and your sentences are sluggish. Choosing the best word will make your writing clearer, more vivid and memorable.

1 Strong nouns

A strong noun gives your readers a clear visual image, so check that you really need to use an adjective to give specific meaning to a noun. Ask yourself, 'Is there a noun that says exactly what I want to say without having to use this adjective?'

Often, without realising it, we use a weak noun as a result of getting into the habit of using a nominalisation – a noun that has been derived from a verb. The noun is usually accompanied by a weak verb, so replacing the nominalisation with the original verb strengthens the sentence by making it more direct and specific.

The decision/the reaction   EXAMPLE

Rather than 'make a decision', we 'decide'; rather than 'show a reaction' we 'react'.

Here are more examples. As you come across others, add them to the list.

Derive a conclusion	–	conclude
Present an argument	–	argue
Have admiration	–	admire
Conduct a review	–	review
Make a discovery	–	discover
Put up a resistance	–	resist
Conduct an investigation	–	investigate
Have a belief	–	believe
Enter into discussion	–	discuss
Give a demonstration	–	demonstrate
Made the arrangement	–	arranged

2 Strong verbs

As we said above, verbs give our writing movement. A strong verb ensures that our argument moves along in a clear direction, so our readers can understand and see where we are taking them. Therefore, dig deeper into the meaning you want to express. If your verb fails to express exactly what you want to say, rather than shore it up with an adverb, replace it. It will invigorate your writing, making your ideas and arguments clearer.

Verbs like 'think', 'talk' and 'say' tend to be weak verbs: they don't say precisely what we want to say. There are verbs we all get used to using without asking ourselves whether that really is the verb we want to use. When you come across them in your own writing, list the alternatives, so you can check to see if these more accurately say what you want to say. Here are five to get you started.

Weak verb	Strong verbs
Criticise	censure, condemn, disparage, compare, appraise, consider, judge, discern, estimate, evaluate, appraise, rate, conjecture, ponder, review
Talk	converse, communicate, discuss, confer, negotiate, inform, confide, speak, utter, confess, acknowledge, concede, criticise, pronounce, dictate, recite
Say	state, declare, announce, maintain, mention, assert, affirm, express, pronounce, communicate, disclose, convey, divulge, report, claim, suggest, insist
Argue	discuss, debate, dispute, question, reason, challenge, claim, insist, maintain, assert, contend, uphold, suggest, imply, allege
Develop	derive, progress, promote, generate, undertake, initiate, cultivate, instigate, start, establish, originate, foster, extend, elaborate, broaden, amplify, augment, enlarge

Qualifiers

In the previous chapter we described the importance of using just the right qualifier to convey accurately the strength of our ideas and the evidence that supports them. When we overstate the strength of a claim, it is likely to be rejected, while understating it robs it of the significance that it deserves. So, it is worth having by your side a table that lists the full range of qualifiers that you are most likely to use so you can choose the best one.

The following table is divided between those qualifiers that we use in absolute, universal claims to express certainty and the equivalent qualifiers that express degrees of uncertainty. Add to them each time you come across a new qualifier that you think might be useful.

Certainty	Uncertainty
All/every	many, most, some, majority, numerous, countless, abundant, copious, profuse, multitude,
None/no	few, minority, some, not many, hardly any, sparse, rare, scarce
Always	often, frequent, recurrent, repeated, common, incessant, perpetual, usual, sometimes, customary, habitual
Never	infrequent, uncommon, sporadic, occasional, rare, seldom, sometimes, intermittent
'To be' (it is, it was, I am, I was, we are, we were)	may be, may have been, might be, might have been, conceivably, perhaps, possibly, could have been, can be, perchance, appears, seems, indicates
Will	may, might, could, possible, likely, probable, feasible, plausible
Will not	improbable, unlikely, doubtful, unforeseeable, implausible, unimaginable, inconceivable, contingent on
Definite	probable, possible, potential, viable, arguable, feasible, attainable, likely, presumable, foreseeable
Indefinite	unlikely, improbable, doubtful, questionable, debatable, controvertible

To check that you are choosing the best qualifiers, it helps to read through your essay and highlight them, so you can decide whether they accurately convey what you intended. You may find you are using some of them to intensify your meaning, either strengthening a word or toning it down, because you haven't spent enough time choosing the best word in the first place.

Transitions

As we discovered in Chapters 19 and 20, when we learnt how to plan an essay, and in the writing stage, particularly in Chapters 26 and 32, topic sentences and transitions, those words and phrases we use to create connections between our ideas, are the essential tools we need to construct our arguments. They represent the scaffolding of our arguments, the signposts that indicate what we are doing and which way we are developing our arguments, so the reader can follow them confidently without getting lost.

We use them to indicate the logic of what we are doing, whether we are striking a contrast, extending or concluding an argument, explaining something, identifying the causal relations between two things, drawing attention to similarities between two sets of arguments, or just summarising the points we have made. In the table below you can find transitions that will meet most of your needs.

Similarities	In the same way, Likewise, Similarly, Correspondingly, By the same token, Equally, For the same reason, Complementing this
Contrast	However, On the other hand, Yet, But, But at the same time, Despite, Even so, For all that, In contrast, In spite of, On the contrary, Otherwise, Although, Whereas, Unlike, By way of contrast, Conversely, Having said that, That said, Nonetheless, There again, All the same, Contrastingly
Illustration	For example, For instance, That is, In other words, In particular, Namely, Specifically, Such as, Thus, To illustrate, As an illustration, As an illustration, In this instance/context, A case in point, A clear example of this
Extension/ addition	Similarly, Moreover, Furthermore, In addition, By extension, What is more, Above all, Further, In the same way, Also, Apart from, Besides, As well as, Indeed, Not only this but, In fact, Equally important, Reinforcing this point
Logical sequence	Therefore, Consequently, As a result, Thus, Hence, Accordingly, So, This means, To conclude, As a final point, Eventually, Finally, In the end, Lastly, It follows that, Given these points, It follows then
Chronological sequence	Then, After that, It follows, Subsequently, Eventually, Previously, Next, Before this, Afterwards, After this, Then, Following this, Meanwhile, At the same time
Emphasis	Above all, After all, Equally important, Especially, Indeed, In fact, In particular, Most important, Of course, Namely, Notably
Causal relations	As a result, Consequently, For that reason, So, Accordingly, Owing to this, Due to this, Because of this, Under these circumstances, Since, As, Hence, Thus, As a consequence, Therefore, As a result, Subsequently
Temporal relations	In future, In the meantime, In the past, At first, At the same time, During this time, Earlier, Eventually, Meanwhile, Now, Recently, Simultaneously, Now, Shortly, Recently, Thereafter, Consequently
Summarising	Finally, In brief, In conclusion, In short, In simpler terms, In summary, On the whole, To summarise, To conclude, So, Thus, To sum up, Overall, Briefly, Given these points, In all, In summary, Altogether, Thus, Hence, Throughout it all
Qualification	However, Nevertheless, Even though, Still, Yet, Nonetheless, Whereas, Admittedly, Despite this, Notwithstanding this, Albeit, Although, In spite of this, Regardless of this, And yet
Alternatives	Alternatively, On the other hand, Rather, As an alternative, Otherwise, Then again, Instead, Apart from that, On the contrary, In another way, Contrastingly, Conversely, On the other side, In contrast, In many ways, In different ways
Explanation	That is to say, In other words, Namely, This means, To put it in another way, To put it simply, That is, By way of explanation, To explain

Compound transitions

However, as we discovered in Chapter 32, the more you use them the more likely you are to notice others in your reading, which you can add to your list. You will also be able to create your own compound transitions by combining words and phrases. These will help you catch all the subtleties in an argument that might otherwise have escaped you. They will allow you to navigate exactly the right passage through your arguments with just the right changes in emphasis and direction.

Conjunction	And moreover, And although, And in one respect, And once, And so, And while some, And as it is, And even though
Extension	So even though, In this way, From that angle, By the same token, On that account, Given this
Emphasis	Not surprisingly, Of course, And moreover, Most important, Even more, In particular
Contrast	But instead, But at the same time, And yet, But even, But then again, But perhaps, Yet still, But while, Even though, But even so, And though, But even if, But otherwise, Yet even
Chronological sequence	Following this, And after that, But then, So began, But so far, More recently, But at the same time, And while, And there continues to be, In so doing
Illustration	Consider for instance/for example

Summary

1 Whenever we use more words than we need to convey our ideas we clutter up our arguments, obscure their structure and make it difficult for readers to understand our points.

2 Nouns and verbs are the most important words in a sentence. Nouns give our sentences a clear image, the sound foundations on which we develop our ideas, while verbs give our sentences their movement, their momentum.

3 By choosing the best qualifier we can avoid overstating the strength of our argument and having it rejected, or understating it and robbing it of the significance it deserves.

4 Transitions are the scaffolding of our arguments, indicating the logic of what we are doing, so readers can follow them confidently without getting lost.

In the next chapter

Now that you've finished writing your essay, before you put it aside until you're ready for revision, you need to deal with all the material that you've borrowed from the texts you've used. In the next chapter you will be shown how to avoid the problems of plagiarism and how to decide when you need to cite your sources.

For more material to practise on, critical thinking problems and complete annotated essays that show the effects of everything we have discussed in the writing stage over the previous 12 chapters, go to the companion website at www.howtowritebetteressays.com.

35

Plagiarism

In this chapter you will learn:

- about the dangers of plagiarism and how to avoid them;
- how to decide when you need to cite sources and when you don't need to – the six-point code;
- how to organise yourself to lessen the chances of plagiarism.

By definition, the research we undertake to write an essay involves us in borrowing material in one form or another. So, before we pack away our notes, relieved that we've done most of the hard work, we need to remind ourselves that we have certain ethical responsibilities to meet. We have an obligation to acknowledge all those who have helped us by giving us material in the form of ideas, quotations, figures and anecdotes. Failure to do this will mean we have committed just about the worst form of academic dishonesty.

To many students it seems strange to frown upon plagiarism when one of the central purposes of education is to get you to read, understand and then use in your own work the accumulated body of scholarship in your subject. But it is not so much using it that is the problem, but the way we use it.

Why is it wrong to plagiarise?

There are two main reasons why it is wrong to plagiarise. The first is ethical. We have a moral obligation to acknowledge anybody who has helped us, particularly when they have invested so much thought and care into their work, which we might otherwise have had to do ourselves. Whenever you use the work of others, remind yourself again of Sir Isaac Newton's famous acknowledgement: 'If I have seen further it is by standing on the shoulders of giants.' In one way or another we all have to stand on the shoulders of giants.

Reasons why plagiarism is wrong

1. We have a moral obligation to acknowledge those who helped us.
2. There is little educational value in it: we fail to process the ideas and make them our own.

However, in contrast to the first reason, the second is quite simply that it is just not in our interests to plagiarise. By passing off someone else's work as our own we could fail on the grounds of having cheated. This is academic deception. But, equally serious, there is just little educational value in it. Copying work and presenting it as our own avoids the task of processing these ideas and making them our own by testing them against, and integrating them within, our own thought structures. If we fail to do this, there is little point in education at all.

What is plagiarism exactly?

There can't be many university students who are unaware of the meaning of this. But still there are things we do that we don't always recognise as plagiarism.[1] Therefore, we ought to have a clear idea of the various activities this includes. In its simplest form it is the attempt to present someone else's ideas or arguments as your own. This might be using an idea you've read in one of your sources without acknowledging it, copying paragraphs directly into your own work without quotation marks or a reference, or just quoting from a paper without quotation marks, even though you may have cited the paper appropriately elsewhere. In effect, it involves any activity which amounts to you taking credit for work that is someone else's.

> Plagiarism: taking credit for work that is someone else's.

Fortunately, most examples of plagiarism are not deliberate. Some students are just unaware of the rules of acknowledgement. Others fail to organise their work well enough, so that when they come to research their essays they take their notes in a rushed and careless manner. As a result they blend their own ideas with those they take from the texts they use. They fail to put these ideas into their own words, so that the paraphrases and summaries that find their way into their essay are not sufficiently different from the original.

- Plagiarism is taking credit for work that is not yours.
- Some of it comes about because we're unaware of the rules of acknowledgement.
- Students who rush their notes and fail to restructure what they read, or express it in their own words, are most likely to plagiarise.
- They leave insufficient time to process the ideas, and rework them without referring back to the original.

The problem is, as we saw in Chapter 10, that the solution can be almost as harmful in its impact on a student's work as plagiarism itself. In other words, we come to believe that the only way to avoid plagiarism is to give a reference for every idea not only quoted or paraphrased, but borrowed in any possible way. This gives us the impression that there is nothing new in education and our role is just to recycle received opinion. In this way, by demonstrating that our ideas are not original, we hope to make them invulnerable: as they have been thought by others, their authority gives our arguments the protection we cannot. Education, then, appears to be more concerned with *what* we think than with *how* we think.

Even so, there are other sources of advice, more tolerant of our own ideas, and in this we begin to see the depth and complexity of the problem. The *Greats Handbook* at Oxford advises students:

> The examiners are looking for your own ideas and convictions, and you mustn't be shy of presenting them as your own: whether you are conscious of having inherited them from somebody else doesn't matter one way or the other.[2]

So, where should you draw the line?

It's simply not enough to tell students, as one university does, that they must use references whenever 'the knowledge you are expressing is not your own original thought'.[3] This would mean that you are left giving references for just about all the ideas you will ever use. You've probably used words like 'gravity' or 'ideology' many times before, but they are not your original thoughts. Does this mean you must provide a reference from Newton's *Principia* or Marx's *The German Ideology*, respectively, each time you use them? You may know that the distance from London to Edinburgh is 378 miles or that Jupiter has 16 moons, but you have never measured or counted them yourself, so should you give the reference to the person who has, each time you use this information? Of course not. So, where should you draw the line?

With specific information or data in the form of facts, statistics, tables and diagrams, it's easier to decide. You will have found them in a specific publication, which you will need to cite, so your reader will know who gathered the information and where to find it. The same applies to any information, or set of ideas, that have been organised in a distinctive way. The information may have been known to you, but you have never seen it presented in this form or argued in this way. And in this lies the crucial principle:

> Whenever the author has given something distinctive to the information or its organisation, cite the source.

In citing the source you are acknowledging the author's distinctive contribution. By the same token, this applies to a phrase or passage that you use verbatim. It has its own distinctive form, which you must acknowledge. This is true even of a single word, if this is distinctive to the author's argument.

Common knowledge

But with most ideas and thoughts the situation isn't so clear-cut. There may be nothing distinctive about them or their organisation. So you may believe, quite reasonably, that although you got the ideas from a source you've read, you can use them without acknowledgement.

One justification for this is that all knowledge in the public domain, all 'common knowledge', need not be referenced. But this seems to do little more than give the problem a different name. So, what is 'common knowledge'? This brings us back to our original distinction. Common knowledge is all those facts, ideas and opinions that are not distinctive of a particular author, or a matter of interpretation. They may be familiar ideas or just easily found in a number of common reference works, like dictionaries, basic textbooks, encyclopaedias or yearbooks.

Common knowledge

PRACTICE EXERCISE

36

Read the following statements and decide which of them are common knowledge and, therefore, need not be referenced.

1   The French Revolution began in July 1789.
2   Professor Robert Katz maintains that a good manager needs not just technical and human skills, but conceptual skills too.
3   34 per cent of all journalists believe that official government sources cannot be relied upon.
4   All public companies have an obligation to submit their accounts to an annual audit.
5   Quantum mechanics deals with the motion and interaction of particles.
6   Of the thousands executed after being sentenced to capital punishment in America a large number were far from incurable.
7   Global warming will bring about a massive downturn in global economies of between 5 and 20 per cent.
8   The carotid artery, found on the side of the neck, carries blood to the brain.
9   Einstein once said, 'God is subtle but he is not malicious.'
10 Surrealism is a twentieth-century movement in art and literature, which aims to express the unconscious mind by depicting the phenomena of dreams.

Answer

The statements that are common knowledge are 1, 4, 5, 8, 10.

It wouldn't even be necessary to give a reference for a distinctive contribution made by someone in a particular discipline, if this is well known within that discipline. In politics or sociology, for example, it wouldn't be necessary to give a reference for Marx's concept of 'alienation', or in philosophy for Kant's 'categorical imperative', but if you were to refer to an author's particular interpretation of either, this would need a reference.

EXAMPLE

Take the word 'paradigm', meaning a dominant theory in an area of study, which sets the conceptual framework within which a science is taught and scientists conduct research. It was first used in this sense by T. S. Kuhn in his seminal work *The Structure of Scientific Revolutions* (1962). Today the term has spread throughout the social sciences and philosophy. But in none of these areas would you be expected to cite the reference to Kuhn, if you were to use the term, so common has it become within each of these disciplines.

Other types of common knowledge come in the form of common or familiar opinion. It may seem to you undeniable that the vast majority of your fellow citizens are in favour of staging the next Olympic Games or the World Cup in your country, but no survey may ever have been done or referendum held. Similarly, it might generally be held that the elderly should receive special treatment, like free bus passes and medical help. In appealing to such common knowledge you would have to judge how familiar it was. The rule is: *If in doubt, cite.*

Common knowledge

1 Familiar ideas found in reference works.
2 Ideas well known within a particular discipline.
3 Common or familiar opinion.

To sharpen up your ability to distinguish between those ideas that are common knowledge and need not be referenced, and those that need to be cited as defined by the six-point code, go onto the companion website (www.howtowritebetteressays.com), where you will find questions you can tackle.

The six-point code

To make it easier for you to decide exactly when you need to cite, use the following simple six-point code. This is another of those notes worth sticking to the side of your computer screen or pinning to the noticeboard above your desk. Wherever you keep it, make sure it's just a glance away.

When to cite

1 **Distinctive ideas**   Whenever the ideas or opinions are distinctive to one particular source.
2 **Distinctive structure or organising strategy**   Even though you may have put it into your own words, if the author has adopted a particular method of approaching a problem, or there is a distinctive intellectual structure to what's written, for example to an argument or to the analysis of a concept, then you must cite the source.
3 **Information or data from a particular source**   If you've gathered information from a source in the form of facts, statistics, tables and diagrams, you will need to cite the source, so your readers will know who gathered the information and where to find it.
4 **Verbatim phrase or passage**   Even a single word, if it is distinctive to your author's argument. You must use quotation marks and cite the source.
5 **If it's not common knowledge**   Whenever you mention some aspect of another person's work, unless the information or opinion is widely known, you must cite the source, so your readers can follow it up.
6 **Whenever in doubt, cite it!**   It will do no harm, as long as you're not citing just to impress the examiner in the mistaken belief that getting good grades depends upon trading facts, in this case references, for marks.

Minimising the chance of an oversight

Nevertheless, even with this simple code and every good intention, there is always the possibility that you just might overlook the need to cite a source. Most examples of plagiarism are probably accidental oversights of this kind. The solution, for the most part, can be found in what we've said in previous chapters.

How can I avoid it?

1 **Organise your work to give you sufficient time**

    It's more than likely that most of these oversights come about through poor organisation. If we start working on our essay just days before it is due to be handed in, we're likely to cut corners as we take notes and gather our material. At this point it's all too easy to blend the author's ideas in with our own, thereby overlooking the need to cite the source. Organising our time is the most effective way of minimising this danger. For useful advice on how you can do this effectively, go onto the companion website (www.howtowritebetteressays.com).

2 **Process the ideas, imposing your own organisation and structure on them. Rewrite them using your own words**

    In Chapter 12 we examined the importance of actively processing the ideas we read and note, not only taking out structures, but criticising and evaluating the ideas we read. This, too, can minimise the chances of an oversight. Not only does it reduce the amount you're likely to borrow, but, more importantly, you will integrate the ideas into your own thinking, imposing your own distinctive organisation and structure on them.

3 **Interpret the question carefully, arming yourself with your own ideas, so you can avoid being dictated to by the author**

    However, as we saw in Stage 1, processing the ideas, in turn, depends upon interpreting the question in the first place. Having analysed the implications of the question and revealed not only what you know, but the questions you want answered in the texts, you can avoid being dictated to by your authors. Armed with your own ideas, you're less likely to adopt their ideas wholesale.

4 **Mark out clearly in your notes the ideas you borrow**

    As you note down material from your sources, you can take simple, practical steps to avoid oversights. The most important of these is just to mark out clearly in your notes the ideas you borrow to distinguish them from your own. For example, it will help if you can put the material you borrow from your sources in a different colour, if not on different sheets of paper, or even in different computer files.

5 **Record the details of the source to remind you that you are borrowing from it**

    For similar reasons, and to save you time when you come to search for the details of a reference, record at the top of the page the title of the text, the author's name, the page numbers and the date of publication. This will not only save you the nightmarish stress that comes from trying to track down a single reference to a quotation, or an idea, that you took down hastily, but it will also serve to remind you that you are working with a source. This is often all we need to take more care to separate our ideas from those of our source and to record accurately what we borrow.

Summary

1 Plagiarism is taking credit for work that is not yours.
2 We have an ethical obligation to acknowledge those sources we have used.
3 There is little educational value in plagiarism.
4 If the author has given something distinctive to the information or its organisation, cite it.
5 Minimise the risk of doing it by processing and reorganising the ideas into your own structures and words.

In the next chapter

Now that you know how to avoid plagiarism and how to decide which of your sources you need to cite, you can turn to the techniques involved in citing your sources and compiling a bibliography and a reference list, both of which should enhance your essay for you and your reader.

Notes

1 One of the most useful and comprehensive accounts of referencing and plagiarism is Gordon Harvey, *Writing with Sources: A Guide for Harvard Students* (Cambridge, MA, 1995). I am indebted to this for the more perceptive distinctions that follow. You can find it at: http://www.fas.harvard.edu/~expos/sources. Also look at two excellent Palgrave Macmillan texts: Richard Pears and Graham Shields, *Cite Them Right* and Kate Williams and Jude Carroll, *Referencing and Understanding Plagiarism*.
2 *Greats Handbook* (Oxford: University of Oxford, 2000), p. 42.
3 Jan Regan, *Essay and Report Writing: What is Expected of You* (Lismore: Southern Cross University, 2000), p. 9.

36

Referencing and Bibliographies

In this chapter you will learn:

- the various ways of citing sources;
- how to create reference lists and useful bibliographies;
- how to acknowledge uncited sources.

Now that we've dealt with the most difficult judgements that we need to make in managing our sources, we're left with the simpler problems of how we cite each reference and list the details of each text we use.

The different systems for citing

There are a number of systems governing the way we cite references. All seem to insist on their own conventions with the strength of religious fervour. Some insist a comma be used in places where others use a semicolon. Many expect the date of publication to appear at different points and would be scandalised if it appeared elsewhere. So, check with your department to see if they have certain expectations, a system they would like you to use. You might refer to your course guide, or its equivalent. Failing that, ask your tutor.

Most tutors won't mind what system you use as long as it meets three cardinal objectives: it must be clear, accurate and consistent. Remind yourself why you're doing this: first, to give credit to the author for the original ideas; and second, to give your readers clear and sufficient detail for them to locate the exact reference for themselves. To get the details consistently right, you may find it helpful to use referencing software, like *RefWorks* or *EndNote*.

- Three objectives: to be clear, accurate and consistent.
- Aims: to give credit to our sources and give sufficient detail for our readers to follow them up.

Footnote or endnote system

This is probably the most well-known system, certainly the most elegant. Each reference is cited in the text by a number, which refers to either a footnote at the bottom of the page, or a list of references at the end of your essay. Its main advantage, beyond its simplicity, is that it doesn't disrupt the text as much as other systems that enter the details of the reference in the actual text itself. These tend to clutter up the text, breaking the flow of ideas as you read. What's more, the footnote or endnote system has the advantage that most word-processing programs create and position footnotes or endnotes automatically for you.

Footnotes

When you write a footnote, it's usual to abbreviate authors and titles. In doing this you can choose from two alternative styles, but the same advice follows as before: choose one and stick to it – be consistent. You can either cite the full title on the first occasion you cite the work and then cite the abbreviated title each time after that, or you can adopt what's known as the Harvard, or the 'name–date', system. Using this, you cite in the note the author's name, the date of publication, and the relevant page. In both cases the full details of all the titles referred to would appear in the reference list and bibliography.

Abbreviation system

In this system the first reference to a book would appear as:

P. Rowe, *The Craft of the Sub-editor* (Cambridge, 1997), p. 37.

Later references to the same book could be abbreviated to:

Rowe, *The Craft*, pp. 102–3.

A reference to a journal article would appear as:

Brian T. Trainor, 'The State, Marriage and Divorce', *Journal of Social Work*, vol. 9, no. 2 (1992), p. 145.

A later reference to the same article could be abbreviated to:

Trainor, 'The State', *JSW*, pp. 138–9.

The Harvard system

Under this system the same references would appear as:

Rowe, 1997, p. 37.
Rowe, 1997, pp. 102–3.
Trainor, 1992, p. 145.
Trainor, 1992, pp. 138–9.

Endnotes

This is by far the simplest of the three systems. The numbers inserted into the text refer to a numbered reference list at the back of the essay. As with the footnotes system, repeated references to a text can be abbreviated, but in this case you use three well-known Latin abbreviations. When you first meet these they can seem arcane and forbidding, but use them once or twice and you will see how much time and effort they can save.

Say your first reference was as follows:

1   P. Rowe, *The Craft of the Sub-editor* (Cambridge, 1997), p. 37.

A number of references later you may want to refer to this text again. In this case you would use the Latin abbreviation 'op. cit.', meaning 'in the work cited', instead of repeating the detailed description of the text, which you've already given. Let's say it was the fifth reference on your list:

    5   Rowe, op. cit., pp. 102–3.

If, in the next reference, you wanted to refer to the same text again, this time you would use another Latin reference, 'ibid.', meaning 'in the same place':

    6   Ibid., p. 84.

If, then, in the next reference, you wanted to refer again to the same page of the same text, after 'ibid.' you would use the Latin abbreviation 'loc. cit.', meaning 'in the passage just quoted':

    7   Ibid., loc. cit.

In-text citing

Like the second form of footnotes, in-text citing uses the Harvard system, but puts the name of the author, the year of publication, and the page number in the actual text itself in parentheses, after the material you've borrowed. Then a list of these references appears at the end of the essay, where the full details of the texts, to which these abbreviations refer, can be found.

On some occasions you may decide that the author's name will appear in the actual text with only the year of publication and the page number in brackets. The following examples illustrate the various ways this can be done.

> Perhaps artists need to feel politically motivated against oppressive regimes in order to etch their identity clearly against a social and political reality they deplore. In the words of Theodore Roethke, 'In a dark time, the eye begins to see' (1966, p. 239).

> Perhaps artists need to feel politically motivated against oppressive regimes in order to etch their identity clearly against a social and political reality they deplore. After all, 'In a dark time, the eye begins to see' (Roethke, 1966, p. 239).

> As Roethke (1966) points out, perhaps artists need to feel politically motivated against oppressive regimes in order to etch their identity clearly against a social and political reality they deplore. After all, 'In a dark time, the eye begins to see' (p. 239).

Paraphrasing

When you paraphrase an author's words, only the author and the year need to be included. For example:

> Certain diets that reduce the levels of serotonin in the brain appear to produce higher levels of aggression. Historically, periods of famine, and carbohydrate and protein malnutrition, have been associated with significant increases in crime and violence (Valzelli, 1981).

> Valzelli (1981) argues that those diets responsible for reducing the levels of serotonin in the brain appear to produce higher levels of aggression. Historically, periods of famine, and carbohydrate and protein malnutrition, have been associated with significant increases in crime and violence.

If your material comes from more than one source by the same author

In this case arrange your sources chronologically, separated by a comma.

> Homelessness was shown to have increased as a result of the change in legislation and with the tighter monetary policy that doubled interest rates over a period of two years (Williams, 1991, 1994).

If the author has published more than one work in a single year, then cite them using a lower-case letter after the year of publication.

> Williams (1994a, 1994b) has shown that higher interest rates, while doing little to arrest the decline in value of the currency, have seriously damaged companies engaged in exports and increased the levels of home repossessions.

When a reference has more than one author

When it has two or three authors, give all the surnames, separated by commas, with the last one separated by the word 'and'.

> Recent evidence has shown that cinema attendance in the 1950s declined less as a result of the impact of television, than through increasing affluence and mobility (Brown, Rowe and Woodward, 1996).

> Computer analysis has shown that the hundred most used words in the English language are all of Anglo-Saxon origin, even the first words spoken when man set foot on the moon in 1969 (Lacey and Danziger, 1999).

> If there are more than three, cite them all the first time – for example: (Brown, Kirby, Rowe and Woodward, 1991) – but, when you cite them again, use just the first name followed by 'et al.' (and all the others) – for example: (Brown et al., 1991).

When an author cites another author

In this case, if you want to use the comments of the cited author, then you acknowledge both authors, but only the author of the text in which you found the comments is listed in the reference list.

> In describing recent studies that tended to show that men become dangerous when their personal aggressiveness is unnaturally contained, Masters (1997, p. 37) cites a comment by Anthony Storr, who says, 'Aggression is liable to turn into dangerous violence when it is repressed or disowned.'

> Anthony Storr (cited in Masters, 1997, p. 37) argues that, 'The man who is able to assert himself in a socially acceptable fashion is seldom vicious; it is the weak who are most likely to stab one in the back.'

When a number of authors present the same idea

In this case arrange the authors in alphabetical or chronological order, separated by semicolons.

> If a child does not receive love from its parents in the early years it will neither integrate their standards within its behaviour, nor develop any sense of moral conscience (Berkowitz, 1962; Farrington, 1978; Rutter, 1981; Storr, 1972).

Acknowledging uncited sources

Before we finish with referencing, consider just one more source that might need acknowledging. At times some of our best ideas come from discussions we have with friends, colleagues and tutors. Many of these may just be informal occasions when an idea might fire your imagination, or you might try out an idea on a tutor, who shows you how to develop it further and in ways you hadn't even thought of. Alternatively, an idea might come from one isolated comment in a lecture, or an example that opens up possibilities you hadn't seen before. Or you may just get inspiration from a novel you've read, or an article you might idly skim while you wait for someone.

All of these sources can play an important part in generating your ideas and giving them shape. So, if they have played a significant role, think about whether you need to acknowledge this. If the help is of a general nature, say the original insight that motivated your thinking in the first place, or an idea that revealed for you the way to tackle the problem raised by the essay, then you can place a reference number after the title or when you state the main idea. You can then pick this up at the bottom of the page or at the top of the list of endnotes with a few words acknowledging your debt. Alternatively, you may just be acknowledging the source of a particular point, one of many in your essay. In this case the note will appear in the middle of the sequence of footnotes or endnotes.

The following are examples of the sort of comments you might make, although there is almost no limit to the sort of help you might acknowledge.

> I am particularly indebted to Dr David Dockrill for many of the ideas on transubstantiation in this section.

> My understanding of intentionality is largely influenced by discussions I have had with Dr Joe Mintoff.

> I have benefited from Dr John Wright's criticisms of the first draft of this passage.

> I owe this example of the Prisoners' Dilemma to Prof. C. A. Hooker, who used it in his lectures on Commercial Values at the University of Newcastle in the first semester 2000.

Bibliographies and reference lists

At the end of your essay it's usual to give both a bibliography and a reference list, although in some pieces of work you may just be asked for a reference list alone. This contains only those authors and works you've referred to in the essay, while a bibliography is a list of all the material you've consulted as background for the topic.

The latter can be very useful both to you and to your readers. Later you might want to check back on certain points or expand and develop some of your ideas. The aim of the bibliography is to tell your readers in the clearest possible way what you've used, so don't pad it out with items to impress them. Nevertheless, it will no doubt help you in your future assignments if you make it as comprehensive as possible. If it's helpful, divide it into primary and secondary material. Primary material includes government reports and statistics, research material, historic documents and original texts, while secondary material includes books, articles and academic papers, which usually discuss or throw light on the primary material.

Why compile a bibliography?

- Because you may want to develop some of your ideas later.
- To give your readers an indication of what you have used.

If you've been systematic from the start, the bibliography is quite easy to compile. But if you haven't recorded your sources carefully, then it can be quite a nightmare. You will find that the habit of recording the details of your sources at the top of the page before you take notes, or, better still, using a section in your index-card system to compile a bibliography, will make the job much more straightforward.

For each source use just one card or one document, if you are using a computer or online system, and record all the details you need. You will even find that recording your own impressions of the usefulness of the text in one or two sentences will help you when you come to research other assignments, for which this source might be useful. These impressions will be lost to you within a short time, so by recording them as soon as you finish with the text you will know exactly how useful it is and what you can use it for in the future.

Listing the sources

Whether you're compiling a reference list or a bibliography, as we said before, the key is to be consistent. There are different conventions governing the way you list the texts, but as long as you follow a regular sequence for citation, there should be no problem. Below you will see one of the most common methods of citation. As you list them, arrange your references alphabetically, and where there is more than one book by the same author, arrange these chronologically under the author's name.

- *For books or other free-standing publications*: first names or initials of the author, the author's surname, full title of the work (in italics or underlined), place of publication, name of the publisher, and date (in brackets).

  Where you're using a later edition than the first, indicate the date of the first publication.
- *For periodical articles*: first names or initials of the author, the author's surname, the name of the article (in quotation marks), the title of the periodical (in italics or underlined), volume number of the periodical (if published in volumes), the year of publication (in brackets unless no volume number is given), the page numbers of the article.

i.e.

> N. Author, *Title of Book* (place of publication: publisher, and date).
> N. Author, 'Title of Chapter', in *Title of Book*, ed. X. Editor and Y. Editor (place of publication: publisher, and date), pp. ••–••.
> N. Author, 'Title of Article', *Title of Periodical*, vol. 2, no. 1 (date), pp. ••–••.

Of course, if you are compiling a reference list and you're using endnotes, you will also have to include the page reference to locate the passage or quotation you have used.

Compiling a reference list

PRACTICE EXERCISE

Arrange the following list of sources into a reference list, using the method of citation we have just outlined.

Once you've completed it, compare your list with the answer given below.

37

List of sources

1   Author: R. E. Robinson and J. Gallagher
     Title: *Africa and the Victorians: The Official Mind of British Imperialism*
     Publisher: Macmillan
     Date and place of publication: 1962, London

2   Author: Peter Singer, ed.
     Title: *Ethics*
     Publisher: OUP
     Date and place of publication: 1994, Oxford

3   Author: Charles Darwin
     Title: *On the Origin of Species*
     Publisher: John Murray
     Date and place of publication: 1859, London

4   Author: Leo Alexander
     Title of the article: Medical Science under Dictatorship
     Title of the periodical: *New England Journal of Medicine*
     Volume number: 241
     Year of publication: 1949
     The page numbers of the article: 39–47

5   Author: Peter Singer
     Title: *The Expanding Circle*
     Publisher: OUP
     Date and place of publication: 1981, Oxford

6   Author: Allen Wood
     Title: Marx against Morality, in *A Companion to Ethics*, ed. Peter Singer, pp. 511–24
     Publisher: Blackwell
     Date and place of publication: 1994, Oxford

7   Author: Peter Curwen
     Title of the article: High-Definition Television: A Case Study of Industrial Policy versus the Market
     Title of the periodical: *European Business Review*
     Volume number: vol. 94, no. 1
     Year of publication: 1994
     The page numbers of the article: 17–23

8   Author: John C. Ford
Title of the article: The Morality of Obliteration Bombing
Title of the periodical: *Theological Studies*
Year of publication in the periodical: 1944
Title of volume of essays in which reprinted: *War and Morality*
Editor: Richard A. Wasserstrom
Date and place of publication: 1970, Belmont
The page numbers of the article: 1–18

9   Author: Peter Singer
Title: *Practical Ethics*
Publisher: CUP
Date and place of publication: 1979, Cambridge

10   Author: Geoffrey Parker
Title of the article: Mutiny and Discontent in the Spanish Army of Flanders, 1572–1607
Title of the periodical: *Past & Present*
Volume number: vol. 58
Year of publication: 1973
The page numbers of the article: 38–52

Answer

1   Leo Alexander, 'Medical Science under Dictatorship', *New England Journal of Medicine*, vol. 241 (1949), pp. 39–47.

2   Peter Curwen, 'High-Definition Television: A Case Study of Industrial Policy versus the Market', *European Business Review*, vol. 94, no. 1 (1994), pp. 17–23.

3   Charles Darwin, *On the Origin of Species* (London: John Murray, 1859).

4   John C. Ford, 'The Morality of Obliteration Bombing', *Theological Studies* (1944); reprinted in Richard A. Wasserstrom (ed.), *War and Morality* (Belmont: 1970), pp. 1–18.

5   Geoffrey Parker, 'Mutiny and Discontent in the Spanish Army of Flanders, 1572–1607', *Past and Present*, vol. 58 (1973), pp. 38–52.

6   R. E. Robinson and J. Gallagher, *Africa and the Victorians: The Official Mind of British Imperialism* (London: Macmillan, 1962).

7   Peter Singer, *Practical Ethics* (Cambridge: Cambridge University Press, 1979).

8   Peter Singer, *The Expanding Circle* (Oxford: Oxford University Press, 1981).

9   Peter Singer (ed.), *Ethics* (Oxford: Oxford University Press, 1994).

10   Allen Wood, 'Marx against Morality', in *A Companion to Ethics*, ed. Peter Singer (Oxford: Blackwell, 1994), pp. 511–24.

Reference list and bibliography

IN YOUR OWN WORK

Now that you've completed this exercise, compile your reference list and a bibliography for the essay you've chosen to work on in these assignments.

11

Summary

1 Whatever system you choose, make sure your referencing is clear, accurate and consistent.
2 Consider whether you should acknowledge uncited sources that may have played an important part in generating and shaping your ideas.
3 Remember, your bibliography is useful not just to your readers, but to you too in your future assignments.
4 So, although you should avoid padding it out to impress readers, make it as comprehensive as possible for your own benefit.

In the next chapter

With your essay completed, along with the reference list and bibliography, it's time to put it aside for a day or two, so that you can come back with a fresh mind to revise it.

But before we move on to the revision stage, there is one form of writing that presents challenges that are different from those a student confronts in the conventional essay. This is reflective writing, which is being adopted as part of the assessment for an increasing number of courses. In the next chapter we will examine the problems it presents and the best way of tackling this form of writing.

Note

1 For the most detailed account of many of the systems used, refer to Gordon Harvey, *Writing with Sources: A Guide for Harvard Students* (Cambridge, MA, 1995). Available at: http://www. fas.harvard.edu/~expos/sources

37

Reflective Writing

In this chapter you will learn:

- how to structure your reflective writing assignments;
- how to analyse your responses, so that you can identify what is significant in them;
- about the differences in style between reflective writing and the conventional essay.

A growing number of courses are asking students to think and write reflectively about their studies and their experience on professional placements. In the past, our education and training led us to believe that useful knowledge comes from just one source: theoretical, academic research, which we then apply in our professional lives. But over recent years we have come to realise the importance of practical knowledge, represented in the patterns of ideas and behaviour that we create as we adapt what we have learnt to meet the demands of the task and circumstances we face.

The point worth remembering is that our knowledge and expertise in anything is not just passive, a simple set of templates and rules that we apply; it is dynamic, continually adapting to the context in which it is used. To make the best use of this we need to reflect on what we have learnt.

What do we mean by reflective writing?

The most obvious characteristic that distinguishes this from the normal essay is that it is more personal. You will be reflecting on something deeply in terms of your own reactions to it: what you think and feel about it. It's a form of self-monitoring that brings you the same type of self-knowledge and awareness that we discussed in Chapter 18 when we examined the value of keeping your own journal and notebook. Your personal reactions are the subject of this, not the texts that you read and the evidence you gather for your normal essay. You might reflect on:

- An action you have taken
- A decision you have made
- An event that has occurred on your placement
- A project that you have completed alone or with others
- An idea – something you have found particularly interesting
- An object – a work of art or an example of modern architecture

You are reflecting on this to reveal your reactions and what you've learnt from it. So choose something that gives you the opportunity to learn. It may be an incident on your placement that really went well or something that didn't go according to plan. Your aim is to reveal both its weaknesses and strengths, along with your feelings and anxieties about it.

The structure

To reveal what you've learnt, ask yourself some simple routine questions and structure your answer around them. Your department might require you to work according to a certain structure, but if not, you will find the following structure useful to follow:

1 Description
2 Analysis
3 Outcome
4 Evaluation
5 What have I learnt?

1 Description

The most common mistake is to spend too much time on the description. To avoid this, plan what you want to write by listing the key facts that explain all we need to know and organise them in the order that will produce the clearest and most logical explanation. Although in some cases not all of these questions will be relevant, ask yourself,

1 What was it exactly – object, event, project, decision, idea, problem?
2 When did it occur?
3 Who was involved?
4 What actually happened?
5 How was it resolved?
6 Why was it significant?

Student teacher – the history class   EXAMPLE

'This was the first class I had ever taught. The plan was that I would teach the first hour before the break and the teacher, who normally taught this class and was observing me, would teach the second half. The topic that Friday morning was British economic policy during the inter-war years and I had decided to take the Gold Standard and its impact. This was a GCSE class for mature students returning to college. My tutor warned me that he thought this was too difficult a topic for the students, who were still unsure of themselves as students and lacked confidence in their abilities.'

In this example the student has explained what it was, when it occurred, who was involved and the facts that made it significant, without analysing what happened.

Writing your description

Think of an event, project or idea, from which you learnt a great deal. Now, in no more than 100 words, write a description of it, including all those details that we need to know if we are to understand it clearly. Omit everything that is not description: analysis, criticism and evaluation – all this will come later. This is harder than it might seem, so start by listing all those things that are essential. Once you have your list, organise the ideas and then write a clear, logical description of it.

2 Analysis

In this section you are now processing these facts by breaking them down into the key features of how you felt about it. You will find it helpful to break this down into two sections: how you felt about it at the time and how you feel about it now. Say you are analysing your feelings about a work of art, how did you feel about it when you first saw it; how do you feel about it now?

The most important aspect of any process of analysis is that it involves a measure of distance, so while you are discussing your feelings and responses, you're also presenting them dispassionately. Your aim is to identify as much significance as you can in your reactions and feelings. You will already know why you think this is significant, otherwise you wouldn't have chosen it as your subject in the first place. But to help you see even more, look for the following things:

1   *Elements* – how many different elements were there to my reaction to the situation?
    –   how many different things did I have to take into account in making my decision?
    –   how many different levels were there to my response to the work of art?
2   *Connections* – how similar or dissimilar is it from other events, projects, ideas, that I have worked on?
3   *Significance* – what is it about this, rather than similar things I could have written about, that has influenced my choice?

Student teacher – the history class

EXAMPLE

'It didn't take long for me to realize that the students were very nervous and afraid that they would not understand. This was not something I had planned for. It made me feel even more nervous with this sea of uncomprehending faces looking at me. I was now even more worried about my tutor's warning that he thought the Gold Standard was too difficult for them. Now I realize what a good idea it was to plan to explain the workings of it by reducing it to very familiar terms. This seemed to work and they began to relax a little. Then, to my great relief, they began asking questions, which seemed to suggest that they were feeling more confident about the situation.'

3 Outcome

In this section you are examining how things worked out: how did you respond; how did others respond? For example, if you were tackling a problem, how was it resolved and how did people respond to the solution?

Student teacher – the history class   EXAMPLE

'After the class my tutor seemed pleased that it had worked as well as it had, but I realized that I had to plan my lessons in future with much more awareness of the feelings and reactions of the class. My own feelings of panic faced by a class also made me aware that I had to have a clear, simple lesson plan to follow, otherwise the panic would easily throw me and leave me confused about what I was doing.'

4 Evaluation

In this section your aim is to assess critically the way you dealt with the subject of your reflection and how you reacted to it. You are asking yourself what was good and bad about the experience and whether it could have been handled better. Like analysis, this calls for a more detached, dispassionate approach, so get into the habit of addressing two key issues:

1 *The way the situation or problem was handled*
   On reflection, what were the different ways of tackling it? This may call for a theoretical response for which you may need to call upon the work of authors whose work you have read and discussed. Once you have outlined the different ways it could have been tackled, ask yourself whether there was a better way than the one you chose.
2 *The roles played in tackling it*
   If the task involved working with others, were the different roles defined clearly, were they distributed in the best way and could you and others have performed your roles better?

Student teacher – the history class   EXAMPLE

The student teacher will have to assess critically whether he, his tutor and, indeed, the class performed their different roles effectively. He might conclude that this time he had a class that was much better and more responsive that he might expect in the future. He might feel that his tutor's warnings were very helpful and that he will have to pay more attention to this sort of advice in the future.

5 What have I learnt?

The quality of this last section depends upon the work you've done in the previous sections. If you have been able to elevate yourself above personal, subjective reactions by analysing your responses well and then critically evaluating them, you will be much clearer about the valuable lessons you need to learn from the experience. Ask yourself questions like,

1 What do I need to learn to do things differently in the future?
2 What things would have helped to bring about a better outcome?
3 Why did the problem arise in the first place?

You may need to use the analyses and perspectives of authors you have discussed in your course to elevate your ideas above the personal level.

Engineering students' group project   EXAMPLE

In this project the students were asked to find a solution to an engineering problem using alternative technology.

'The most interesting thing that I learnt from the project is just how creative people can be in a group if they are given the freedom to put forward their ideas without the fear of criticism. But the other side of the coin is how difficult it then is to manage all these ideas to get the best outcome. I now realize that good ideas are not enough; you have to have someone who is prepared to lead the team, take the difficult decisions about who does what and then make sure that everyone does what they've agreed to do.'

Differences in style between this and the conventional essay

Although in reflective writing and in the conventional essay you are talking about *your* ideas and arguments, in the conventional essay you may still be expected to hide this beneath a veil of anonymity by avoiding personal pronouns, like 'I', 'my' and 'we'. However, this disguise is impossible to maintain convincingly in reflective writing. You cannot hide the fact that these are *your* ideas, arguments, reactions and feelings by inventing some anonymous individual as the source. Therefore, your style is likely to be more personal and subjective.

This means that it is acceptable to use personal pronouns. Still, beyond that, everything else remains the same. The temptation in such informal writing, where you are talking about your reactions and feelings about situations, is to use the language you would use when writing or chatting to a friend. So, make sure you avoid the following:

1 Abbreviations
2 Colloquialisms
3 Empty clichés
4 Incomplete sentences
5 Poorly constructed paragraphs

Remember that you are writing something that will be read by your tutor. Your aim should be to make your meaning perfectly clear without any danger of confusion. Rather than resort to colloquialisms, like 'cool', to describe something, pin your idea down ('cool' in what way?): make sure you know exactly what you want to say and then search for just the right word to convey it clearly. In all your writing remember,

If you leave room for doubt, you leave room to lose marks.

Getting the best out of your reflective writing

As you can see, reflective writing is an exercise in which you are able to stand back from your learning experiences and draw valuable lessons with the help of those, like your tutors, who have greater experience. But to get the best out of it you need to reflect deeply on your experiences and use the expertise that's available to you. Often the weakest reflective essays are those that fail to elevate themselves above the personal, subjective level and, therefore, fail to see these valuable lessons.

Summary

1 Reflecting upon our learning experiences is an important source of knowledge about the way we adapt what we have learnt to meet the demands we face.
2 To reveal this in an effective, logical structure we need a simple set of routine questions to answer.
3 The most successful reflective writing comes from elevating our reflections above the merely personal by analysing and revealing their significance.

The next stage

In the next stage you will learn how to revise your work without killing off your most creative ideas and without breaking up the fluency of your prose. Indeed, you will see how effective revision can be in giving your work the sort of polish that elevates it from being just a good piece of work into one that is interesting and thought provoking.

Revision

Introduction

Now that you've written your essay you will realise that one of the most difficult problems is to remind yourself of all those things we've talked about to improve your style, while at the same time writing as freely as possible. The key to doing this successfully is to separate the writer from the editor.

The writer v. the editor

In this stage you will learn to use these two distinctly different sets of skills without fearing that one is getting in the way of the other. This reinforces, again, the importance of breaking up essay writing into its distinct stages. Separating the writing and revision stages frees our hand, allowing us to write without the burden of having to produce the final polished version all in one go. Knowing that we can polish up our prose later, we can be more creative. It allows our ideas to flow and our minds to explore all the contrasts and connections between our ideas that give our writing impact.

But to do this effectively we have to learn to shift the focus from the writer to the editor without endangering our best ideas. The rich insights we saw in our ideas, which engaged our interest and commitment when we first began to plan and write them, are likely to engage our readers too. Therefore, we have to learn to edit our work without killing the very thing that's likely to grab our readers and make them think.

> We have to learn to shift the focus from the writer to the editor without endangering our best ideas.

To help you in this, and to make revision simpler and more manageable, you will learn to revise with a purpose: with a clear strategy of those things you want to work on in each revision, rather than attempting to revise everything at the same time. To make this easier, you will be shown the five-stage revision strategy, the first two revisions of which deal with the structural features of the essay, while the last three deal with the content.

- To make sure we write fluently and use our most creative ideas, we must separate the writer from the editor.
- Separating writing and revision is the key to this.

- But now we must make sure that revision doesn't kill our richest insights.
- So, revise it more than once, each time concentrating on different things.

Sample essays

To get a clearer idea of the impact of the sort of changes we make in each revision, look at the essay that we have been writing in the preceding chapters in answer to the question: 'Advertisers seek only to ensure that consumers make informed choices.' Discuss. This is the product of all the work we have done interpreting the question and analysing the concept of 'advertising', brainstorming our own ideas, planning the essay, writing the introduction, paragraphs and conclusion and working on our style.

 As you work through each revision, track the changes on the companion website (www.howtowritebetteressays.com) by looking at the essay after it has been through each one. In particular, you can see the effects of the revisions we do in Chapters 39 and 40 to the structure and content respectively, by reading through the two sample essays that follow the relevant chapter. From my explanation at the end of the essay, you will see clearly what we have done and the impact it has had on the essay.

Structure

In the first revision you will be shown how to identify those passages where your talk in print breaks down and it's difficult to continue to read fluently with the right emphasis and rhythm. Once this is done you will move on to the second revision, in which you learn how to revise the structural features of your essays, like the introduction, the conclusion, the logical structure of the essay, and the relevance of your arguments and evidence.

With these two revisions completed you will be keenly aware of the impact the types of changes you've made can have on your essay. By tying in paragraphs to the introduction with clear topic sentences and transitions, an essay that might have been just a loose list of points becomes a taut, cohesive piece of work, in which readers are never in danger of getting lost and every argument counts for marks. Similarly, if you have wrapped the structure up in a conclusion that completes the circle by coming back to issues first raised in the introduction, you will leave readers not only convinced that you have kept your promises, but with the satisfaction that everything has found its appropriate place.

> The aim of the second revision is to create a taut, cohesive essay, in which readers are in no danger of getting lost and every argument counts for marks.

You will also be shown how to revise your evidence, so that you use it to the best effect. If it's relevant and varied you will have made your work more interesting by breaking it up with changes in pace and content. And if you use evidence that allows people to speak for themselves, your readers are likely to be more involved in your work. They can respond empathetically, with their emotions and feelings engaged, which can lend untold support to your arguments. Nevertheless, you have to be sure your evidence does real work and you don't bury your readers beneath too much.

Structure

1 Does it read fluently with the right emphasis and rhythm?
2 Are introductions, paragraphs and conclusions tied in to each other, creating a taut cohesive essay?
3 Is the evidence used effectively? Does it break up the pace and engage the reader?

Content

In the final three revisions our main concern is to remove all unnecessary words and phrases that are likely to obscure the meaning of our sentences. If we fail to remove all of this, the clarity of our thinking will be lost, and our readers will be left wondering what it all means. With it removed, those words we use to carry the greatest significance in our work will no longer be smothered. They will stand out more and have sufficient impact to make our readers think.

As we saw in the last stage, knowing what to leave out is as important as knowing what to include. The readability of our work will increase in proportion to the number of unnecessary words we eliminate. Therefore, in this revision our aim is to ensure that our meaning is being carried by strong nouns and verbs, rather than being shored up with too many adverbs, adjectives and prepositional phrases. Removing these, replacing long words and sentences with shorter ones, and identifying all those sentences that would be better in the active voice, we can make our writing not only clearer and more concise, but more direct.

Content

1 Have we removed all unnecessary words and phrases that obscure our key arguments?
2 Is our meaning being carried by strong nouns and verbs?
3 Have we made it simpler by replacing all long words and sentences?
4 Have we made it more direct and concise by expressing our ideas in the active voice wherever appropriate?

Learning from feedback

Finally, we will learn what we need to do to make the best use of our tutor's comments on our work. This is an important opportunity to develop our understanding and our skills and abilities. But many of us have never been taught what we need to do to make the most of these valuable contributions to our education. Indeed, feedback on essays is more strongly and consistently related to academic achievement than any other form of teacher intervention. This is your opportunity to take up the challenge and begin to get the sort of grades that more accurately reflects your abilities and undoubted potential.

Feedback on essays is more strongly and consistently related to academic achievement than any other form of teacher intervention.

So, in this chapter you will learn what to look for in these comments and how to make the best use of them. You will learn how to prioritise what you need to do and how to organise your responses by using a feedback record. With a well-organised strategy you will begin to realise that the cumulative effects of your responses after each essay are bringing about marked improvements in the quality of your essays.

38

Preserving Your Best Ideas

In this chapter you will learn:

- about the importance of revision in allowing you to be more creative;
- how to shift the focus from the writer to the editor without endangering your best ideas;
- how the five-stage revision strategy makes revision easier and more effective.

Using your mind more effectively

A surprising number of students still seem quite unaware of just how much the writing stage depends for its success on the revision stage. As we thump the page with our last emphatic full stop there are those of us who breathe a deep sigh of relief that the essay's finally done, without a thought for revision, beyond a cursory check to see the spelling is all right.

But, if nothing else, revision has the effect of freeing your hand, allowing you to write without the burden of knowing you have to produce the final polished version all in one go. Knowing that you can polish up your prose later, you can be more creative, allowing your ideas to flow and your mind to make the logical connections and comparisons that give your writing impact.

> Revision frees our hand, allowing us to write more creatively.

In this lies an interesting parallel with the invention of the word processor. Before the modern home computer and the word-processing packages we now use, unless you were prepared to type the whole essay out again, you were condemned to write the final presentable draft in one go. This meant your creative flow was constantly interrupted both for the correction of errors and to give you time to find exactly the word you wanted, along with its correct spelling.

Now, with the word processor, it's possible to divide up the task one step further than we've already done with our stages of writing. By having a planning stage, distinct from the writing stage, we've already separated the two most difficult things in writing: on the one hand, summoning up our ideas and putting them in a logical order, and on the other, choosing the right words, phrases and sentence structures to convey them accurately. But now we can go even further: we can separate the ideas entirely from the choice of words and their correct spelling. You don't even have to worry too much about the sentence structure and punctuation, because these too can be cleaned up later.

- Splitting essay writing up into stages frees us to do one thing at a time.
- We can make use of our most creative ideas without the burden of producing at the same time the final draft.
- Now, with word processing, we can go one stage further and separate the words from our ideas.

Freeing your ideas and creativity

As a result of splitting up the task in this way you can be more creative and use more of your own ideas, many of which, you'll no doubt be surprised to find, like most students when they first do this, are full of insight and intelligence.

We've all had the experience of writing the old way with pen and paper or with a manual typewriter. All too frequently the words would get hopelessly tangled up with the ideas as they began to flow like a torrent. Your mind would make connections, analyse issues, synthesise arguments and evidence, and draw all sorts of interesting contrasts, all of which you would struggle desperately to retain and use. But as fast as you fought to find the right words and their correct spelling in order to capture these ideas, they would be gone and others, equally evanescent, would replace them.

The mind simply moves much faster than our inadequate techniques will allow us to record. Breaking the essay up into stages and using a word processor both give us the same advantages as using pattern notes in the interpretation stage, rather than linear notes: it's a more effective way of keeping up with the mind and using more of its creativity.

> The mind produces ideas faster than our techniques allow us to record.

The same can be said for revision. The importance of this stage lies in the fact that it allows you the freedom to focus more of your attention on the ideas in the writing stage and on your creative use of language. If you make mistakes with your grammar, your spelling or your sentence structures, don't worry, you can pick them up and sort them out in the revision stage.

Cooling off

The shift from the writer in you to the editor, then, involves a shift of focus from the creative activity of converting your ideas into language to a more self-conscious focus on the way you've used words, phrases and structures. The editor inside you should be asking: How does it sound? Is it fluent? Does it move logically from one stage in the argument to another? Are there sections that need more evidence, or more development?

| The writer | Creative activity converting ideas into language. |
| The editor | Self-conscious focus on the way we use words, phrases and structures. |

With this in mind, you've got to allow yourself to undergo a conversion from the writer to the editor, from the artist to the craftsman. To do this, the first thing is to put your essay aside. Allow yourself a cooling-off period of at least a day, so your editor can surface. It's not that you're trying to create objectivity between yourself and what you've written. This would endanger those rich insights you saw in your ideas when you first began to plan and write them. It's these that first engaged your interest and commitment, and they're likely to engage your readers' too. So, if you were to revise in an objective, dispassionate frame of mind, you might kill the very thing that's likely to grab your readers and make them think.

Nevertheless, aware of these dangers, try to approach your work as you believe the examiner or any reader will approach it. Allow yourself to feel the impact of your original insights as you expect the reader to be affected too.

> You're not revising objectively; that would only kill the insights that grabbed you and are likely to grab your readers too.

Revise with a purpose

However, once you begin to revise you will soon find your most difficult problem is that there are so many things to check – so many questions to ask of your work. The only effective way of making this simpler and manageable is to revise a number of times, each time checking on a different range of things.

This may seem a lot of work, but it will certainly pay dividends: each extra revision always improves your work. The effortless feel of talk in print that flows across the page in light elegant prose only comes from multiple revisions undertaken with a clear purpose in mind each time. But that's not to say that this is an endless process. As your writing improves you'll know when it's time to stop and put it aside – you'll know when it's finished.

Summary

1 Splitting essay writing into its different stages allows you to concentrate on them one at a time.
2 Separate the writer from the editor by allowing yourself a cooling-off period.
3 Revise purposefully with a clear idea of the different things you're looking for in each revision.

In the next chapter

What follows is a strategy of five revisions, each one looking for different things. You may find you want to do more than five, because you can see there are still improvements coming through each time, but you should regard five as the minimum. In the next chapter we will tackle the first two revisions, which deal with the structural features of the essay.

Revising the Structure

In this chapter you will learn:

- about the importance of listening to your essay being read aloud, to identify those passages you will need to work on;
- how to revise the structural features of your essay, like the introduction, the conclusion and the logical structure of the essay;
- how to make sure your arguments and evidence are relevant and effective.

First revision – revising for reassurance

This is the lightest of all revisions. After we've finished writing an essay most of us are keen to read it through to see how it sounds. We like to be reassured that it reads well, so we can give ourselves a mental pat on the back. This may sound like aimless self-indulgence that we should train ourselves to do without, but, in fact, this sort of revision and the reassurance it brings does have a valuable point to it.

It allows us to set down a marker: not only are we reassured that it reads well and it's interesting, but we're also clearer about those areas we need to work on to improve it. More often than not these may just involve a clumsy word or passage that needs tidying up, but they can be more serious.

> This allows us to set down a marker: to identify those sections we need to work on.

They may indicate that you haven't thought through your arguments clearly enough, or your ideas have developed further since you wrote the passage and you now see the issues differently. This revision is not just about making sure what you've written is clear from the outside, but also about ensuring that your writing expresses clearly the ideas on the inside. If you were not entirely clear about them when you wrote the passage, then your writing is likely to be unclear, too. Either way, at this stage you just need to mark the passage so that you can come back to it later.

After the cooling-off period, then, read it through for reassurance. But as you read through, tolerate your mistakes. Don't stop and start working on them. Just jot down notes on mistakes and weak areas that you must look at later.

IN YOUR OWN WORK

First revision

Take the essay you completed in the last exercise: 'In your own work 11'. First, read it through to yourself, then get a friend to read it to you. As he or she reads it, note those passages where your talk in print breaks down, where it's difficult to continue to read fluently with the right emphasis and rhythm. Remember, your ear can often pick up awkward passages much more effectively than your eye.

Although you'll pick up other problems as you go through each subsequent revision, this lays down clear markers that these are problem passages and you will have to look at them.

Second revision – the larger questions

In the second revision your main concern is with the larger structural features of your essay – the introduction, the conclusion, the logical structure of the essay, the relevance of your arguments and the evidence you use.

With this in mind, as you work through your essay concern yourself just with the following things.

Introduction

Check that you've interpreted the implications of the question clearly and haven't missed anything. Your tutors will want to assure themselves that you have thought this through thoroughly and that you haven't begged questions, taking some things for granted that you shouldn't have. Then, having done this, check that you've outlined the structure, the map of the essay, clearly, so the reader knows not just what you're going to do, but why.

Introduction – checklist

1 Have I interpreted the implications thoroughly?
2 Have I missed anything?
3 Have I outlined the structure, the map, of my essay clearly?

A clear logical structure

Now, as you move on to read the body of the essay, you're checking that you've delivered on all these promises. You must be sure that you've led the reader clearly through the essay. Of course, this is helped if you've organised the material in a clear, logical sequence that the reader can follow. But it also depends on the direction signs you erect in your essay to make sure the reader is never lost.

Keeping this at the front of your mind, in addition to checking that there is a logical sequence in your arguments, a clear pattern to your essay, also check your transitions and topic sentences. If your structure is clear, you won't need transitions for every paragraph, but if in doubt use them. They help the reader follow the route you're taking without getting derailed and sidetracked. The same can be said of topic sentences – they allow the reader to see clearly what the following paragraph is going to be about. But check that everything else in the paragraph supports it.

Structure – checklist

1 Have I arranged the material logically?
2 Is there fluency between each paragraph?
3 Have I omitted transitions where they are needed?
4 Do my topic sentences introduce the subject of each paragraph clearly?

A clear logical structure

'Advertisers seek only to ensure that consumers make informed choices.'
Discuss.

 Go on to the companion website (www.howtowritebetteressays.com) and read the unrevised essay on the question above. As you read it check that in the introduction the writer has interpreted the question, revealing its implications, and has laid out the map of the essay clearly.

Then, as you read through, check the topic sentences and transitions of each paragraph, noting wherever they fail to indicate the logic of the arguments that follow in the paragraph and their relevance to the interpretation of the implications of the question in the introduction. Do they make clear the topic of the paragraph and indicate the direction the writer is developing the argument? Are all the paragraphs relevant and has the writer created a cohesive structure that moves fluently and logically from one paragraph to another? Note the passages that you think need to be changed.

Once you have done this, read through the sample essay that follows this chapter to see what I thought needed to be changed. Read the comments that I have made at the bottom of the essay to explain why I have changed things in the way I have.

Your arguments

Having checked that you have made clear the relevance of what you're doing through the overall structure of your essay, now look at the content of each paragraph. Read the arguments contained in each paragraph, checking two things. First, make sure that all the arguments bear directly on the map of the essay outlined in the introduction. If they don't, it will dilute the overall approach of the essay and it will tend to confuse the reader. Second, check that you have developed each argument sufficiently and that they are clear. If there are difficult passages that could be clearer, rewrite them. This will include most of those you identified as a problem in the first revision.

Arguments – checklist

1 Does each argument develop out of the map of the essay?
2 Has each argument been developed clearly?
3 Have they been developed in enough depth?
4 Have I dealt with all the implications identified in the introduction?

Your evidence

As you read these arguments you should also be concerned that you've supported them with enough evidence. But make sure you haven't used too much – remember, pruning all unnecessary detail means that what remains stands out. It's the art of knowing what not to say. For similar reasons, make sure you haven't given the reader irrelevant information. This will blur the focus of your arguments and weaken the structure of your essay.

Now, make sure your evidence is specific. If you're developing arguments that employ generalisations, perhaps involving fairly abstract concepts, your examples should be as specific as possible, so that they pin down your arguments. Not only have your examples got to support your arguments, but they must illustrate them vividly. This will make them more believable and interesting – they will grab and hold your reader's attention.

Finally, check that, wherever possible, your arguments have *shown* your readers what you mean, rather than simply *told* them. For this, make sure you've used enough quotations and anecdotes. They will make your writing more readable, but they must make the point you want them to make. Therefore, make certain they all do *real* work. And remember, like other forms of evidence, too many are as bad as too few.

Evidence – checklist

1 Is there enough?
2 Is there too much?
3 Is it relevant?
4 Is it specific?
5 Do I *show* rather than *tell*?

Your conclusion

Having checked all of this, when it comes to your conclusion it should be plain sailing. The key thing you must be certain of is that the introduction and conclusion relate to each other, giving your essay a tight cohesion. If you haven't achieved this, then rewrite it so that you come back to the issues you raised, and the anecdote you may have used, in the introduction. But avoid raising any new issues that weren't raised in the body of the essay. The key to conclusions is to let your readers know that you have delivered on all the promises you made in the introduction.

Conclusions

'Advertisers seek only to ensure that consumers make informed choices.'
Discuss.

Go back onto the companion website (http://www.howtowritebetteressays.com)
and read the conclusion of the unrevised essay. Has it been tied in with the
introduction, giving the essay a tight cohesion? Does it sum up the main arguments of the
essay, or does it go beyond the preceding discussion with unrepresentative conclusions? Note
how you would change it. Then read the conclusion in the sample essay that follows this chapter
and my explanation of why I decided to change it as I have.

Conclusion – checklist

1 Do the introduction and conclusion relate to each other?
2 Have I avoided raising new issues?
3 Have I delivered on the promises I made in the introduction?

Revision – the structure

Now revise your essay carefully again. This time go through each of the stages
outlined here.
   Start with the introduction, checking all those things we've talked about. Once
you've done this, tick off the items on the introduction checklist. Then move on to
the logical structure, checking the logical sequencing of the arguments, the topic sentences and
the transitions. Tick them off on the structure checklist and then move on to consider the
arguments, evidence and conclusion, ticking these off on the remaining checklists.

Summary

1 Read your essay through to reassure yourself and to identify those passages that
   need to be reworked.
2 Check that you have thought through and written each argument clearly.
3 In the second revision work through each checklist, revising where necessary
   the structural features of your essay.

In the next chapter

Before you move onto the next revision, read the sample essay that follows this chapter where you can see the impact that revising the structural features of your essay has on the logic and the coherence of the essay. With this done you should feel more confident that all your ideas, what's on the inside, are now clearly and logically developed in your essay. You can now turn to the outside, the language and style through which you've expressed these ideas.

Sample essay 1: Revising the structure

'Advertisers seek only to ensure that consumers make informed choices.'
Discuss.

Most advertising executives are willing to defend their profession by arguing that all they are doing is informing the public and in doing so protecting the democratic freedoms of individuals, in particular their freedom of choice. To a certain extent, of course, this is true: without advertising we would be less informed about new developments in technology, in fashion and in medical advances. Even government warnings about the dangers at work and in the home depend upon advertisements. But the key to this is the claim that this is the 'only' thing they do, when most of the public suspect their paramount concern is to manipulate consumers into buying products that they may not want or need.

As this suggests, at least part of the advertiser's role is to provide consumers and the public with information. But this goes to the heart of what we mean by an 'advertisement'. Few of us would doubt that in some sense a railway timetable is an advertisement, after all it is telling the customer what is for sale and how to buy it. Yet there are no catchy jingles urging you to 'Let the train take the strain.' Nor are there any persuasive messages offering to let children travel free if the parents take the whole family to the beach. It is simply informative: it gives you information on the routes and the stations the train will stop at on the way; it tells you the departure and arrival times; and it tells you on what platform you can find the train.

Given this, it might not be unreasonable to conclude that advertisements can, after all, be purely informative. Yet we still might be right in thinking suspiciously that behind all this information lies a covert message intended to persuade us that we ought to travel by train because it is more convenient, efficient and less stressful than the alternatives. We could argue that by putting out this sort of information the intentions of the managers of the train companies are not just to give us information, but to so impress us with their efficiency and the convenience of travelling by train, that we will travel this way more frequently.

1 Indeed the intentions of advertisers may be the central defining characteristic that enables us to decide what is and what is not an advertisement, including those that are presented as just informative. A small sign nailed to a village tree announcing where and when the local village fete will take place might be giving just information, but beneath it lies a covert message, an appeal to people, who might be reading it, to come along and support local causes in their fund raising activities. The information may just be the surface appearance. What matters is the underlying intention of those who wrote the advertisement – to persuade us to adopt a certain course of action.

2 Nevertheless the statement in the question seems to be right at least in one respect. It is possible to argue that almost all advertisements, with the exception of a few, are informative, indeed, as we have already seen, some appear to be wholly

concerned with this, although government bodies releasing warnings about smoking or the use of domestic fire alarms, are clearly intent on changing our behaviour, they are still concerned to give the public what they believe is vital information.

The same can be said of many commercial companies. Although their intention is to persuade us to buy their products, they are an important provenance of information about new products and technology, like computer equipment and software, new developments in digital technology, and the latest improvements in telecommunications, like smart phones. Other advertisements are a source of information on the latest designs in fashion or in equipment, like washing machines, dishwashers and microwaves, that we use every day.

3 But where the question appears to go too far is in arguing that informing the consumer is the 'only' thing that advertisers do. They may give us information on the latest technology, but they are also covertly suggesting that we cannot afford not to keep up with the latest developments. Similarly, while they inform us of the latest designs in fashions and household equipment, they are also persuading us that we cannot afford to let ourselves be left behind by our friends and neighbours, who will be clamouring for these products.

And, of course, in most of the advertisements we see in our papers or on television these messages are not the subtle, covert subtext of a simple statement of information. Indeed, if we cannot free ourselves of their influence, most of us can, at least, recognise the different strategies employed overtly by advertisers to manipulate our thinking and shape the choices we make.

4 Probably the most obvious of these is the selective use of information to promote their products. They will tell you, if you are thinking of making a purchase, what is good about their product, but pretermit any evidence that suggests it is not all that they claim it to be. An advertising company will tell you that the car they are promoting accelerates from 0 to 60kph in just six seconds, but they are likely to omit to tell you that recent research has revealed that it has an alarming tendency to rust severely within five years of purchase. Similarly, a manufacturer of computer printers might be keen to tell you that theirs is the most advanced printer on the market, but be really nervous about telling you that their print cartridges cost on average five times as much as any other printer.

5 Even more, we are probably all aware of examples of advertisers using comments and information taken out of context to promote their product, particularly when they are taken from reports that are critical of it. A report from a consumer association might heavily criticise a product for one reason or another, but if it contains just a single sentence of praise, this is likely to find its way into promotional literature. A publisher or a theatre promoter is likely to comb through an unfavourable review looking carefully for any isolated expression of a favourable comment that can be used to promote the book or play they are producing.

However, advertisers have developed still more effective forms of manipulation for the consumer, particularly in their exploitation of the sex, status and prejudices of the consumer. As our understanding of the psychology of the individual has grown so too has the advertiser's capacity to tap into our deepest motivations by associating their product with our strong feelings, desires and prejudices they can by-pass our reason, short circuiting our ability to make conscious choices. Cars, clothes, perfume, even alcohol are all promoted by associating them in the consumer's mind with sexual desires. The advertiser works to establish a close contiguity between driving a certain car, wearing a certain perfume and drinking a certain drink, and a full, active social and sexual life.

In the same way our desire for status and our respect for authority have bestowed on advertisers an effective way of deceptively taking advantage of our feelings to promote all manner of products. For example, our respect for the authority of science has convinced many advertisers that the only way of promoting washing machines, vacuum cleaners, dishwashers or detergents is to have a figure dressed in a laboratory coat, supposedly putting the product through rigorous tests and declaring authoritatively that it is the most successful product of its kind on the market. The same strategy can be extended to popular and respected public figures. Sportsmen and women, and TV personalities have, in their time, sold anything from mobile phones, health drinks and clothes to deodorants and shampoos.

So, rather than promoting consumers' freedom to choose, this appears to do quite the opposite. By appealing to their strong tastes and feelings advertisers successfully by-pass consumers' reason and their capacity to make rational choices. The most successful form of this has been subliminal manipulation, where messages have been recorded onto sound tracks at low speeds. These can only be picked up by the subconscious, when the tape is played at normal speed, without individuals knowing that they have been manipulated. The same can be achieved visually by inserting isolated frames into a reel of film to suggest and stimulate certain behaviour.

In one experiment in the 1970s managers in some US supermarkets recorded subliminal messages onto the music played throughout the store in order to reduce shoplifting. Messages, like 'I will not steal', 'I will be honest', were so successful in altering behaviour that shoplifting fell by 30% in a matter of weeks. If the same strategy were to be employed to improve the turnover of the store or to promote a certain range of products, this would amount to a serious invasion of the individual's freedom to choose.

But in fact most advertisers do not have to go to these lengths to switch off the thinking process. It is enough just to appeal to a convincing, though distorted, picture of what is taken for common-sense or accepted values in our societies. Archetypal characters and scenarios are created to evoke predictable responses that advertisers believe we will all share. Those promoting slimming products try to convince us that everyone wants and desires to be slim, that it is associated with success, and that if you are overweight this is a sign of social failure and self-indulgence. We are induced to believe that for most people, if dishes come out of the dishwasher unclean or the kitchen floor is not spotless, these are major life crises.

Appeals are made to some imagined social consensus: to 'basic' or 'shared' values, it is assumed we all want to drive the latest and fastest car on the road and our lives will be unfulfilled unless we have a 'multi-valve engine' and 'ABS braking' and to sustain these appeals myths have to be created by the media. It is thought we are all in a desperate race to keep up with our neighbours and that we fret endlessly about what people will say if they see us out in last year's fashions. We are all expected to share the myth that the average housewife is constantly paranoid about the whiteness of her wash and the cleanliness of her floors.

6 In the light of this the arguments of most advertising executives that the only thing advertisers are doing is informing consumers, thereby protecting their freedom of choice, appears implausible. As we have seen, to convince a manufacturer that they can deliver more customers advertisers need to do more than just inform – they need to escape the unpredictability of the consumers' freedom to choose by switching off their thinking process. If they do inform, it can hardly be claimed that this is the 'only' thing they do. Perhaps all that can be said in their favour is that the alternative of government manipulation would be worse still.

Notes

Look at the original, unrevised essay on the companion website (http://www.howtowritebetter essays.com) and compare it with the changes I have made in this revision.

1   The transition here from one paragraph to the next is too abrupt. We need to create a clearer, more fluent connection that ties this paragraph in with the previous paragraphs and indicates the logic of what we will be doing in this new paragraph. For this we need a transition that will indicate the logic of what we are doing and a new topic sentence. 'Indeed' indicates that we are reinforcing a point made in the previous paragraph, while the rest of the topic sentence indicates that we are extending it in a new direction.

2   In this paragraph the topic sentence works well, but it needs a transition to indicate the connection with the previous paragraph and the logic of what we will be doing in this paragraph. So, I have added the transition 'nevertheless' to indicate that we are qualifying what was said in the previous paragraph.

3   In this paragraph we need a transition that indicates that we are establishing a contrast with what has been said so far, so I have changed the topic sentence slightly. Topic sentences like these are important because they remind the reader of the question and tie what you are doing in with your interpretation of the question in the introduction and with the map of the essay that you outlined there. In this way, by tying in your paragraphs with the introduction, you create a cohesive essay in which all the parts fit tightly together.

4   This paragraph doesn't seem to have a topic sentence at all. Notice how it pitches you into the middle of the argument with the words 'They will tell you …' without giving you any idea of how it fits into the structure as a whole. So, I've added the highlighted topic sentence.

    The most interesting thing about this is the use of the demonstrative pronoun, 'these' as the transition that links the topic sentence with the previous paragraph. As I said in Chapter 32, demonstrative pronouns, such as 'this', 'these' and 'those', slipped into a topic sentence create a bridge between two paragraphs, while hardly disturbing the flow of ideas.

5   In this paragraph I've added the words 'Even more' at the beginning to act as a transition that links these two paragraphs and indicates to the reader the logic of what I am doing. In other words, in this paragraph I am extending and reinforcing the argument.

6   As you can see, this conclusion attempts to sum up the arguments developed in the essay. To do this well you have to identify what you believe to be the most important issues the essay raises and then come to a measured judgement that reflects the balance of the essay.

    In the original conclusion in the unrevised essay on the companion website (http://www. howtowritebetteressays.com), the writer has ignored important issues and come to a judgement that doesn't reflect the balance of the essay. Consequently, I have rewritten the conclusion. You can, of course, come to a different conclusion, but your summary of the most important issues must accurately reflect the substance of the essay.

Revising the Content

In this chapter you will learn:

- about the importance of checking factual accuracy, spelling and grammar;
- how to make the revision of your style simple and straightforward, yet comprehensive;
- how to make your writing more vivid;
- how to use the checklists to make sure you haven't overlooked anything;
- about the importance of the appearance of your essay to the final mark.

In the next two revisions your attention shifts to the smaller questions, such as factual accuracy, grammar and the use of words. Although this means you'll be focusing on fewer things, this is a more meticulous and slower read.

Third revision – checking the details

In the third revision your concern is for the accuracy of your facts and quotations. Particular care needs to be taken in checking these. If you lose your readers' trust over these details it may infect all of your work. They may conclude that they must be cautious about everything you say.

In addition, you will also be checking your spelling and grammar. Don't assume that such things are unimportant trifles. Making these simple mistakes will not only affect your grade, but might ultimately affect your chances of getting the job you most want. Details matter in all organisations. Not only does poor spelling and grammar strike at their credibility, but employers reasonably conclude that someone who makes fewer mistakes in this will make fewer mistakes doing other things. Karl Wiens,[1] the founder of the software company Dozuki and the CEO of iFixit, makes it plain that 'if job hopefuls can't distinguish between "to" and "too", their applications go into the bin … If it takes someone more than 20 years to notice how to properly use "it's", then that's not a learning curve I'm comfortable with.'

To remind you of the most common mistakes keep the following table close by as you revise your work and add to it the mistakes you commonly make.

Spelling and grammar – some of the most common mistakes

Grammar

advice (noun)/advise (verb)
    the same applies to practice/
    practise, device/devise,
    prophecy/prophesy, licence/
    license, etc.
	distinct/distinctive

	imminent/immanent
	impracticable/impractical
	infer/imply
affect (verb, never a noun)/ effect (verb and a noun)	ingenuous/ingenious
	invidious/insidious
alternate/alternative	judicial/judicious
choose/chose	loose/lose (loose = slack, free, untied)
complement/compliment	mitigate/militate
continual/continuous	phenomenon (singular)/phenomena (plural)
criterion (singular)/criteria (plural)	principle/principal
definite/definitive	stationary/stationery
dependant (noun)/dependent (adjective)	too/to (too = as well, in addition)
deprecate/depreciate	who/whom
discreet/discrete	

Possessives

hers, not her's	whose, not who's
its, not it's	your, not you're
one's, not ones	yours, not your's
theirs, not their's	

Spelling

acceptable, not acceptible	definitely, not definately
accommodation (2 c's and 2 m's)	develop, development
bureaucratic, not beauracratic	embarrass, embarrassment
commit, committee, committed	exceed, not excede
conscience, conscientious, conscious	fulfil, not fulfill
correspondence, not correspondance	harass, not harrass
deceit, not deciet	imitate, not immitate
irresistible, not irresistable	programme, program (for computers only)
liaise, liaison	receive, not recieve
maintenance, not maintainance	refer, reference, referred
manoeuvre, not manouvre	relevant, not relevent
occasion, occasionally	remit, remittance
occur, occurred, occurrence	separate, not seperate

offence, offensive	supersede, not supercede
omit, omission, omitted	tendency, not tendancy
parallel, not paralell	transfer, transferred
perceive, not percieve	travel, traveller
permit, permission, permitted	tyranny, not tyrrany
personal, personnel	until, not untill
privilege, not priviledge	

You must be sure that if you break the rules of grammar, it's deliberate – that you're doing it for reasons of style, to produce a certain effect – and it's not the result of a lack of knowledge. But whether you keep to the rules or decide to break them, the key is clarity: it must be the best way of making your meaning clear.

Checking the details – checklist

1 Is the content accurate?
2 Are the grammar, punctuation and spelling correct?
3 Have I distinguished clearly between my own ideas and those of others?
4 Have I acknowledged all sources and references?
5 Have I omitted any text from my bibliography?

Fourth revision – style

For most of us this is the most difficult and confusing of all revisions. There's just so much we need to focus on. To make it easier, just work from a simple list of things you're looking for. Eventually, you may want to include other things that you come to realise are significant problems in your writing. But at this stage just confine yourself to the following simple list of the most important things that you need to pay attention to – they will have an immediate impact on your writing, making it light, interesting and easy to read:

1 Unnecessary material
2 Long sentences
3 Long words
4 Strong nouns and verbs
5 The active voice

It's worth reminding yourself that the more you take out at this stage, the more readable your work becomes. What remains becomes more vivid, grabbing and keeping the interest of your reader. In view of this you will almost certainly need several revisions of this type. I find the more of these revisions I can do the better it becomes, until I reach a stage when I realise all too clearly that I need do no more.

Unnecessary material

As you go through your work, keep asking yourself if there are any unnecessary words, phrases, sentences or even paragraphs that ought to be removed. Again, remind yourself that the readability of your work will improve in proportion to the unnecessary material you eliminate.

EXAMPLE

In the advertising essay you might have a sentence like the following:

A small sign nailed to a village tree announcing where and when the local village fête will take place might be giving just information, but beneath it lies a covert message, an appeal to people, who might be reading it, to come along and support local causes in their fundraising activities.

By taking out the unnecessary words the meaning is made clearer, sharper and more direct.

A small sign nailed to a village tree announcing where and when the local village fête will take place might be giving just information, but beneath it lies a covert appeal to come along and support local causes in their fundraising activities.

Long sentences

With long sentences you run the risk of confusing, even losing, your readers, who will then be unable to give you marks for your good work. They may even lose patience with you as they struggle to find their way through the unfamiliar terrain of your thinking. To guard against this, cut up every long, complex sentence that can be reduced to two or more shorter sentences.

EXAMPLE

Although it's not impossible to understand the following sentence, its meaning is difficult to track at times. But once you've broken it down into three sentences, it presents no problem at all.

Appeals are made to some imagined social consensus, to 'basic' or 'shared' values, it's assumed we all want to drive the latest and fastest car on the road and our lives will be unfulfilled unless we have a 'multi-valve engine' and 'ABS braking' and to sustain these appeals myths have to be created by the media.

Appeals are made to some imagined social consensus: to 'basic' or 'shared' values. It's assumed we all want to drive the latest and fastest car on the road, and our lives will be unfulfilled unless we own a 'multi-valve engine' and 'ABS braking'. And to sustain these appeals, myths have to be created by the media.

Long words

Much the same advice goes for long words, although they have a different effect on your writing. They may not confuse your readers quite as much as long sentences; nevertheless, they can leave them wondering whether you really meant to say what you did, and will often make your writing sound unnecessarily pompous. It makes sense, then, wherever possible to replace long obscure words with short and simple ones.

The following example presents no problem in understanding what is meant, but it does sound slightly pompous:

> Our constant demand for material possessions and a higher standard of living has bestowed on politicians an effective way of influencing the way we vote.

It would be simpler and more direct to say:

> Our constant demand for material possessions and a higher standard of living has given politicians an effective way of influencing the way we vote.

This next example not only sounds pompous, but leaves you wondering whether you are clear about what the writer really meant to say:

> An advertiser will work to establish a close contiguity between driving a certain car, or drinking a certain drink, and a full, active social life.

Once you've substituted a more familiar word, the meaning is immediately clearer:

> An advertiser will work to establish a close association between driving a certain car, or drinking a certain drink, and a full, active social life.

Unnecessary material, long sentences and long words

'Advertisers seek only to ensure that consumers make informed choices.' Discuss.

 In this exercise re-read the first unrevised version of the essay on the companion website (www.howtowritebetteressays.com). This time look for unnecessary material that might be obscuring the meaning and blunting the impact of what is being argued. At the same time, reorganise any long complex sentences that pose the risk of confusing and losing the reader. Similarly, replace long words that may leave the reader wondering whether the writer really meant to say this.

Once you have done this, read through the sample essay that follows this chapter to see what I thought needed to be changed. Read my explanation at the bottom of the essay.

Strong nouns and verbs

Enough has already been said about the importance of writing with strong nouns and verbs, rather than shoring them up with adjectives and adverbs. So, check that you have used strong nouns and verbs with the minimum of modifiers. And constantly remind yourself that the fewer verbs you have to modify with adverbs, and nouns with adjectives, the better your writing will be.

EXAMPLE

You might argue,

> A manufacturer of computer printers will be keen to tell you that theirs is the most advanced printer on the market, but be really nervous about revealing that their print cartridges cost on average five times as much as those for any other printer.

But your meaning will be clearer if you argue,

> A manufacturer of computer printers will be keen to tell you that theirs is the most advanced printer on the market, but be reluctant to reveal that their print cartridges cost on average five times as much as those for any other printer.

'Nervousness' manifests itself in many different forms. So, in the first sentence, where you really wanted to identify one particular form that was relevant to the printer manufacturer, it was too vague to do this. In fact, shoring it up with the word 'really' didn't help much either, because, although you might be interested in the intensity of nervousness, what you really wanted to convey was the type of nervousness involved.

EXAMPLE

In the following sentence there are examples of both weak nouns and weak verbs. By substituting stronger, more specific words, see how the sentence gains in clarity and directness.

> Theatre promoters are likely to comb through unfavourable reviews looking carefully for any isolated expression of a favourable comment that can be used to promote their plays.

> Theatre promoters are likely to comb through unfavourable reviews in search of any isolated expression of approval that can be used to promote their plays.

Strong nouns and verbs

PRACTICE EXERCISE

'Advertisers seek only to ensure that consumers make informed choices.' Discuss.

As you did in the previous exercise, go onto the companion website (www.howto writebetteressays.com) and read the first unrevised version of the essay. In practice exercise 32 you identified all the nouns and verbs that needed to be replaced. Now, think of stronger alternatives that could replace them without the need for adjectives and adverbs.

When you have finished, read the sample essay that follows this chapter and my comments at the bottom.

The active voice

The same can be said of the active as opposed to the passive voice – we have already spent some time stressing the importance of the active voice in making your points clearer, by making them more concise and direct. Therefore, as you revise, ask yourself whether you have used the passive voice on only those occasions when what is done or the receiver of the action is more important than the doer. Wherever possible make the doer the subject of the sentence.

EXAMPLE

In the following example the most important information is what was actually done, rather than by whom. So, re-forming the sentence in the passive form makes the point more effectively.

In the 1970s managers in some US supermarkets, in order to reduce shoplifting, recorded subliminal messages onto the music played throughout the store.

In the 1970s subliminal messages were recorded onto the music played throughout some US supermarkets by managers, who wanted to reduce shoplifting.

Style – checklist

1 Have I removed all unnecessary words, phrases, sentences and paragraphs?
2 Have I cut up all the long complex sentences that can be cut up?
3 Have I replaced all long, obscure words with short and simple ones?
4 Have I removed all unnecessary modifiers in favour of good strong nouns and verbs?
5 Have I written in the active voice wherever possible, making the doer of the action the subject of the sentence?

Revising the content

PRACTICE EXERCISE

Read the following passage and then revise its content by going through the stages we've outlined above. Wherever you find unnecessary material, long sentences, long words, weak nouns and verbs, and passages that should be in the active or passive voice, revise them. Then go through the checklist to see if you've covered everything.

When you've finished, check your revised version against the answer given below.

Revising the content

Cultural change in modern Europe

In the second half of the nineteenth century as labour and information moved more rapidly and easily across borders new pressures for change were generated bringing with them unprecedented social and cultural fragmentation rarely seen before. Towns grew at inconceivable rates into vast cities drawing workers in from the countryside to interact with the new foreign migrant labour flooding in from all over Europe, developing a new urbane, cosmopolitan culture, fuelled by rising literacy and a popular press with mass readership. Not only were traditional social classes changing with movement up and down the social structure, but cultures and traditional customs were being threatened by an exodus away from the rural areas into cities, and by international, cosmopolitan influences that flowed across borders.

The forces for uniformity in tastes, culture and fashion that touched just about every European society that engaged in trade and commerce were fuelled by the revolution in communications alone. Consumers demanded the best of what they bought irrespective of where it was produced, so architecture, clothes and fashions were discovered to be increasingly the same and, except where they were consciously prolonged, national styles slowly faded. Even in the 1930s it was already apparent that a time was approaching when it would be impossible to tell one country's towns and cities from another and, add to this the impact of dance music, the cinema and the wireless, even the cheap recreational literature that more and more drew its inspiration from the US, and it became clear to a growing number of people that their social and cultural identity, once a source of patriotic pride and a sense of belonging, was disappearing beneath a uniform, cosmopolitan culture, that was constantly changing.

Answer

Cultural change in modern Europe

In the second half of the nineteenth century as labour and information swept across borders, new pressures for change were generated, bringing with them unprecedented social and cultural fragmentation. Towns grew at inconceivable rates into vast cities drawing workers in from the countryside to interact with the foreign labour flooding in from all over Europe. Here a new cosmopolitan culture developed, fuelled by rising literacy and a popular mass press. Not only were traditional social classes changing with movement up and down the social structure, but cultures and customs were being threatened by movement away from the countryside into cities, and by cosmopolitan influences that flowed across borders.

The revolution in communications alone was fuelling forces for uniformity in tastes, culture and fashion that touched just about every European society that engaged in commerce. Consumers demanded the best product irrespective of where it was produced. Architecture, clothes and fashions were increasingly the same. Except where they were consciously prolonged, national styles slowly faded. Even in the 1930s it was already apparent that a time was approaching when it would be impossible to tell one country's towns and cities from another. Add to this the impact of dance music, the cinema and the wireless, even the cheap recreational literature that more and more drew its inspiration from the US, and it became clear to a growing number that their social and cultural identity, once a source of patriotic pride and a sense of belonging, was disappearing beneath a uniform, cosmopolitan culture, that was constantly changing.

Fifth revision – revise by ear

Finally, your last revision! This appears to come back to your first, because you're reading your work through to see how it sounds. You're interested in its flow and rhythm. Hopefully, it should read like talk in print, with light effortless prose that glides across the page with a pace and rhythm that holds the reader's attention.

Unfortunately, most of us get so close to what we write and the thought patterns our sentences represent, that we find it's difficult to read it as another person would. If you have this problem, ask a friend to listen while you read it out aloud or, better still, ask your friend to read it out aloud to you.

Does it read like talk in print with light effortless prose?

This is the best test of all: if it doesn't come across fluently to someone who has never seen or heard it before, then it will need to be changed. This reading will certainly identify clumsy sentences or where you might have dealt with your ideas in an illogical order. The other advantage is that, because you're not reading it yourself, you'll be free to note where in your work it was difficult to understand the meaning of what was written. Failing this, if you haven't got a compassionate friend, or you're afraid to risk your friendship in this way, then record it and play it back to yourself as if you were listening to it for the first time.

- We can be too close to our sentences and thought patterns to recognise our mistakes.
- Our essay should glide across the page effortlessly.
- Get a friend to read it to you to see if it does.

But beyond the question of whether your work can be read and understood easily by someone reading it for the first time, think about one other thing. You may want to change the pace of your work at certain times in order to make your points more effectively. You may want to speed up or slow down in some sections by varying the length of sentences. Long sentences are very comforting and reassuring. They may be best suited to the development of the core elements of your arguments, which need to be analysed and elaborated carefully. But when you want to be abrupt, to grab your reader's attention with a vivid piece of detail, or an insight that you feel is a key point to get across, use a short sentence – don't let it get drowned in the words that surround it.

Revise by ear – checklist

1 Does it read well for someone reading it for the first time?
2 Is the pace and rhythm right for the arguments I want to make?

Using the checklists

As we've seen in previous stages, it always helps if you have a simple, clear strategy to work with: even though you may know what you're looking for, it helps to have a checklist so you can deliberately ask yourself questions which you just might overlook. It will also help you to assess how well you've completed each stage of the process, so you can see where you need to spend more time in the next assignment. With these advantages in mind, get into the habit of using checklists and try to answer the questions as you think your tutors might answer them when they assess your work.

Appearance

Does your essay have a neat, professional appearance?

Amid every other consideration, this last question appears to be the least significant. And, of course, it is, or it should be. But first impressions count, however unfair this may seem. Despite every effort made to ensure that each essay is subjected to the same objective criterion for assessment, marking still contains an element of subjectivity. Most people find it difficult to shake off their first impressions as they read an essay.

What's more, there may be an inductive truth here. There are people who are convinced that experience shows that a sloppily presented essay is more than likely to be sloppily argued. It's likely to lack sufficient attention to detail in terms of accuracy and the evidence used to support arguments convincingly. Whether these views have any credence or not, you can avoid the danger of dropping a grade by making sure your essay is clearly and neatly presented, with as few mistakes in it as possible. Your work must look like the work of a fastidious person.

Revision – the content

IN YOUR OWN WORK

Take the essay you've been working on and go through the final three stages revising the content.

In your first revision look for all the unnecessary words, phrases and sentences. Check for readability. If sentences are long, cut them up into shorter, more manageable lengths. Remember, the key is to keep your readers engaged and not to lose them.

On the second revision check for strong nouns and verbs, and where you find too many adjectives and adverbs see if you can think of stronger nouns and verbs that would make these unnecessary. The same goes for the active and passive voices in your writing. Check wherever you've used the passive voice that it is more effective than the active voice would be.

Then, once you've completed that, move on to the last revision. Get someone to read your essay to you, so that you can see how well it sounds.

Summary

1 Check the accuracy of your facts and quotations, otherwise you might lose your reader's trust.
2 As you revise your style have beside you a simple checklist of those things you're looking for.
3 Remember, the more you take out the more readable your essay becomes.
4 In the last revision get a friend to read it to you so you can see where the fluency breaks down or where the sequence of ideas seems illogical.
5 Does your essay look like the work of a fastidious person?

In the next chapter

Working through these different revisions will have revealed the sort of problems you will need to address in future essays. You will also realise that there are simple things you need to concentrate on as you work on each essay, which will help you generate your own ideas and express them in a way that more accurately reflects your abilities. You should find both of these concerns reflected in your tutor's comments when you get the essay back. Indeed, there is lot to learn from your tutor's comments. In the next chapter we will look at what we can do to make the most of this advice.

Note

1   http://blogs.hbr.org/cs/2012/07/i_wont_hire_people_who_use_poo.html

Sample essay 2: Revising the content

**'Advertisers seek only to ensure that consumers make informed choices.'
Discuss.**

Most advertising executives are willing to defend their profession by arguing that all they are doing is informing the public and in doing so protecting the democratic freedoms of individuals, in particular their freedom of choice. To a certain extent, of course, this is true: without advertising we would be less informed about new developments in technology, in fashion and in medical advances. Even government warnings about the dangers at work and in the home depend upon advertisements. But the key to this is the claim that this is the 'only' thing they do, when most of the public suspect their paramount concern is to manipulate consumers into buying products that they may not want or need.

As this suggests, at least part of the advertiser's role is to provide consumers and the public with information. But this goes to the heart of what we mean by an 'advertisement'. Few of us would doubt that in some sense a railway timetable is an advertisement, after all it is telling the customer what is for sale and how to buy it. Yet there are no catchy jingles urging you to 'Let the train take the strain.' Nor are there any persuasive messages offering to let children travel free if the parents take the whole family to the beach. It is simply informative: it gives you information on the routes and the stations the train will stop at on the way; it tells you the departure and arrival times; and it tells you on what platform you can find the train.

1 Given this, it might not be unreasonable to conclude that advertisements can, after all, be purely informative. Yet we still might be right in suspecting that behind all this information lies a covert message intended to persuade us that we ought to travel by train because it is more convenient, efficient and less stressful than the alternatives. We could argue that by putting out this sort of information the intentions of the managers of the train companies are not just to give us information, but to so impress us with their efficiency and the convenience of travelling by train, that we will travel this way more frequently.

2 Indeed the intentions of advertisers may be the central defining characteristic that enables us to decide what is and what is not an advertisement, including those that are presented as just informative. A small sign nailed to a village tree announcing where and when the local village fete will take place might be giving just information, but beneath it lies a covert message, an appeal to people to come along and support local causes in their fund raising activities. The information may just be the surface appearance. What matters is the underlying intention of those who wrote the advertisement – to persuade us to adopt a certain course of action.

3 Nevertheless the statement in the question seems to be right at least in one respect. It is possible to argue that almost all advertisements, with the exception of a few, are informative. Indeed, as we have already seen, some appear to be wholly concerned with this. Although government bodies releasing warnings about smoking

or the use of domestic fire alarms, are clearly intent on changing our behaviour, they are still concerned to give the public what they believe is vital information.

4 The same can be said of many commercial companies. Although their intention is to persuade us to buy their products, they are an important source of information about new products and technology, like computer equipment and software, new developments in digital technology, and the latest improvements in telecommunications, like smart phones. Other advertisements are a source of information on the latest designs in fashion or in equipment, like washing machines, dishwashers and microwaves, that we use every day.

5 But where the question appears to go too far is in arguing that informing the consumer is the 'only' thing that advertisers do. They may give us information on the latest technology, but they are also covertly suggesting that we cannot afford not to keep up with progress. Similarly, while they inform us of the latest designs in fashions and household equipment, they are also persuading us that we cannot afford to let ourselves be left behind by our friends and neighbours, who will be clamouring for these products.

And, of course, in most of the advertisements we see in our papers or on television these messages are not the subtle, covert subtext of a simple statement of information. Indeed, if we cannot free ourselves of their influence, most of us can, at least, recognise the different strategies employed overtly by advertisers to manipulate our thinking and shape the choices we make.

6 Probably the most obvious of these is the selective use of information to promote their products. They will tell you what is good about their product, but omit any evidence that suggests it is not all that they claim it to be. An advertising company will tell you that the car they are promoting accelerates from 0 to 60kph in just six seconds, but they are likely to omit to tell you that recent research has revealed that it has an alarming tendency to rust severely within five years of purchase. Similarly, a manufacturer of computer printers might be keen to tell you that theirs is the most advanced printer on the market, but be reluctant to reveal that their print cartridges cost on average five times as much as any other printer.

7 Even more, we are probably all aware of examples of advertisers using comments and information taken out of context to promote their product, particularly when they are taken from reports that are critical of it. A report from a consumer association might heavily criticise a product, but if it contains just a single sentence of praise, this is likely to find its way into promotional literature. A publisher or a theatre promoter is likely to comb through an unfavourable review in search of any isolated expression of approval that can be used to promote the book or play they are producing.

8 However, advertisers have developed still more effective forms of manipulation, particularly in their exploitation of the sex, status and prejudices of the consumer. As our understanding of the psychology of the individual has grown, so too has the advertiser's capacity to tap into our deepest motivations. By associating their product with our strong feelings, desires and prejudices they can by-pass our reason, short circuiting our ability to make conscious choices. Cars, clothes, perfume, even alcohol are all promoted by associating them in the consumer's mind with sexual desires. The advertiser works to establish a close association between driving a certain car, wearing a certain perfume and drinking a certain drink, and a full, active social and sexual life.

9 In the same way our desire for status and our respect for authority have given advertisers an effective way of exploiting our feelings to promote all manner of products. For example, our respect for the authority of science has convinced many advertisers that the only way of promoting washing machines, vacuum cleaners, dishwashers or detergents is to have a figure dressed in a laboratory coat, supposedly putting the product through rigorous tests and declaring authoritatively that it is the most successful product of its kind on the market. The same strategy can be extended to popular and respected public figures. Sportsmen and women, and TV personalities have, in their time, sold anything from mobile phones, health drinks and clothes to deodorants and shampoos.

10 So, rather than promoting consumers' freedom to choose, this appears to do quite the opposite. By appealing to their passions and feelings advertisers successfully by-pass consumers' reason and their capacity to make rational choices. The most successful form of this has been subliminal manipulation, where messages have been recorded onto sound tracks at low speeds. These can only be picked up by the subconscious, when the tape is played at normal speed, without individuals knowing that they have been manipulated. The same can be achieved visually by inserting isolated frames into a reel of film to suggest and stimulate certain behaviour.

11 In one experiment in the 1970s subliminal messages were recorded onto the music played throughout some US supermarkets by managers, who wanted to reduce shoplifting. Messages, like 'I will not steal', 'I will be honest', were so successful in altering behaviour that shoplifting fell by 30% in a matter of weeks. If the same strategy were to be employed to improve the turnover of the store or to promote a certain range of products, this would amount to a serious invasion of the individual's freedom to choose.

12 But in fact most advertisers do not have to go to these lengths to switch off the thinking process. It is enough just to appeal to a convincing, though distorted, picture of what is taken for common-sense or accepted values in our societies. Archetypal characters and scenarios are created to evoke predictable responses that advertisers believe we will all share. Those promoting slimming products try to convince us that everyone wants to be slim, that it is associated with success, and that if you are overweight this is a sign of social failure and self-indulgence. We are induced to believe that for most people, if dishes come out of the dishwasher unclean or the kitchen floor is not spotless, these are major life crises.

13 Appeals are made to some imagined social consensus: to 'basic' or 'shared' values. It is assumed we all want to drive the latest and fastest car on the road and our lives will be unfulfilled unless we have a 'multi-valve engine' and 'ABS braking'. And to sustain these appeals myths have to be created by the media. It is thought we are all in a desperate race to keep up with our neighbours and that we fret endlessly about what people will say if they see us out in last year's fashions. We are all expected to share the myth that the average housewife is constantly paranoid about the whiteness of her wash and the cleanliness of her floors.

In the light of this the arguments of most advertising executives that the only thing advertisers are doing is informing consumers, thereby protecting their freedom of choice, appears implausible. As we have seen, to convince a manufacturer that they can deliver more customers advertisers need to do more than just inform – they need to escape the unpredictability of the consumers' freedom to choose by switching off their thinking process. If they do inform, it can hardly be claimed that this is the 'only' thing they do. Perhaps all that can be said in their favour is that the alternative of government manipulation would be worse still.

Notes

Now that we have revised the structural features of the essay on the companion website, we can revise the content. Take Sample Essay 1 and compare it with the further changes I have made in this revision.

1   In this sentence the verb 'thinking' is not sufficiently specific, therefore, it has to be shored up with the adverb 'suspiciously'. As a result, the idea that is created is not as sharp and direct as it could be; we are not immediately clear about the meaning that the author wants to convey. By substituting the stronger verb 'suspecting' immediately the meaning is clear and the sentence is sharper and more direct.

2   In this paragraph the words 'who might be reading it' have been taken out. This phrase is unnecessary: it adds no meaning to the sentence. We already know that it can only appeal to people if they read it. As a result, not only is the point of the sentence expressed more economically, but it means the really significant words are no longer smothered by the unnecessary phrase, so they stand out and have a more direct impact. The key part of this sentence is 'an appeal to people to come along and support local causes', which stands out a lot better now that it is not diluted by the unnecessary phrase.

3   This paragraph is dominated by one very long, rambling sentence. Its complex structure makes it difficult to navigate successfully, so you get easily lost. As a result, you end up unsure whether you have, in fact, understood everything. Breaking it up into three shorter sentences makes it much easier to understand. The simpler sentences are easier to navigate, so at the end of the paragraph you are much more confident that you understand the point that is being made.

4   In this paragraph the word 'provenance' is replaced by the much simpler word 'source'. As a result, the meaning is much clearer. Replacing complex, more obscure words with simpler words makes it much easier to understand what you are saying. If, for example, you use the word 'utilize' instead of the simpler word 'use', then you are piling on unnecessary layers of complication that will make it more difficult for your reader to understand you.

5   In this paragraph 'latest developments' has been replaced by 'progress'. The problem is that the noun 'developments' is too general. It's not specific enough and, therefore, it fails to create a clear image. To make up for this, the writer has had to shore it up with the adjective 'latest', which, as you can see, waters the idea down. As a result, it loses impact. By replacing it with 'progress' a clearer and more specific image is created, one that has more impact and meaning. It's not just the latest developments that are the issue here, but the whole idea of progress and whether this is necessarily a good thing.

6   In the second sentence of this paragraph the phrase 'if you're thinking of making a purchase' has been deleted. Not only do these words contribute nothing to the sentence, they obscure the important words, making the meaning of the sentence less clear and concise. By removing the unnecessary words we produce a sentence that is sharper and more direct.

   The word 'pretermit' has been replaced by the simpler word 'omit'. As a result, it is easier to understand the meaning of the sentence as it edges closer to the rhythms and the language of spoken English.

   In the last sentence of the paragraph 'really nervous' has been replaced by 'reluctant'. To describe the manufacturer as being 'really nervous' about revealing this information doesn't convey accurately the type of nervousness he feels. The word is too general. It needs a more specific word that identifies exactly what he feels. By substituting the word 'reluctant', the meaning is immediately clearer.

7   In the second sentence of this paragraph the phrase 'for one reason or another' has been deleted. It adds no meaning to the sentence and only serves to distract our attention

from the more important words that carry the key ideas of the sentence. As a result of removing this phrase the sentence is sharper and more direct.

In the last sentence of the paragraph the words 'a favourable comment' have been replaced by the single noun 'approval'. This might not convey more meaning than 'a favourable comment', but it is more economical. Consequently, it doesn't bury the meaning of the sentence under unnecessary words, making it clearer.

8   In the first sentence of this paragraph the words 'for the consumer' have been deleted. They add no meaning to the sentence, which is perfectly clear without them.

The following sentence is long and rambling. The structure is difficult to follow, so it's easy for the reader to get lost. To safeguard against this, it would help to break it up into smaller sentences and use punctuation to indicate the logical of what's being said. Once you have broken it up into three sentences and used commas to indicate the structure it is a lot easier to navigate the ideas and the argument.

In the final sentence of the paragraph the word 'contiguity' has been replaced by the simpler word 'association'. This makes the meaning of the sentence a lot clearer.

9   A similar problem arises in the first sentence of the following paragraph. The writer has decided to use the word 'bestowed' for the simpler alternative 'given'. Using 'given' in this sentence immediately makes the meaning clearer.

However, the sentence still needs work on it to make it perfectly clear. The clumsy phrase 'deceptively taking advantage of' can be replaced by the single word 'exploiting' and the sentence suddenly becomes clear, direct and economical.

10 In this paragraph the writer has used the weak noun 'tastes' and has had to shore it up with the adjective 'strong' in an attempt to make his meaning a little clearer. The problem is that the word needs to be more specific and definite to make the meaning clear. It is too general: 'tastes' can mean a number of things. As a result, the meaning of the sentence is unclear and loses its impact. By replacing the noun and its adjective with the single, more specific noun 'passions' a clearer image is produced, one which carries much more meaning. The point is that it's not just tastes that the writer is discussing, but passions – a particular type of taste which is much stronger than all the rest, at times even irresistible.

11 The first sentence of this paragraph is a good example of where the passive form of the sentence is much more effective than the active form. The key question is what is the most important aspect of the sentence that needs to be stressed? If it is the doer of the action – in this case, the managers – then the active form is the most effective. It will make your points clearer, by making them more concise and direct. However, when what is done – in this case, recording subliminal messages – is more important than the doer of the action, the passive form makes the point more effectively, because it puts what is done at the beginning of the sentence, rather than the doer. With this example, clearly the most important aspect is what was done – the recording of the subliminal messages.

12 In the middle of this paragraph the words 'and desires' have been deleted. They add nothing to the sense of the sentence – what someone 'wants' is what they 'desire'. They clutter up the sentence, so by removing them we make the sentence clearer and more direct.

13 This paragraph begins with a long, complex sentence. It needs to be broken up and punctuated clearly, so readers can navigate their way through it safely without getting lost. In fact, when you look at it closely, it's clear that you don't need to do more than break it up into three sentences. You can then understand clearly what is being argued.

Learning from Feedback

In this chapter you will learn:

- how important feedback on essays is to your academic achievement;
- the sort of feedback you need, if it is to be effective;
- how to organise yourself to get the most out of feedback;
- how to prioritise your responses to feedback.

Now that you have worked through the five stages of essay writing you will know how to get the most from your abilities in every essay you write. But there is one more thing to do. At the beginning of this book we discussed the question 'Why Write Essays?' and one of the reasons I gave was that this provides your tutor with the opportunity to comment on your work and for you to use those comments to develop your understanding and your skills and abilities.

Importance of feedback

Like most of us, at times you have no doubt just glanced at the grade on an essay that your tutor has returned and filed it away, either content with it or so fed up and disillusioned, because you didn't understand why you should be getting such grades, that all you wanted to do was forget all about it. But your tutor's feedback represents a challenge to make the changes that will bring the sort of grades that more fairly reflects your abilities and potential. This is your opportunity to reflect on your learning, to assess your skills and how you work, and to clarify the areas in which you need to improve.

Feedback on essays is more strongly and consistently related to academic achievement than any other form of teacher intervention.

Although the importance of this sort of feedback has been underrated with stories of teachers returning essays with hastily scribbled comments such as 'Good work' or 'Could do better', it is in fact one of the most critical elements in the learning process. Numerous studies over the last 30 to 40 years have shown that feedback on essays is more strongly and consistently related to academic achievement than any other form of teacher intervention. In fact, they also suggest that, if we want to promote learning and help students reach their potential, it makes more sense to provide less teaching and more feedback. Even so, if this feedback is to work, it must meet a certain criteria:

1   **Goal-related** – the characteristics of a good essay should be clear to you – you should know what you are aiming to produce;

2   **Tangible results** – you must be able to see clearly how your essay is being assessed in relation to this goal;

3   **Useful and specific** – you must be able to understand the advice and use it to make concrete changes;

4   **Personal, not general advice** – the advice must be tailored to *your* particular work and not just about the subject of the essay or about essays in general;

5   **Consistent** – you can only change the way you work and make continuous progress if you know the advice you are getting is consistent from one essay to another.

Therefore, the first thing you must do, if it doesn't meet these criteria, is ask. Most tutors are more than happy to clarify exactly what they meant, because they know how important feedback is to your progress. They are keen to make it clearer by digging deeper to analyse what is really going on in order for you to begin to tackle it. So, mark those things you don't understand and ask your tutor about them.

The things to look for

Some tutors can seem unremittingly negative and critical. If you are confident and have a strong character, you will work well with this sort of tutor. But most tutors realise that criticism alone is not enough; that they need to identify students' strengths as well as their weaknesses. As a plant flourishes through light rather than darkness, we flourish more through praise than criticism.

The best comments, therefore, strike a balance between the two: a tutor will lift and motivate you by highlighting your achievements and the progress you have made, but will then point you in the direction in which you can achieve even more progress by noting those things that you need to work on. With a clear idea of what is possible and the confidence that you have the ability to achieve it, you are much more likely to steel yourself with uncompromising determination to address these problems and do better in the next essay so that you begin to do justice to our potential.

In detail, therefore, the following are the sort of comments you need to be looking for, so you can take note of them and begin to work on the issues:

Things to look for

---

1   Corrections
2   Ability range
3   Structure
4   Style
5   Ideas to think about
6   Follow-up work

---

1   Corrections

The obvious things that tutors identify are the mistakes you might have made, so you can correct them, or at least look again at the particular section of the essay affected.

This includes assessing the content of your essay: how well you have researched the topic and covered all the issues raised. Tutors are looking to see whether you have covered the subject well, done sufficient research and shown clear evidence that you understand the issues raised by the topic. They want to see whether you can use the complex ideas involved skilfully and with clear understanding. All of these problems need to be considered while your ideas are still fresh in your mind. So, note them on the 'Feedback record' below and make time to work on them.

Similarly, your tutor may have drawn attention to logical mistakes in your arguments, the sort that we examined in Chapter 16. You will need to note these in the same way to make sure that, if they are recurring problems, you have a way of identifying them by going through previous feedback records and checking that you have corrected them before you hand in future essays. The same is the case with simple mistakes in punctuation and grammar, the sort we listed in Chapter 40. Many of these are recurring problems, so you need a system to identify and correct them each time you finish an essay.

Content – factual mistakes – have you done sufficient research – do you show clear understanding?
Logical mistakes
Punctuation and **grammar mistakes**

2 Ability range

In Chapters 8 and 9 we discussed the importance of making sure that in the essay you do what the question asks you to do: that you make sure the type of essay you are writing matches the range of abilities the question wants to see you use.

EXAMPLE

'Are there any circumstances where the individual is justified in refusing to obey a law?'

This question asks you to analyse the circumstances in which you might be justified in refusing to obey a law and to discuss the issues this raises. Therefore, it would be irrelevant to outline the main types of law, describe the campaign of civil disobedience launched by the suffragettes in 1906 or give an account of the ideas of Socrates, Henry Thoreau or Martin Luther King.

In Chapter 1 we discussed the importance of not uncritically accepting the terms of the question. When a question asks you to discuss, critically evaluate or analyse issues it will want you to show that you can use your analytical abilities to identify the subtle implications that the question raises, to unravel the complexity of the problems you are discussing and all the possible disagreements. In your discussion it will want you to show that you can play devil's advocate by discussing both sides of the problem, particularly the side for which you have least sympathy. So, the feedback on your essay may draw attention to the following problems:

Analysis – you might not have developed a clear and comprehensive analysis of the issues and the implications of concepts;

Discussion – as a result you might have missed important implications that you should have examined in your discussion;

Playing devil's advocate – you may not have used your imagination to explore issues from both sides. As a result your discussion may appear one-sided;

Critical evaluation – in turn you might have only taken into account a limited range of the evidence and arguments that you should have examined and evaluated.

3 Style

Most tutors will point out how you can improve your style to help you express your ideas simply and clearly. In Chapters 29–31 we discussed the important elements of style – simplicity and economy. If phrases and words can be left out and ideas expressed more simply and economically, you will run less risk of losing the reader and, equally important, the significant words and ideas will stand out. Remember what we said in Chapter 32:

> The readability of your work increases in proportion to the unnecessary words you eliminate.

So, your tutor is likely to point out how you can express your ideas more accurately and clearly: sentences that can be improved; words and phrases that can be simplified; transitions that can be used to indicate the logic of what you are doing so you don't lose the reader; and a more careful choice of words that accurately convey the strength of your evidence.

- **Long and complex sentences**
- **Choice of words**
- **De-clutter sentences**
- **Active/passive voice**
- **Transitions and logical indicators**
- **Evidence**

4 Structure

Without exception tutors will comment on whether the essay answers the question relevantly and comprehensively. Therefore, they are likely to indicate how your plan could be reorganised to answer the question in a simpler, more straightforward and relevant way. They will give you advice on how you could improve your use of introductions, conclusions and paragraphs to improve the logic of the essay so that each part fits together forming a tight, cohesive piece of work. They will also offer you advice on how you can make this logic clearer, so that you are never in danger of confusing and losing the reader.

- **Introduction**
- **Paragraphs**
- **Conclusion**

5 Ideas to think about

Tutors will rarely pass up the opportunity to help you develop your ideas by suggesting new ideas, fresh examples or different opinions. They might open up different perspectives, different ways of looking at a problem that you hadn't seen. As a result, you may realise that there are new avenues to be pursued and questions to be answered. All of these need to be considered while your ideas are still fresh in your mind. They are your opportunity to deepen your understanding of the key issues raised by your essay and develop your own arguments and ideas.

- **Ideas and arguments**
- **Opinions**
- **Different perspectives**
- **New examples and evidence**
- **New avenues** to be pursued and **questions** to be answered

6 Follow-up work

Along with this your tutor is likely to suggest further reading: a journal article or a passage from a text that explores an idea you have raised. You may have developed an idea that describes an unusual way of looking at a problem or interpreting a body of evidence. Tutors are generally keen to fuel their students' interests and encourage them when they develop their own insights and ideas.

Responding to feedback

1 Recording them – the Feedback record

As you realise by now, like most other aspects of learning, you will get the greatest benefit from these comments if you organise yourself to respond to them effectively. The first thing is to record them separately from your essay, so that you have a clear record in front of you of the things you need to work on. Use the 'Feedback record' below: photocopy it or download a copy from the companion website (www.howto writebetteressays.com). This will make it clear what you have to do. It won't be lost somewhere within the notes you've taken, which often results in oversights and missed opportunities.

Moreover, many of the comments a tutor will make will be spread throughout your essay. By condensing all of these onto a single form for each essay, you will have a record of those things you need to be more aware of in future essays and a clear set of notes to work on as you develop your ideas further.

Feedback record

PRACTICE EXERCISE

Fill out feedback records for each of your last three essays. In particular, note the ideas your tutor gives you to think about. If you haven't worked on these ideas, write them up in your journal and develop them further to reveal their significance. As you'll see below, the more time you give to this the more likely you are to come up with your own ideas and insights.

In addition, look for recurring problems: logical mistakes, grammar and spelling mistakes, and problems with your style and structure. These are often the result of habits we have developed, which make it difficult for us even to notice them at times. They may be spread throughout your essays, so you will have to go through them checking all of your tutor's comments.

Feedback record	
Date	
Essay title	
Corrections	
Ability range	
Style	
Structure	
Ideas to think about	
Follow-up work	

2 Using your journal

If your tutor leaves you with fresh ideas to pursue, this might involve further reading, or at least developing your own response in your journal, where you can develop your ideas freely without thinking that someone is looking over your shoulder. The key to this, as we've seen, is to give your thinking the opportunities it needs to grow and develop. Each discrete stage of the writing process provides fresh opportunities, as do your journal and notebook, so that when you come to look back over them you can see just how far you have come, how much more you understand, and how better equipped you are to research and write about those things that interest you.

> You will no longer be expressing ideas that are not yours in a language that is not your own.

What's more, by giving your thinking the opportunity it needs to grow and develop in this way, you will more effectively process these ideas and make them your own by evaluating them in the context of your own beliefs, values and ideas. Rather than expressing ideas that are not yours in a language that is not your own, these will be *your* ideas and *your* arguments, which will be more convincing as a result.

- Each discrete stage of the writing process provides fresh opportunities for your ideas to grow and develop.
- By giving your thinking the opportunity to grow in this way you will more effectively process these ideas and make them your own.

Prioritising the issues raised

All of this feedback might seem a little overwhelming, but it need not be. Some things can be dealt with simply, such as grammar and spelling problems. It makes sense, therefore, to deal with these first so that you are organised to recognise them and correct them before you hand in future essays.

Some of the other problems may be due to the way you organise your time. You may need to reorganise your timetable so that you make sure you always tackle the thinking stages of essay writing (the interpretation of the title, planning and writing) at those times you work best. Alternatively, some of the problems may be due to not having enough time to do sufficient research. Whatever it is, plotting out the five stages of essay writing over a longer time frame, so that you allow your ideas time to develop, will result in a deeper understanding of the issues, genuine insights of your own and more convincing and compelling arguments. Look at the time management section of the companion website (www.howtowritebetteressays.com).

> Allow one issue to dominate your thinking to the exclusion of all others.

Once you have the simpler problems out of the way, you can concentrate on the more complex issues, those that your tutor is telling you that you need to think about. But don't set yourself too much to do. Most of us make the most surprising discoveries and solve the most difficult problems by allowing one issue to dominate our thinking to the exclusion of all others. Allow problems to take over your thinking, become totally preoccupied and reap the rewards.

Summary

1 Feedback on essays is more strongly and consistently related to academic achievement than any other form of teacher intervention.
2 Use the five-point criteria to ask the questions you need to ask to get the most out of your feedback.
3 As a result of developing and processing your ideas in your journal you will make them your own and express them more convincingly.
4 Allowing one issue to dominate our thinking to the exclusion of all others can produce the most surprising insights and discoveries.

Finally

Now that you have completed your essay and taken as much from it as you can to make sure your future essays benefit from the lessons you have learnt, you should need no convincing that you are capable of producing an essay that not only does justice to your ideas, but leaves your readers knowing they have read something that is interesting, well argued and thought provoking. Remember, you have the abilities to think and write perceptively. All you need are the skills that we have learnt in this book to open up and develop these abilities.

Conclusion

We started this book by drawing attention to the value of writing essays, both in what you can learn from them and in terms of the abilities and skills you develop along the way. Now that we've worked through each of the stages, it should be possible to see more clearly the benefits that can be derived if each of these stages is done well.

Stage 1: Interpretation of the question

In the first stage you were shown ways of developing the skills you need to analyse the most difficult concepts. As a result, you should now feel confident that you can reveal not just the key issues involved in any question, but also the sort of insight which marks your work out as interesting and original. What's more, you should now be able to build on this with the brainstorming skills you learnt in this stage. These will help you mobilise your ideas, arming you with your own thoughts, so you're no longer tyrannised into accepting uncritically the opinions of the authors you read.

Stages 2 and 3: Research and Planning

In these stages you were shown how to develop the sort of intellectual skills that will give you the confidence to tackle any assignment no matter how difficult. Having researched the topic, not only will you have learnt a great deal about it and many of the peripheral issues, but you will have developed the capacity to use your research skills with more flexibility to meet a wider range of intellectual tasks. Moreover, by planning your essay you created a structure of ideas you can draw upon not only in your written work, but in discussions and examinations. Around this you can now build your own understanding of the subject.

Stages 4 and 5: Writing and Revision

As to your ability to capture your ideas in writing that is clear, fluent and interesting, now that you've worked your way through the writing and revision stages you will know that by separating the writer from the editor you can use the skills involved in each much more effectively. Having done this once, you should be able to repeat it in all your work, producing essays that are clearly structured, logically argued and written in clear, light prose that holds the reader's attention. You will know now, having worked through each of the five stages of revision, that you can allow yourself to write freely, knowing that you can significantly improve your essay later, when you let the editor in.

Learn to value your own unique contribution

Finally, remember, you can never do a perfect job. To do this you would have to wait until all the facts are in – and, of course, they never will be. All you can do is add to our understanding of what we *do* know. *Your* insights and *your* interpretation of the facts add to this understanding: they are just as valuable as anyone else's. Therefore, be bold – don't be cowed by the fear of authority.

Bibliography

Dorothea Brande, *Becoming a Writer* (London: Macmillan, 1984). Even professional writers admit they are indebted to this book for its help in freeing their most creative insights.

Tony Buzan, *Use Your Head* (London: BBC, 1979). One of the first to popularise pattern notes, or 'mind maps'.

Stuart Chase, *Guides to Straight Thinking* (New York: Harper, 1956).

Stella Cottrell, *The Study Skills Handbook*, 3rd edn (Basingstoke: Palgrave, 2008).

Edward de Bono, *Parallel Thinking* (London: Penguin, 1994).

Edward de Bono, *Serious Creativity* (London: HarperCollins, 1995).

Jean M. Fredette (ed.), *Handbook of Magazine Article Writing* (Cincinnati: Writer's Digest Books, 1990). Learn from the professionals – this is full of sound practical advice from professional writers.

Bruno Furst, *The Practical Way to a Better Memory* (Marple: Heap, 1977). One of the most renowned books on concentration and memory training.

John Peck and Martin Coyle, *The Student's Guide to Writing* (Basingstoke: Palgrave, 1999).

William Strunk and E. B. White, *The Elements of Style* (New York: Macmillan, 1979). Once known as 'the little book', this sold over two million copies in its first edition – learn how to write clearly and concisely.

Robert H. Thouless, *Straight and Crooked Thinking* (London: Pan, 1958).

John Wilson, *Thinking with Concepts* (Cambridge: Cambridge University Press, 1963).

Index